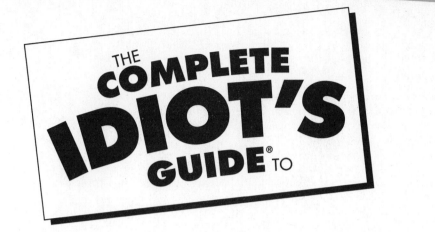

THE **COMPLETE IDIOT'S GUIDE®** TO

Creating a Website

by Paul McFedries

ALPHA

A member of Penguin Group (USA) Inc.

For Karen and Gypsy

ALPHA BOOKS

Published by the Penguin Group

Penguin Group (USA) Inc., 375 Hudson Street, New York, New York 10014, USA

Penguin Group (Canada), 90 Eglinton Avenue East, Suite 700, Toronto, Ontario M4P 2Y3, Canada (a division of Pearson Penguin Canada Inc.)

Penguin Books Ltd., 80 Strand, London WC2R 0RL, England

Penguin Ireland, 25 St. Stephen's Green, Dublin 2, Ireland (a division of Penguin Books Ltd.)

Penguin Group (Australia), 250 Camberwell Road, Camberwell, Victoria 3124, Australia (a division of Pearson Australia Group Pty. Ltd.)

Penguin Books India Pvt. Ltd., 11 Community Centre, Panchsheel Park, New Delhi—110 017, India

Penguin Group (NZ), 67 Apollo Drive, Rosedale, North Shore, Auckland 1311, New Zealand (a division of Pearson New Zealand Ltd.)

Penguin Books (South Africa) (Pty.) Ltd., 24 Sturdee Avenue, Rosebank, Johannesburg 2196, South Africa

Penguin Books Ltd., Registered Offices: 80 Strand, London WC2R 0RL, England

Publisher: *Marie Butler-Knight*
Editorial Director: *Mike Sanders*
Senior Managing Editor: *Billy Fields*
Acquisitions Editor: *Tom Stevens*
Senior Development Editor: *Christy Wagner*
Production Editor: *Kayla Dugger*

Copy Editor: *Amy Borrelli*
Cartoonist: *Steve Barr*
Cover Designer: *Bill Thomas*
Book Designer: *Trina Wurst*
Indexer: *Celia McCoy*
Layout: *Chad Dressler*
Proofreader: *Laura Caddell*

Contents at a Glance

Contents

Introduction

Many years ago (we're talking last century), after having meandered around the web's nooks and crannies for quite awhile, I got this sudden urge to have my own website. *Sheesh*, I thought to myself, *all these people are doing this wild web stuff that just seems so, well, cool. I want in!* So I scoured the web and bookstores for information on creating a website. What I found were a bunch of highfalutin manuals written in a turgid style that made website creation sound like some esoteric business best left to people with advanced engineering degrees.

When I was done, however, one thing was blindingly obvious: creating a website is actually pretty easy! So why were there no books out there shouting this from the rooftops? I resolved to take matters into my own hands and write just such a book. The result was the first edition of *The Complete Idiot's Guide to Creating a Web Page*, which saw the light of day back in 1996.

Sounds great! But why are you calling me an idiot?

Well, when it comes to producing content for the World Wide Web, a "complete idiot" is someone who, despite having at least the normal complement of gray matter, wouldn't know HTML from H. G. Wells. This is, of course, perfectly normal and, despite what many so-called Internet gurus may tell you, it does not imply any sort of character defect on your part.

So I might as well get one thing straight right off the bat: the fact that you're reading *The Complete Idiot's Guide to Creating a Website* does *not* make you an idiot. On the contrary, it shows that …

- You have discriminating taste and settle for nothing less than the best. (And it shows you don't mind immodest authors.)

- You have a gift for self-deprecation (which is just a fancy-schmancy way of saying you don't take yourself—or any of this Internet malarkey—too seriously).

- You're determined to learn this HTML thing, but you don't want to be bothered with a lot of boring, technical details.

- You realize it doesn't make sense to learn absolutely everything about HTML. You just need to know enough to get your web page up and running.

- You're smart enough not to spend your days reading 5 bazillion pages of arcane (and mostly useless) information. You do, after all, have a life.

In this book, I teach you how to create beautiful websites in no time flat. I understand that the very idea of trying to create something that looks as good as what you see on the web sounds like an intimidating challenge. However, it's my goal in this book to show you that it's really quite simple and that *anyone* can build a website with their bare hands. We even try to have—*gasp!*—a little irreverent fun as we go along.

You'll also be happy to know that this book doesn't assume you have any previous experience with website production. This means you start from scratch and slowly build your knowledge until, before you know it, you have your very own tract of web real estate. All the information is presented in short, easy-to-digest chunks you can easily skim through to find just the information you want.

How to Use This Book

I'm assuming you have a life away from your computer screen, so *The Complete Idiot's Guide to Creating a Website* is set up so you don't have to read it from cover to cover. If you want to know how to add a form to your website, for example, just turn to the chapter that covers working with forms. (Although, having said that, beginners will want to read at least Chapter 1 before moving on to more esoteric topics.) To make things easier to find, I've organized the book into five more or less sensible sections:

Part 1, "Building a Website with Your Bare Hands," helps you get your website labors off to a fine start by showing you everything you need to know to get a site up and running. First you learn some solid basics and move on to learn how to create interesting site designs using tables; how to spruce up your site with lists, news feeds, and free content; and how to enhance your site with e-mail links, forms, chat rooms, and forums.

Part 2, "Designing Your Website," takes your website from good to great. You learn how to design a nice site, set up your site for easy and sensible navigation, and be sure people with mobile web browsers can access your site.

When your site is up to scratch, it's time to get it on the web, and **Part 3, "Publishing Your Website,"** helps you do just that. You learn how to check your site for errors, publish your site to the web, run your own web server, and let the world know that your website is open for surfing.

Part 4, "Automating Your Website with JavaScripts," shows you how to add tiny little programs to your website to give your pages that interactive boost. I start with this JavaScript thing everyone always blathers on about. I also give you quite a few examples of scripts you can plop right inside your pages. I also show you a bunch of other examples that do all kinds of amazingly useful things.

Most web welders are happy just to put up their pages and leave it at that. But a few want to generate some extra cash from their hard work, and that's what I show you how to do in **Part 5, "Turning Your Website Skills into Cash."** You learn how to get started as a professional web designer, make money from festooning your site with ads, earn cash by adding links to affiliate programs on your site, and set up a store to sell things.

Finally, at the end of the book, I've included a glossary of Internet, World Wide Web, and HTML terms that should help you out if you come across a word or phrase that furrows your brow. Also back there is more information about what you'll find on this book's CD (more on this is coming right up!).

About the CD

The book's major bonus is the CD that's glued onto the back cover. This little plastic Frisbee contains tons of website-related knickknacks, including all the examples I use in the book, some sample website templates, and lots more.

Extras

Happily, there's more to this book than 17 chapters of me yammering away. To round out your website education and make your site publishing adventures a bit easier, I've included a few other goodies:

Webmaster Wisdom
These boxes contain notes, tips, and asides that provide you with interesting and useful (at least theoretically!) nuggets of web page lore.

def•i•ni•tion

This type of box defines words and phrases every budding webmaster needs to know.

Page Pitfall

These boxes contain cautionary tales that warn you of web page traps to avoid and hurdles to jump over.

Acknowledgments (The Giving Credit Where Credit Is Due Department)

English essayist Joseph Addison once described an editor as someone who "rides in the whirlwind and directs the storm." I don't know if that's true for editors in some of the more sedate publishing nooks (novels and cookbooks and such), but I think it applies perfectly to the rigors of computer book editing. Why? Well, the computer industry (and the World Wide Web in particular) is so fast paced that any kind of editorial (or authorial) dawdling could mean a book will be obsolete before it even hits the shelves.

The good folks at Alpha Books avoid premature book obsolescence by subjecting each manuscript to a barrage of simultaneous edits from a number of specialists (I call it "gang editing"). So a process that normally might take months is knocked down to a few short weeks. This means you get a book that contains timely and relevant information, and a book that has passed muster with some of the sharpest eyes and inner ears in the business. My name may be the only one that appears on the cover, but tons of people had a big hand in creating what you now hold in your hands. Of those I worked with directly, I'd like to extend warm thanks to Acquisitions Editor Tom Stevens, Senior Development Editor Christy Wagner, Production Editor Kayla Dugger, Copy Editor Amy Borrelli, Technical Editor Don Passenger, and Software Specialists Rebecca Harmon and Bill Thomas.

The members of the editorial team aren't the only people who had their fingers in this publishing pie. Flip back a few pages and you'll find a list of the designers, illustrators, indexers, and other professionals who worked long and hard to produce this book. I tip my authorial hat to all of them. I'd also like to thank the thousands and thousands of readers who have written to me over the years to offer compliments and suggestions. Your couple of cents' worth is always appreciated.

Special Thanks to the Technical Reviewer

The Complete Idiot's Guide to Creating a Website was reviewed by an expert who double-checked the accuracy of what you'll learn here, to help us ensure that this book gives you everything you need to know about creating a website. Special thanks are extended to Don Passenger.

Don has been a reader of Paul's books for many years in addition to his official title of technical editor on many of his tomes. Don's site, htmlfixit.com (developed with a fellow McFedries reader), is a great resource for aspiring website creators. He offers domain hosting and site design services through bestfoot.com.

Trademarks

All terms mentioned in this book that are known to be or are suspected of being trademarks or service marks have been appropriately capitalized. Alpha Books and Penguin Group (USA) Inc. cannot attest to the accuracy of this information. Use of a term in this book should not be regarded as affecting the validity of any trademark or service mark.

Part 1

Building a Website with Your Bare Hands

This is, as you know, a book about websites. However, all websites—from the sprawling sites maintained by your average corporate colossus, to the simple sites put together by your average dude or dudette—have at least one thing in common: they consist of web pages. The site might have just a few pages, or it might have a few thousand. Either way, the humble page is the fundamental unit of any website. In other words, when you're building your own website, you build it one web page at a time. That means you need to know how to construct a page with the sweat of your own brow. The chapters in Part 1 show you how to do just that.

Building Blocks:
The Basic Tags

In This Chapter

◆ Web page editing made easy

◆ Getting comfy with tags and HTML

◆ Understanding the basic blueprint for all web pages

◆ Adding text, images, and links to your page

◆ Adding fonts and colors

Building a web page from scratch using your bare hands may seem like a daunting task. It doesn't help that the codes you use to set up, configure, and format a web page are called the Hypertext Markup Language (HTML for short), a name that could only warm the cockles of a geek's heart. But even though the name HTML is intimidating, the codes used by HTML aren't even close to being hard to learn. There are only a few of them, and in many cases they even make sense!

Don't believe me? I can't say that I blame you. However, just work through this chapter, which introduces you to the basic HTML codes and shows you how to build up your page one little bit at a time. By the time you're done with this chapter, you'll have an honest-to-goodness web page fully constructed and ready for action.

The Basics of Creating a Web Page

One of the most surprising things about creating web pages is that you don't need a fancy-schmancy software program to get it done. In fact, you can do it using the least fancy and least schmancy program known to mankind: a humble text editor such as Notepad in Windows or TextEdit in Mac OS X. That may seem improbable to you now. After all, web pages have colors, fonts, images, and links. How can a text editor do all that?

> **Webmaster Wisdom**
>
> This chapter only gives you the minimum you need to know about HTML. If you've got a hankering to know more, may I not-so-humbly suggest my book *The Complete Idiot's Guide to Creating a Web Page and Blog,* which goes into all this stuff in a satisfying amount of detail.

The secret is the HTML knickknacks that you sprinkle liberally throughout your text. For example, suppose you want a particular word to appear in italics for emphasis. HTML has a code for italics, so you just surround the word with the proper code. (Yes, impatient one, you'll learn what that code is later in this chapter.) You don't see the italics right away because the text editor doesn't know what to do with HTML. However, a web browser such as Internet Explorer, Firefox, or Safari knows *exactly* what to do. When you load your page into the browser, the program sees your code and promptly displays the word in italics, no questions asked.

Firing Up a New Text File

When you're ready to start building a web page, your first step is to create a new text file. To do that, not surprisingly, you need to fire up your favorite text editor:

- If you have Windows XP or Vista, launch Notepad by selecting **Start, All Programs, Accessories, Notepad.**

- If you have Mac OS X, open **Finder,** click **Applications,** and double-click **TextEdit.**

- If you have another text editor, launch it the way you normally do.

Both Notepad and TextEdit display a brand-new text document automatically when you start each program. If you ever need to start a new document by hand, select **File, New.** TextEdit creates a new file automatically, but it's not the plain text file you need. To convert the file to plain text, select **Format, Make Plain Text.** Notepad creates the plain text file automatically.

If you prefer, you can use a word processor such as WordPad, the program that comes with most versions of Windows, or Microsoft Word. Again, launch the program and a new document will be staring at you in a few seconds (or choose **File, New** to do it yourself).

If you take the word processor route, don't use the program's commands to format the document in any way (such as adding italics or centering paragraphs). Not only do you run the risk of having a browser choke on these extra formatting codes, but every web browser on the face of the earth will completely ignore your efforts. Remember, the only way to make a browser do your bidding and display your web page properly is to use the appropriate HTML codes.

Also, don't save the file in the word processor's native format. Be sure to save the file as pure text, sometimes referred to as ASCII text. More on this in a sec.

Saving HTML Files

Using a text editor (or a word processor) to create a web page sounds relatively straightforward, but there are a couple traps you need to avoid to ensure everything works out okay in the end. Here are some notes to bear in mind:

The Save command. You save a file by selecting the program's **File, Save** command. The first time you do this with a new file, the Save As dialog box shows up. You use this dialog box to specify three things: the file name, the file type, and the file's location on your hard disk. The next few notes discuss some tidbits about the name and type.

Use the right file extension. For garden-variety web pages, your file names must end with either the .htm or the .html file extension (for example, mypage.html). When you name your file, be sure to specify either .htm or .html.

> ### Webmaster Wisdom
>
> What's the different between .htm and .html? Not much. Windows and OS X treat both extensions as a web page file, so you're free to use either one.

Use lowercase file names only. The majority of web servers (computers that store web pages) are finicky when it comes to uppercase letters versus lowercase letters. For example, the typical server thinks that index.html and INDEX.HTML are two different files. To be safe, always enter your file names using only lowercase letters.

Don't use spaces. Most versions of Windows and the Mac are happy to deal with file names that include spaces. Internet Explorer is also space savvy. However, some other browsers get *really* confused if they come upon any file name that has one or more spaces. So avoid using spaces in your file names. If you want to separate words in file and directory names, use an underscore (_) or a hyphen (-).

Use the right file type. While in the Save As dialog box, you need to select the correct "file type" for your HTML file. How you do this depends on what program you're using:

♦ If you're using Notepad, use the **Save as type** list to select **All Files (*.*).** This ensures that Notepad uses your .htm or .html extension (and not its normal .txt extension).

♦ If you're using Windows WordPad, use the **Save as type** list to select **Text Document.** You also need to surround your file name with quotation marks (for example, "index.html") to ensure that WordPad uses your .htm or .html extension.

♦ If you're using Microsoft Word, use the **Save as type** list to select **Text Only (*.txt).** Again, surround your file name with quotation marks.

When you've done all that, click **Save** in the Save As dialog box to save the file. (If you're using WordPad, the program might ask if you're sure you want to save the file in "Text-Only format." Say "Duh!" and click **Yes.**)

Browsing the Results

Earlier I mentioned that when you add HTML codes to your text file, the text editor doesn't show you what the results will look like. To see your page in action, you need to load it into your favorite web browser. This is great because it means you can test-drive your page without first having to put it on the web. Here's the basic method you'll use to build your pages:

1. In your text editor or word processor, either start a new file (if one isn't started for you already) or use the **File, Open** command to open an existing file.

   When you run the **File, Open** command, the Open dialog box probably won't show your HTML files. To see them, use the **Files of type** list to select **All Documents (*.*).** (Some programs use **All Files (*.*)** instead.)

Page Pitfall

If you're using Microsoft Word, you may not see the HTML tags at first because Word hides them from you. In Word 2003, you need to select the **View, HTML Source** command to see the tags. In Word 2007, you must jump through a few more hoops. First, select **Office, Word Options,** click **Advanced,** scroll down to the **General** section, activate the **Confirm file format conversion on open** check box, and click **OK.** Now when you open your HTML file, you see the Convert File dialog box. Select **Plain Text** and click **OK** to see your tags.

2. Add some text and HTML stuff (I'll define what this "stuff" is in the next section) to your file.

3. Select the program's **File, Save** command to save the file using the points I mentioned earlier.

4. Load the file into your browser of choice to see how things look. As a public service, here are the appropriate instructions for loading a file from your hard disk using Internet Explorer, Firefox, and OS X Safari:

   ♦ *Internet Explorer.* First, if you're using Internet Explorer 7, press **Alt** to see the menu bar. Select **File, Open** (or press **Ctrl+O**), click the **Browse** button in the Open dialog box that appears, pick out the file you need, and click **Open.** You can reload the file by selecting the **View** menu's **Refresh** command, or by pressing **F5.**

   ♦ *Firefox.* Select **File, Open File** (or press **Ctrl+O**) to display the Open File dialog box, select the file, and click **Open.** To reload, select **View, Reload,** or **Ctrl+R.**

   ♦ *Safari.* Select the **File, Open File** command (or press ⌘**+O**), use the Open dialog box to choose your file, and click **Open.** You can reload the page by selecting **View, Reload Page,** or by pressing ⌘**+R.**

5. Lather. Rinse. Repeat steps 2 through 4.

Getting the Hang of HTML

I keep going on and on about this HTML hoo-ha, so it's about time I stopped talking about it and started showing you what it's all about. At its most basic, HTML is nothing more than a collection of codes—called *tags*—that specify how you want your web page to look. In general, tags use the following format:

```
<tag>This here's the text that the tag modifies</tag>
```

What you have here is a couple codes—`<tag>` and `</tag>`—with a bit of silly text in between. The `tag` part is a code that specifies the type of effect you want. Most of these codes are one- or two-letter abbreviations, but sometimes they're entire words. You always surround these codes with angle brackets `<>`; the brackets tell the web browser that it's dealing with a chunk of HTML and not just some random text.

For example, let's start with a simple sentence that might appear in a web page:

```
Okay, listen up people because this is important!
```

Suppose you want to punch this up a bit by displaying the word *important* in italics. In HTML, the tag for italics is `<i>`, so you'd modify your web page like so:

```
Okay, listen up people because this is <i>important</i>!
```

Page Pitfall _____

One of the most common mistakes rookie web weavers make is to forget the slash (/) that identifies a tag as an end tag. If your page looks wrong when you view it in a browser, look for a missing slash. Also look for a backslash (\) instead of a slash, which is another common error.

See how I've surrounded the word `important` with `<i>` and `</i>`? The first `<i>` says to the browser, "Listen up, Browser Boy! You know the text that comes after this? Be a good fellow and display it in italics." This continues until the browser reaches the `</i>`. The slash (/) defines this as an *end tag*, which lets the browser know it's supposed to stop what it's doing. So the `</i>` tells the browser, "Okay, okay, that's enough with the italics already!" As you'll see, there are tags for lots of other effects, including bold, paragraphs, headings, page titles, links, and lists. HTML is just the sum total of all these tags.

Laying the Foundation: A Bare-Bones Web Page

Okay, it's high time we got the lead out and transformed this discussion from the theoretical to the practical. In this section, I show you the tags that serve as the basic blueprint you'll use for all your web pages.

Your HTML files will always lead off with the `<html>` tag. This tag doesn't do a whole lot except tell any web browser that tries to read the file that it's dealing with a file that contains HTML doodads. Similarly, the last line in your document will always be the corresponding end tag: `</html>`. You can think of this tag as the HTML equivalent for "The End." So each of your web pages will start off with this:

```
<html>
```

and end with this:

```
</html>
```

The next items serve to divide the page into two sections: the head and the body. The head section is like an introduction to the page. Web browsers use the head to glean various types of information about the page. A number of items can appear in the head section, but the only one that makes any real sense at this early stage is the title of the page, which I talk about in the next section.

To define the head, add `<head>` and `</head>` tags immediately below the `<html>` tag you typed in earlier. So your web page should now look like this:

```
<html>
<head>
</head>
</html>
```

The body section is where you enter the text and other fun stuff that the browser will actually display. To define the body, place `<body>` and `</body>` tags after the head section (that is, below the `</head>` tag):

```
<html>
<head>
</head>
<body>
</body>
</html>
```

Hmm. It's not exactly a work of art, is it? On the excitement scale, these opening moves rank right up there with watching the grass grow and tuning in to C-SPAN on a slow news day. Let's just file this stuff in the "Necessary Evils" section and move on to more interesting things.

Webmaster Wisdom

Most of the time it makes no difference if you enter your tag names in uppercase or lowercase letters. The HTML powers that be prefer to see HTML tags in lowercase letters, so that's the style I use in this book, and I encourage you to do the same so your website is compliant with the current HTML standards.

Page Pitfall

A common page error is to include two or more copies of these basic tags, particularly the `<body>` tag. For best results, be sure you use each of these six basic structural tags only one time on each page.

Adding a Title

When you surf the web, you've probably noticed that your browser displays some text in its title bar at the top of the window. That title bar text is, not surprisingly, the web page title, which is a short (or sometimes long) phrase that gives the page a name. (In tabbed browsers such as Internet Explorer 7, Firefox, and Safari, the title also appears in the tab.) You can give your own web page a name by adding the `<title>` tag to the page's head section.

To define a title, surround the title text with the `<title>` and `</title>` tags. For example, if you want the title of your page to be "My Home Sweet Home Page," enter it as follows:

```
<title>My Home Sweet Home Page</title>
```

Note that you always place the title inside the head section, so your basic HTML document now looks like this:

```
<html>
<head>
<title>My Home Sweet Home Page</title>
</head>
<body>
</body>
</html>
```

Figure 1.1 shows this document loaded into the Internet Explorer 7. Notice how the title appears in the browser's title bar and also in the tab.

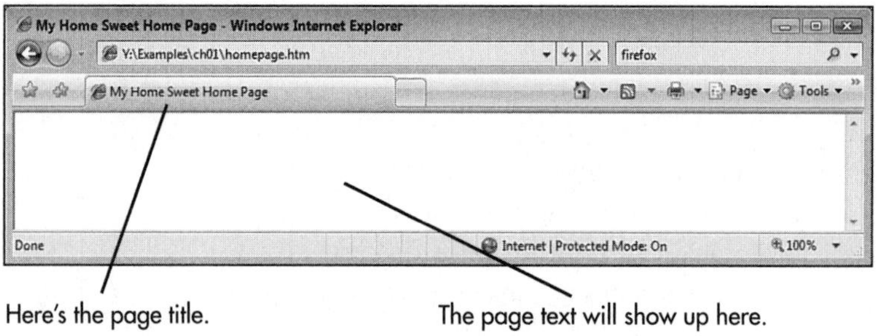

Figure 1.1

Tabbed web browsers display the title in the title bar as well as in the tab.

Here's the page title.   The page text will show up here.

Here are a few things to keep in mind when thinking of a title for your page:

- Be sure your title describes what the page or blog is all about.

- Don't make your title too long. If you do, the browser might chop it off because there's not enough room to display it in the title bar or tab. Fifty or sixty characters are usually the max.

◆ Use titles that make sense when someone views them out of context. For example, if someone really likes your page, that person might add it to his or her list of favorites or bookmarks. The browser displays the page title in the favorites list, so it's important that the title makes sense when he or she looks at the bookmarks later on.

◆ Don't use cryptic or vague titles. Titling a page "Link #42" or "My Web Page" might make sense to you, but your readers might not appreciate it.

Giving 'Em Something to Read: Adding Text

With your page title firmly in place, you can now think about putting some flesh on your web page's bones by entering the text you want to appear in the body of the page. For the most part, you can simply type the text between the `<body>` and `</body>` tags, like this:

```
<html>
<head>
<title>My Home Sweet Home Page</title>
</head>
<body>
This text appears in the body of the web page.
</body>
</html>
```

Before you start typing willy-nilly, however, there are a few things you should know:

You might think you can line things up and create some interesting effects by stringing together two or more spaces. Ha! Web browsers chew up all those extra spaces and spit them out into the nether regions of cyberspace. Why? Well, the philosophy of the web is that you can use only HTML tags to lay out a document. So a run of multiple spaces (or white space, as it's called) is ignored.

Tabs also fall under the rubric of white space. You can enter tabs all day long, but the browser ignores them completely.

Browsers also like to ignore the carriage return. It might sound reasonable to the likes of you and me that pressing **Enter** (or **Return**, if you're using a Mac) starts a new paragraph, but that's not so in the HTML world. I talk more about this in a bit.

Page Pitfall

The angle brackets < and > can't be displayed directly in HTML pages because the browser uses them to identify tags. If you need to use them, replace < with `&lt;` and replace > with `&gt;`.

If HTML documents are just plain text, does that mean you're out of luck if you need to use characters such as ©, ™, and £? Luckily, no. HTML has special codes for these kinds of characters. I talk about them a bit later in this chapter.

Word processor users, it bears repeating that it's not worth your bother to format your text using the program's built-in commands. The browser cheerfully ignores even the most elaborate formatting jobs because, as usual, browsers understand only HTML-based formatting. (And besides, a document with formatting is, by definition, not a pure text file, so a browser might bite the dust trying to load it.)

Adding Paragraphs

As I mentioned earlier, carriage returns aren't worth a hill of beans in the World Wide Web. If you type one line, press **Enter,** and type a second line, the browser simply runs the two lines together, side by side.

If you need a new paragraph, you have to stick the browser's nose in it, so to speak, by using the <p> tag. For example, consider the following text:

```
<html>
<head>
<title>My Home Sweet Home Page</title>
</head>
<body>
This text appears in the body of the web page.
This is the second line (not!).
<p>
This is the third line.
</p>
</body>
</html>
```

Figure 1.2 shows how this text looks in the browser. As you can see, the first two lines appear beside each other, despite the fact that they're on separate lines in the original text. However, the third line sits nicely in its own paragraph, thanks to the <p> tag that precedes it. Note, too, that I used the </p> end tag to finish the paragraph.

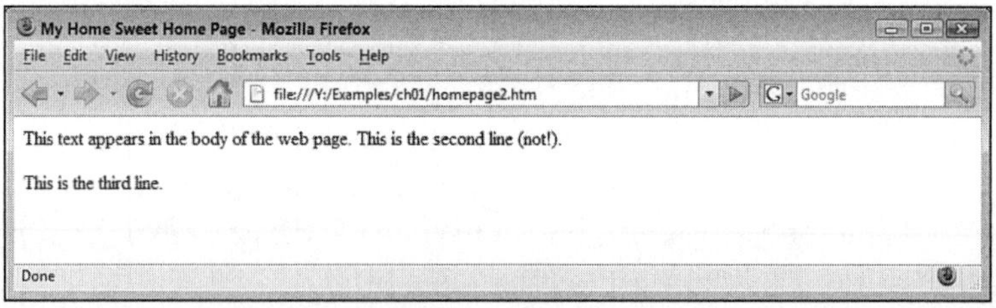

Figure 1.2

Use the <p> tag to create paragraphs in HTML.

My Home Sweet Home Page - Mozilla Firefox
File Edit View History Bookmarks Tools Help
file:///Y:/Examples/ch01/homepage2.htm   Google

This text appears in the body of the web page. This is the second line (not!).

This is the third line.

Done

Adding Headings

Earlier you saw that you can give your web page a title using the aptly named `<title>` tag. However, that title only appears in the browser's title bar and tab. What if you want to add a title that appears in the body of the page? That's almost easier done than said because HTML comes with a few tags that enable you to define headings, which are bits of text that appear in a separate paragraph and usually stick out from the surrounding text by being bigger, appearing in a bold typeface, and so on.

There are six heading tags in all, ranging from `<h1>`, which uses the largest font, down to `<h6>`, which the smallest font. Here's some web page code (see headings.htm on the CD that accompanies this book) that just adds the six headings to a page; Figure 1.3 shows how they look in Safari:

```
<html>
<head>
<title>The Heading Tags</title>
</head>
<body>
<h1>This is Heading 1</h1>
<h2>This is Heading 2</h2>
<h3>This is Heading 3</h3>
<h4>This is Heading 4</h4>
<h5>This is Heading 5</h5>
<h6>This is Heading 6</h6>
</body>
</html>
```

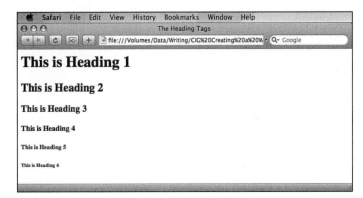

Figure 1.3

The six HTML heading tags.

What's up with all the different headings? The idea is that you use them to outline your document, something like this:

◆ Use `<h1>` for the overall page title.

◆ Use `<h2>` for the page subtitle.

◆ Use `<h3>` for the titles of the main sections of your page.

◆ Use `<h4>` for the titles of the subsection of your page.

As an example, consider the headings I've used in this chapter, and see how I'd format them in HTML. The overall heading, of course, is the chapter title, so I'd display it using, say, `<h1>`. The first main section is the one titled "The Basics of Editing a Web Page," so I'd give its title an `<h2>` heading. That section contains three subsections, "Firing Up a New Text File," "Saving HTML Files," and "Browsing the Results." I'd give each of these titles the `<h3>` heading. Then I come to the section called "Getting the Hang of HTML." This is another main section of the chapter, so I'd go back to the `<h2>` tag for its title, and so on.

The following HTML document (look for headings2.htm on the CD) shows how I'd format all the section titles for this chapter, and Figure 1.4 shows how they appear in the web browser. (Notice that I don't need to use a `<p>` tag to display headings on separate lines; that's handled automatically by the heading tags.)

```
<html>
<head>
<title>Some Example Headings</title>
</head>
<body>
<h1>Building Blocks: The Basic Tags</h1>
<h2>The Basics of Editing a Web Page</h2>
<h3>Firing Up a New Text File</h3>
<h3>Saving HTML Files</h3>
<h3>Browsing the Results</h3>
<h2>Getting the Hang of HTML</h2>
<h2>Laying the Foundation: A Bare-Bones Web Page</h2>
<h2>Adding a Title</h2>
<h2>Giving 'Em Something to Read: Adding Text</h2>
<h3>Adding Paragraphs</h3>
<h3>Adding Headings</h3>
<h2>Giving 'Em Something to See: Adding Images</h2>
<h3>Converting Graphics to GIF or JPEG</h3>
<h3>Adding an Image to Your Page</h3>
```

```
<h3>Wrapping Text Around an Image</h3>
<h2>Giving 'Em Something to Click: Adding Links</h2>
<h2>Fancy Font Formatting</h2>
<h3>Some Basic Text Formatting Tags</h3>
<h3>Combining Text Formats</h3>
<h3>Changing the Font Size</h3>
<h3>Changing the Font Family</h3>
<h2>Coloring Your Web World</h2>
<h3>Working With Colors</h3>
<h3>Coloring Your Page Text</h3>
<h3>Coloring the Page Background</h3>
</body>
</html>
```

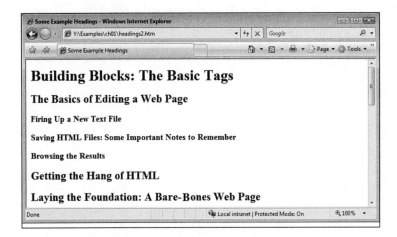

Figure 1.4

Examples of HTML heading tags.

Accessorizing: Displaying Special Characters

You might think that because HTML is composed in text-only documents (documents that include only the characters and symbols you can peck out from your keyboard), nonstandard characters such as © and ™ would be taboo. It's true that there's no way to add these characters to your page directly, but the web wizards who created HTML thought up a way around this limitation. Specifically, they came up with special codes called *character entities* (surely a name only a true geek would love) that represent these and other oddball symbols.

These codes come in two flavors: a *character reference* and an *entity name*. Character references are basically just numbers, and the entity names are friendlier symbols that describe the character you're trying to display. For example, you can display the registered trademark symbol ® by using either the `&#174;` character reference or the `&reg;` entity name, as shown here:

```
Print-On-Non-Demand&#174;
```

Or:

```
Print-On-Non-Demand&reg;
```

Page Pitfall

To ensure that all browsers render your characters properly, use only lowercase letters when typing the entity names.

Note that both character references and entity names begin with an ampersand (&) and end with a semicolon (;). Don't forget either character when using special characters in your own pages.

Table 1.1 lists a few other popular characters and their corresponding codes. For a complete list, see codes.htm on this book's CD.

Table 1.1   A Few Common Characters

Symbol	Character Reference	Entity Name
<	<	<
>	>	>
¢	¢	¢
£	£	£
¥	¥	¥
©	©	©
®	®	®
TM	™	™
°	°	°
¼	¼	¼
½	½	½
¾	¾	¾
×	×	×

Giving 'Em Something to See: Adding Images

Whether you want to tell stories, give instructions, pontificate, or just plain rant about something, you can do all that and more by adding text to your page. But to make it more interesting for your readers, add a bit of eye candy every now and then. To that end, there's an HTML tag you can use to add one or more images to your page.

Images are endlessly useful, and they're an easy way to give your page a professional look and feel. Although I'm sure you can think of all kinds of ways to put pictures to work, here are a few suggestions:

♦ A company logo on a business-related page

♦ Graphics from an ad

♦ Drawings done by the kids in a paint program

♦ Charts and graphs

♦ Fancy fonts

♦ Your signature

Before we get too far into this picture business, I should tell you that, unfortunately, you can't use just any old image on a web page. Browsers are limited in the types of images they can display, and an image that might display fine in, say, Firefox, might not show up at all in Internet Explorer. To be safe, always use either *GIF* or *JPEG* image formats, which all web browsers support.

GIF was the original web graphics format. It's limited to 256 colors, so it's best for simple images like line art, clip art, text, and so on. GIFs are also useful for setting up images with transparent backgrounds and for creating simple animations.

Page Pitfall _____

Although graphics have 1,001 uses, don't include 1,001 images on each page. The majority of surfers use broadband connections nowadays, but many of your readers are still accessing your site from a slow modem link, which means that graphics take forever to load. If you have too many images, most folks give up and head somewhere else.

Webmaster Wisdom

When you work with graphics files, bear in mind that GIF files use the .gif extension, while JPEG files use the .jpg or .jpeg extensions.

JPEG, which gets its name from the Joint Photographic Experts Group that invented it, supports complex images that have many millions of colors. The main advantage of JPEG files is that, given the same image, they're smaller than GIFs, so they take less time to download. This doesn't matter much with simple images, but digitized photographs and other high-quality images tend to be huge; the JPEG format compresses these images so they're easier to manage.

Converting Graphics to GIF or JPEG

What do you do if you've got the perfect image for your web page, but it's not in GIF or JPEG format? You need to get your hands on a graphics program that's capable of converting images into different formats. Here are some you can use:

♦ *Paint Shop Pro.* This excellent all-around graphics program is great not only for converting graphics, but also for manipulating existing images and for creating new images. See www.corel.com.

♦ *Graph-X.* This is a neat little program that's happy to convert a whack of graphics formats into GIF or JPEG. See www.group42.com.

♦ *ACDSee32.* This is a simple program that works best as a graphics viewer. However, it can also convert many different graphics formats into JPEG (but not GIF, unfortunately). A trial version of this program is available on the CD as well. See www.acdsee.com.

♦ *LView Pro.* The latest versions can perform lots of image manipulation tricks, but it's still best as a graphics converter. See www.lview.com.

♦ *PolyView.* A good converter with some interesting graphics features (such as the ability to create a web page from a set of images). See www.polybytes.com.

♦ *Graphic Workshop.* This program has a bit of a clunky interface, but it does a good job of converting graphics. See www.mindworkshop.com/alchemy/gwspro.html.

♦ *IrfanView.* This powerful program can not only convert your images to all the major formats, but it's free, too! See www.irfanview.com.

For most of these programs, you use the same steps to convert an image from one format to another:

1. In the program, select the **File, Open** command and use the Open dialog box to open the image file you want to convert.

2. Select **File, Save As.** The Save As dialog box drops by.

3. In the **Save as type** list, choose either JPEG or GIF. (In some programs, the latter is called CompuServe Graphics Interchange format.)

4. Click **Save.**

Adding an Image to Your Page

Okay, enough of all that. Let's start squeezing some images onto your web page. As I mentioned earlier, there's an HTML code that tells a browser to display an image. It's the `<img>` tag, and here's how it works:

```
<img src="filename" />
```

Here, `src` is short for "source" and `filename` is the name of the graphics file you want to display. Note, too, that the close angle bracket has a slash (/) before it, which is weird. This is a bit of HTML pedantry because the HTML gods decree that all tags must "close," but the `<img>` tag doesn't have a corresponding `</img>` close tag (because there's nothing you'd put between `<img>` and `</img>`). Therefore, you "close" the `<img>` tag by adding the slash.

Okay, let's see an example: suppose you have an image named logo.gif. To add it to your page, you use the following line:

```
<img src="logo.gif" />
```

> **Webmaster Wisdom**
>
> Throughout this book, you'll see that you often populate a tag with extra information, such as the `src` value in the `<img>` tag. These values are called *attributes*.

In effect, this tag says to the browser, "Excuse me? Would you be so kind as to go out and grab the image file named logo.gif and insert it in the page right here where the `<img>` tag is?" Dutifully, the browser loads the image and displays it in the page.

For this simple example to work, bear in mind that your HTML file and your graphics file need to be sitting in the same directory on your computer, assuming you're just testing things at home. (When you put your page online, you have to send the image file to your web host and be sure it's in the same directory as your HTML file.) Many webmasters create a subdirectory just for images, which keeps things neat and tidy. If you plan on doing this, be sure you study my instructions for using directories and subdirectories in Chapter 5.

 Here's some HTML code that adds an image named me.jpg to a web page (look for the file named image.htm on the CD), and Figure 1.5 shows how things appear in a web browser:

```
<html>
<head>
<title>Welcome</title>
</head>
<body>
<img src="me.jpg" />
<h1>Welcome to my Website!</h1>
</body>
</html>
```

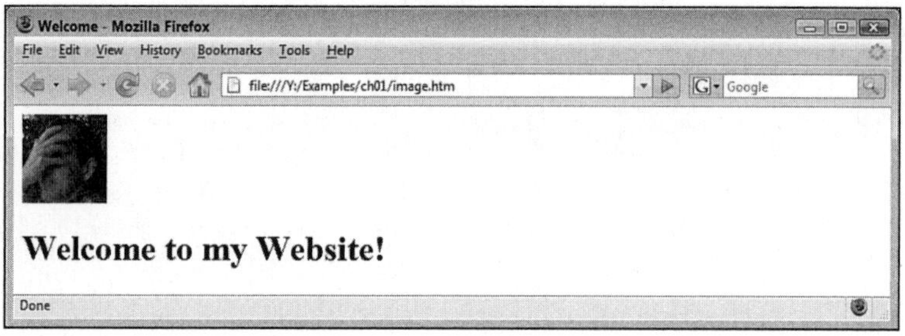

Figure 1.5

A web page with an image thrown in.

> **Welcome to my Website!**

Wrapping Text Around an Image

Most of the pages on your website will be a mixture of text and images, so you'll want to be sure your words and your pictures get along well with each other. For the most part, this means having your prose wrap itself nicely around each image so you don't end up with unsightly gaps. Do this by specifying an alignment option for the image, like so:

```
<img src="filename" align="alignment" />
```

Here, you replace *alignment* with the alignment you want:

♦ `left` aligns the image on the left side of the page, and the surrounding text wraps around the image on the right.

◆ `right` aligns the image on the right side of the page, and the surrounding text wraps around the image on the left.

Here's a bit of HTML code that demonstrates these two alignment options (see the file alignment.htm on the CD)—the first image (news.gif) is aligned on the left, while the second image (angst.gif) is aligned on the right:

```
<html>
<head>
<title>Teen Boy's Vocabulary Down to a Single Word</title>
</head>
<body>
<p>
<img src="news.gif" align="left" />
Area teen Dylan Geronimo now communicates with his parents and teachers
using just the word "whatever." With subtle voice inflections, Mr.
Geronimo can convey the full range of his emotions: sullenness,
disgust, exasperation, and a seething, nameless rage.
</p>
<p>
"It was frustrating, at first," said Betty Geronimo, Dylan's mother.
"It seemed like he was giving us the same answer to every question.
Then we learned the difference between 'whatever' and 'what-EVER'."
<img src="angst.gif" align="right" />
</p>
<p>
The phenomenon is called Adolescent Vocabulary Attrition Syndrome,
according to Hans Longwinded, a language chiropractor. "Speaking
is quite painful for most male teenagers, so they ease the pain by
shedding words."
</p>
<p>
When asked to comment on this story, Mr. Geronimo said, "WHAT-ever."
</p>
</body>
</html>
```

Figure 1.6 gives you a sneak peek of how all this looks in a web browser.

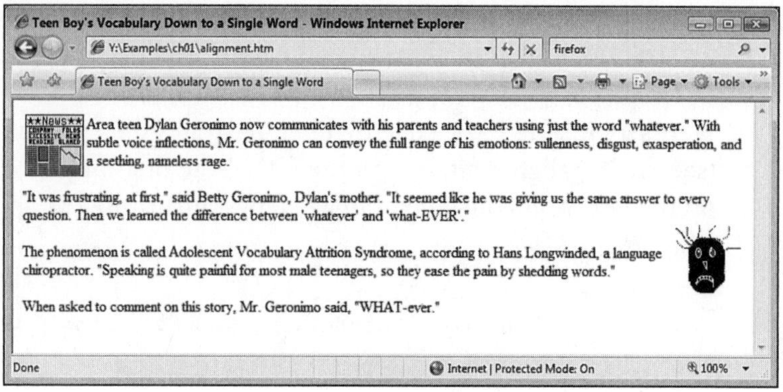

Figure 1.6

A web page with images aligned on the left and right.

Giving 'Em Something to Click: Adding Links

When all is said and done (actually, long before that), your website will consist of anywhere from 2 to 102 pages (or even more, if you've got lots to say). Here's the thing, though: if you manage to cajole someone onto your home page, how do you get that person to your other pages? That really is what the web is all about, isn't it, getting folks from one page to another? And of course, you already know the answer to the question. You get visitors from your home page to your other pages by creating links that take folks from here to there. In this section, you learn how to build your own links and how to finally put the "hypertext" into HTML.

The HTML tags that do the link thing are `<a>` and `</a>`. Here's how the `<a>` tag works:

```
<a href="address">
```

Here, HREF stands for *Hypertext Reference*, which is just a highfalutin way of saying "address." Your job is to replace *address* with the actual address of the web page you want to use for the link. And yes, you have to enclose the address in quotation marks. Here's an example:

```
<a href="http://www.mcfedries.com/creatingawebsite/">
```

You're not done yet, though, not by a long shot (insert groan of disappointment here). What are you missing? Right, you have to give the reader some descriptive link text to click. That's pretty straightforward because all you do is insert the text between the `<a>` and `</a>` tags, like this:

```
<a href="address">Link text goes here</a>
```

Need an example? You got it. See the file link.htm on the CD:

```
Check out this book's <a href="http://www.mcfedries.com/
creatingawebpage/">
➥ home page</a>!
```

➥ is this book's code continuation character, which means the current line is just a continuation of the previous line, so it isn't something you need to add to the code.

Figure 1.7 shows how it looks in a web browser. Notice how the browser highlights and underlines the link text, and when I point my mouse at the link, the address I specified appears in the browser's status bar.

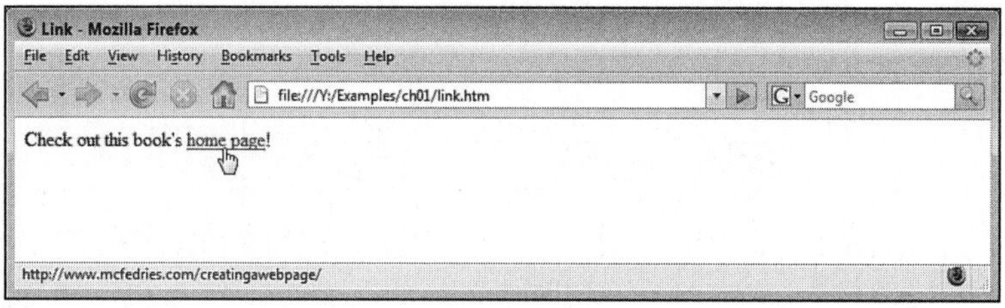

Figure 1.7

How the link appears in the web browser.

Fancy Font Formatting

Except for the odd heading or two, your web page text is embarrassingly plain. Not to worry, though, because the next few sections show you some techniques for sprucing up your text.

Some Basic Text Formatting Tags

The good news about text formatting is that you'll mostly deal with four basic kinds: **bold,** *italic,* underline, and monospace. The bad news is that HTML seemingly has about a billion different tags that produce these formats. However, I'll take mercy on you and only let you in on the easiest tags to use. Table 1.2 shows the tags that produce each of these formats.

Table 1.2   The Basic Text Formatting Tags

Text Format	Begin Tag	End Tag
Bold	<b> (or <strong>)	</b> (or </strong>)
Italic	<i> (or <em>)	</i> (or </em>)
<u>Underline</u>	<u>	</u>
`Monospace`	<tt>	</tt>

Here's a simple example that uses each tab (see texttags.htm on the CD); Figure 1.8 shows how the styles look when viewed with Internet Explorer:

```
Feel free to format your text as <b>bold</b> or <i>italic</i> or
<u>underlined</u> or <tt>monospace</tt>.
```

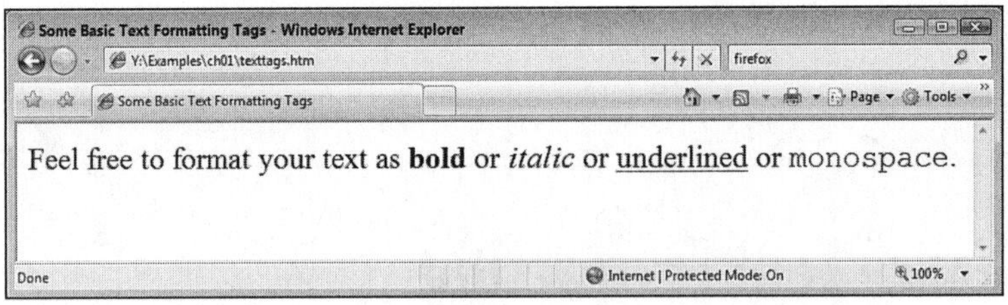

Figure 1.8

A web page showing the four basic text formatting styles.

Combining Text Formats

It's perfectly okay to combine these text formats. So for example, if you need bold italic text, you can get it by throwing the <b> and <i> tags together, like this:

```
<b><i>This'll give you, like, bold italic text</i></b>
```

To ensure everything looks the way you want it, be sure to add the closing tags in the reverse order of the opening tags.

Changing the Font Size

The *font size* is a measure of the relative height used for each character. Although HTML gives you several ways to specify these heights, it's probably best to stick with the traditional *points* measure, where 72 points equals 1 inch.

To set the size, you add the `style` attribute to a tag and include the `font-size` style, which you set to a number that ends with `pt`, like this:

```
<tag style="font-size: Xpt">
```

Here, replace `tag` with the HTML tag you're using, and replace *x* with the font size you want to use. For example, suppose you want all the text in a particular paragraph to display with a 16-point font. Here's how you'd set it up:

```
<p style="font-size: 16pt">
```

Here are a few more examples (see fontsize.htm on the CD); Figure 1.9 shows what the web browser makes of them:

```
<p>This is regular text.</p>
<p style="font-size: 16pt">This is 16-point text.</p>
<p style="font-size: 24pt">This is 24-point text.</p>
<p>
This example shows that you can apply the font size to <span
style="font-size: 20pt">just a few words.</span>
</p>
```

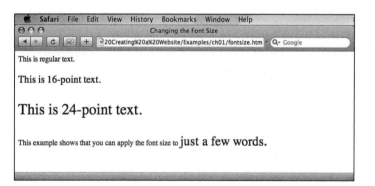

Figure 1.9

Putting the `font-size` style through its paces.

Notice in this example that I used the `<span>` tag. This is a special HTML tag that's handy for specifying chunks of text. The `<span>` tag doesn't do anything on its own. Instead, you almost always populate it with the `style` attribute. In other words, you use `<span>` to apply some style to a few words.

You can also apply a particular style to an entire page or to every page on your site. To learn how all this works, see Chapter 5, in particular the "Using Style Sheets to Design Your Site" section.

Changing the Font Family

The *font family* (or *typeface*) represents the overall look associated with each character. Unlike the other styles, there are no set values you can use. Instead, you usually specify several possibilities and the browser uses the first one that's installed on the user's computer. Here's an example:

```
<p style="font-family: Bookman, Garamond, 'Times New Roman'">
```

Page Pitfall

Bear in mind that the reader sees only a specified typeface if it's installed on his or her computer. If the typeface isn't installed, the reader sees only the browser's default typeface.

Notice that multiple-word family names must be enclosed in single quotation marks.

There are also five so-called *generic* family names you can use:

- ◆ `cursive` displays text in a cursive font (such as Comic Sans MS), which is a flowing style reminiscent of handwriting.

- ◆ `fantasy` displays text in a fantasy font (such as Broadway), which is a decorative style.

- ◆ `monospace` displays text in a monospace font (such as Courier New), which means that each character—from the wide *w* to the skinny *i*—is given the same amount of horizontal space. This is similar to the effect produced by the `<tt>` tag.

- ◆ `serif` displays text in a serif font (such as Times New Roman), which means that each character has extra cross strokes (called *feet* in the typographic biz).

- ◆ `sans-serif` displays text in a sans serif font (such as Arial), which means that each character doesn't have the extra cross strokes. (Although this is a two-word value, it doesn't require quotation marks because it's a built-in value.)

These names are most often used at the end of a list of font families as a catch-all value that renders the text the way you want if the user doesn't have any of the specific font families installed. For example, if you want to display sans-serif text, you might set up your style like this:

```
<span style="font-family: Verdana, Arial, Helvetica, sans-serif">
```

The following HTML file (it's fontfamily.htm on the CD) puts a few families to the test; Figure 1.10 shows how they look in Internet Explorer 7:

```
<html>
<head>
<title>Changing the Font Family</title>
</head>
<body>
<div style="font-size: 18pt">
<p style="font-family: 'Times New Roman'">The Times New Roman Font
Family</p>
<p style="font-family: Verdana">The Verdana Font Family</p>
<p style="font-family: 'Comic Sans MS'">The Comic Sans MS Font Family
</p>
<p style="font-family: Impact">The Impact Font Family</p>
<p style="font-family: 'Courier New'">The Courier New Font Family</p>
<hr>
<p style="font-family: cursive">The cursive Generic Font Family</p>
<p style="font-family: fantasy">The fantasy Generic Font Family</p>
<p style="font-family: monospace">The monospace Generic Font Family</p>
<p style="font-family: serif">The serif Generic Font Family</p>
<p style="font-family: sans-serif">The sans-serif Generic Font Family
</p>
</div>

</body>
</html>
```

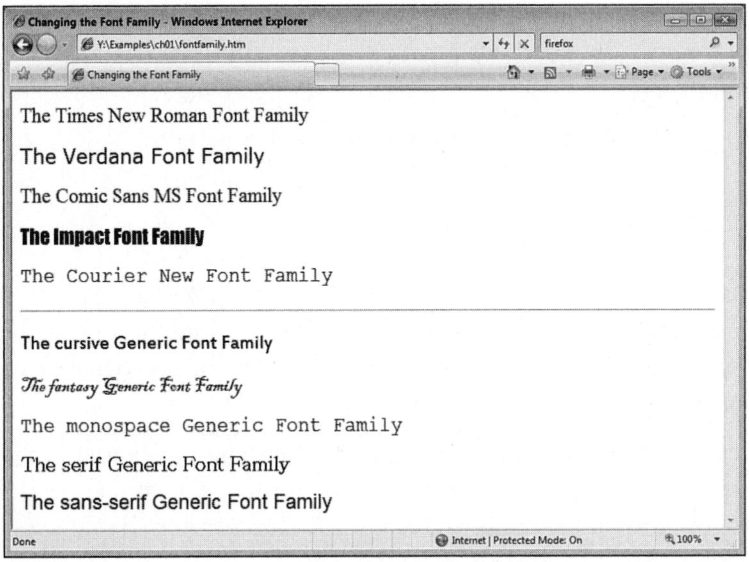

Figure 1.10

A few font families in Internet Explorer 7.

Did you notice the `<div>` tag I used in the preceding example?

```
<div style="font-size: 18pt">
```

The `<div>` tag is a lot like the `<span>` tag in that it specifies a chunk of text. The difference is that you usually use the `<span>` tag for just a few words, but you can use the `<div>` tag for any amount of text you want. Whatever style you specify within the `<div>` tag, that style is applied to all the text that lies between `<div>` and the `</div>` end tag. In the preceding example, all the text between `<div>` and `</div>` is formatted with an 18-point font size.

Coloring Your Web World

Okay, your text is looking pretty good, but there's still one major problem with your page: it's boring black text on a plain white background. Now, don't get me wrong: I'm a black-text-on-a-white-background guy from way back, because I think that color combination is by far the easiest to read, especially on the web. Still, a *little* color is always a good thing because it adds visual interest and tells the world that you're willing to let your hair down a little. So with your hair ready to let loose, the rest of this chapter shows you a few techniques and tricks for adding a splash of color to your page.

Working With Colors

The next sections show you how to change the colors of your text and the page background. You'll find that you often have to work with colors when constructing web pages, so it's probably a good idea to take a minute or two now and get the HTML color techniques down pat.

Most of the time, you specify a color by entering a six-digit code that takes the following form:

```
#rrggbb
```

This sure looks weird, but there's method in its mathematical madness. Here, `rr` is the red part of the color, `gg` is the green part, and `bb` is the blue part. In other words, each code represents a combination of the three primary colors, and it's this combination that produces the final color. These are called *RGB values*.

The truly nerdish aspect of all this is that each two-digit primary color code uses *hexadecimal* numbers. These are base 16 (instead of the usual base 10 in decimal numbers), so they run from 0 through 9, then A through F. Yeah, my head hurts, too. Table 1.3 lists the corresponding RGB values for some common colors.

Table 1.3   RGB Codes for Common Colors

If You Use This Value	You Get This Color
#000000	Black
#ffffff	White
#ff0000	Red
#00ff00	Green
#0000ff	Blue
#ff00ff	Magenta
#00ffff	Cyan
#ffff00	Yellow

Rather than working with these bizarre RGB values, you might prefer to use the standard HTML color names. These color names use nice English words such as "Blue" and "Tan" (as well as plenty of bizarre words such as "Bisque" and "Orchid"). A complete list of the color names, their corresponding RGB values, and a swatch that shows the color are available in the file colors.htm on the CD (note that in each case, the color names are case-sensitive; see Figure 1.11 for a black-and-white version of that document).

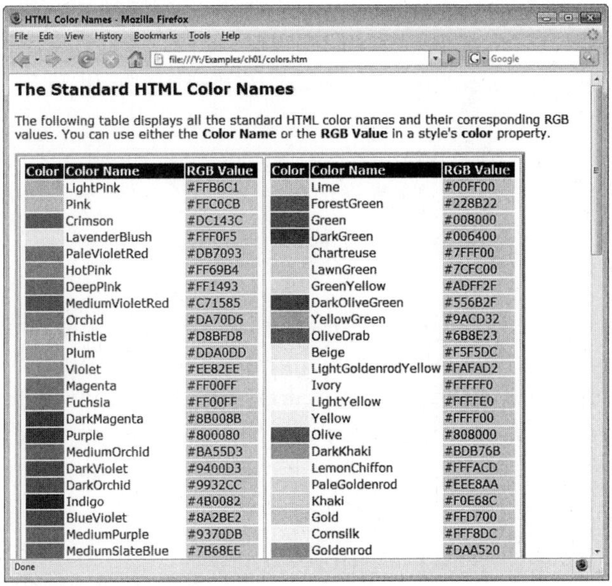

Figure 1.11

HTML colors, color names, and their RGB equivalents.

Coloring Your Page Text

Browsers display your text in basic black, which is readable but not all that exciting. To put some color in your text's cheeks, you can add the `color` style to a tag and set it to one of the color names or a six-digit RGB value.

For example, the following code changes the text between the `<span>` and `</span>` tags to red:

```
<span style="color: #ff0000">This text is
red</span>
```

Here's another example that adds the `color` style to the `<body>` tag, which changes the color for all the body text:

```
<body style="color: ForestGreen">
```

Coloring the Page Background

Depending on the browser you use, web page text and graphics often float in a sea of dull, drab gray, or plain white. It's about as exciting as a yawning festival. To give things a little pep, you can change the background color your page appears on to whatever suits your style. You can apply a background color or image to sections of your page, or even to individual words.

To set a background color, use either a color name or an RGB value:

```
<body style="background-color: blue">
<p style="background-color: #0000ff">
```

The Least You Need to Know

♦ You can create perfectly good web pages and blogs using a lowly text editor such as Notepad (Windows) or TextEdit (Mac). If you prefer to use WordPad, Word, Microsoft Works, or some other word processor, don't use the program's formatting commands, and be sure to save the file as a text file.

♦ When naming your files, use the .htm or .html extension, use only lowercase letters, and avoid spaces like the plague.

♦ Always start your page with the `<html>`, `<head>`, `<title>`, `</title>`, `</head>`, `<body>`, `</body>`, and `</html>` tags.

- ◆ Use the `<b>` tag for bold text, `<i>` for italics, `<u>` for underlining, and `<tt>` for monospace.

- ◆ To add an image to your web page, include the `<img src="`*`filename`*`" />` tag, where *`filename`* is the name of the graphics file.

- ◆ Here's the basic structure of an HTML link:

  `<a href="`*`address`*`">`*`Link text`*`</a>`.

Designing Your Site with Tables

In This Chapter

♦ What are tables, and why are they useful?

♦ Creating simple tables and ever-so-slightly advanced tables

♦ Using tables to create a page with a margin, a page with a header and footer, and a three-column page

♦ Tons of table tips and techniques

If you trudged through the examples in Chapter 1, you may have noticed something peculiar about cobbling together a web page: you don't have much control over where things go! Sure, you can align text and images, but that's boring, not to mention limiting. For the most part, when you add text and the tags from Chapter 1, your content just tumbles down the page, one thing after another.

The good news is that it's possible to add just about any structure you want to your pages. The secret to taking your pages to this higher level is a single HTML tag that creates a *table*. A table adds structure to your page by dividing it into different rectangular sections, into which you can plop whatever content you need. Suddenly, you have the power to lay out your pages exactly the way you want!

Tables are one of the most powerful tools for creating a great site design, and you learn all about them in this chapter. You also learn how to use tables to create three very useful and very common page structures.

Web Woodworking: How to Build a Table

Despite the name, HTML tables aren't really analogous to the big wooden thing you eat on every night. Instead, a table is a rectangular arrangement of rows and columns on your page. Figure 2.1 shows an example table.

Figure 2.1

An honest-to-goodness HTML table.

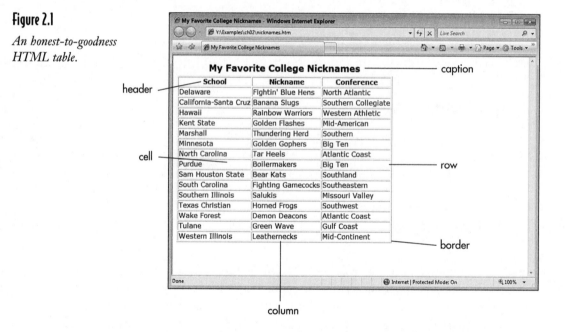

To be sure you understand what's going on (that *is* my job, after all), let's check out a bit of table lingo:

◆ A *row* is a single "line" of data that runs across the table. The table shown in Figure 2.1 contains 16 rows.

◆ A *column* is a single vertical section of data. The table in Figure 2.1 has three columns.

◆ A *cell* is the intersection of a row and column. The cells are where you enter the data that appears in the table.

- A *caption* is the text that appears (usually) above the table and is used to describe the contents of the table.

- *Headers* are the first row of the table. The headers are optional, but many people use them to label each column.

- *Borders* are the lines that surround the table and each cell.

Nothing too rocket science-y there, but also so far nothing too earth-shattering. What advantages do tables bring to the, uh, table? Here are a few:

- Each table cell is self-contained. You can edit and format the contents of a cell without disturbing the arrangement of the other table elements.

- The text "wraps" inside each cell, making it a snap to create multiple-line entries.

- Tables can include not only text, but images and links as well—even other tables!

- Most text tags such as `<b>`, `<i>`, `<h1>`, and so on are fair game inside a table, so you can format the table to suit your needs (with some cautions, as you'll see a bit later).

Okay, it's time to put the table pedal to the HTML metal and start cranking out some tables. The next few sections take you through the basic steps. As an example, I show you how I created the table in Figure 2.1.

Starting Easy: Building a One-Row Table

Tables always use the following basic container:

```
<table>
</table>
```

All the other table tags fit between these two tags. You need to know two things about the `<table>` tag. If you want your table to show a border, one way is to use the `<table border="n">` tag, where *n* is a number (measured in pixels) that specifies the border width. I used 1 (the smallest border) for the table in Figure 2.1. You can use any number you feel like, although in practice, you wouldn't use a border larger than about 5 pixels. If you don't want a border, use just `<table>`.

Webmaster Wisdom

I can't tell you how many table troubles I've solved just by turning on the border to get a good look at the table structure. I highly recommend using a border while constructing your table. You can always get rid of it after you're done.

After completing the previous steps, most of your remaining table chores involve the following four-step process:

1. Add a row.

2. Divide the row into the number of columns you want.

3. Insert data into each cell.

4. Repeat steps 1 through 3 until done.

To add a row, you toss a `<tr>` (table row) tag and a `</tr>` tag (its corresponding end tag) between `<table>` and `</table>`:

```
<table border="1">
<tr>
</tr>
</table>
```

Now divide that row into columns by placing the `<td>` (table data) and `</td>` tags between `<tr>` and `</tr>`. Each `<td></td>` combination represents one column (or more specifically, an individual cell in the row), so if you want a three-column table (with a border), do this:

```
<table border="1">
<tr>
<td></td>
<td></td>
<td></td>
</tr>
</table>
```

Now you enter the row's cell data by typing text between each `<td>` tag and its `</td>` end tag:

```
<table border="1">
<tr>
<td>California-Santa Cruz</td>
<td>Banana Slugs</td>
<td>Southern Collegiate</td>
</tr>
</table>
```

Remember that you can put any of the following within the `<td>` and `</td>` tags:

◆ Text

◆ HTML text-formatting tags (such as `<b>` and `<i>`)

◆ Links

◆ Lists

◆ Images

Tacking On More Rows

When your first row is firmly in place, all you have to do is repeat the procedure for the other rows in the table. For our example table, here's the HTML that includes the data for all the rows:

```
<table border="1">
<tr>
<td>California-Santa Cruz</td><td>Banana Slugs</td><td>Southern
Collegiate</td>
</tr>
<tr>
<td>Delaware</td><td>Fightin' Blue Hens</td><td>North Atlantic</td>
</tr>
<tr>
<td>Hawaii</td><td>Rainbow Warriors</td><td>Western Athletic</td>
</tr>
<tr>
<td>Kent State</td><td>Golden Flashes</td><td>Mid-American</td>
</tr>
<tr>
<td>Marshall</td><td>Thundering Herd</td><td>Southern</td>
</tr>
<tr>
<td>Minnesota</td><td>Golden Gophers</td><td>Big Ten</td>
</tr>
<tr>
<td>North Carolina</td><td>Tar Heels</td><td>Atlantic Coast</td>
</tr>
<tr>
<td>Purdue</td><td>Boilermakers</td><td>Big Ten</td>
</tr>
```

```
<tr>
<td>Sam Houston State</td><td>Bear Kats</td><td>Southland</td>
</tr>
<tr>
<td>South Carolina</td><td>Fighting Gamecocks</td><td>Southeastern</td>
</tr>
<tr>
<td>Southern Illinois</td><td>Salukis</td><td>Missouri Valley</td>
</tr>
<tr>
<td>Texas Christian</td><td>Horned Frogs</td><td>Southwest</td>
</tr>
<tr>
<td>Tulane</td><td>Green Wave</td><td>Gulf Coast</td>
</tr>
<tr>
<td>Wake Forest</td><td>Demon Deacons</td><td>Atlantic Coast</td>
</tr>
<tr>
<td>Western Illinois</td><td>Leathernecks</td><td>Mid-Continent</td>
</tr>
</table>
```

Adding a Row of Headers

If your table displays stats, data, or other info, you can make your readers' lives easier by including labels at the top of each column that define what's in the column. (You don't need a long-winded explanation; in most cases, a word or two should do the job.) To define a header, use the `<th>` and `</th>` tags within a row, like this:

```
<tr>
<th>First Column Header</th>
<th>Second Column Header</th>
<th>And So On, Ad Nauseum</th>
</tr>
```

As you can see, the `<th>` tag is a lot like the `<td>` tag. The difference is that the browser displays text that appears between the `<th>` and `</th>` tags as bold and centered within the cell. This helps the reader differentiate the header from the rest of the table data. Remember, though, that headers are optional; you can bypass them if your table doesn't need them.

Here's how I added the headers for the example you saw at the beginning of the chapter:

```
<table border="1">
<tr>
<th>School</th><th>Nickname</th><th>Conference</th>
</tr>
[The rest of the table code goes here]
</table>
```

Tossing In a Caption

The last basic table element is the caption. A caption is a short description (a sentence or two) that tells the reader the purpose of the table. You define the caption with the `<caption>` tag:

```
<caption align="where">Caption text goes here.</caption>
```

Here, *where* is either `top` or `bottom`; if you use `top`, the caption appears above the table; if you use `bottom`, the caption appears—you guessed it—below the table. Here's the `<caption>` tag from the example (for the complete document, look for nicknames.htm on the CD):

```
<table border ="1">
<caption align="top" style="font-size: 16pt">
<b>My Favorite College Nicknames</b>
</caption>
[The rest of the table code goes here]
</table>
```

Using Border Styles

Shoehorning the `border` attribute inside the `<table>` tag tells the browser to display a border around the table and around each cell. That's fine, but if you want more control over the look of the border, you need to use the various border styles, which come in three flavors: width, style, and color.

The border width is controlled by the following five properties:

◆ `border-top-width` specifies the width of the top border.

◆ `border-right-width` specifies the width of the right border.

- `border-bottom-width` specifies the width of the bottom border.

- `border-left-width` specifies the width of the left border.

- `border-width` specifies the width of all the borders, in this order: `border-top-width`, `border-right-width`, `border-bottom-width`, and `border-left-width`. Separate each property with a space—for example, `border width: 5px 10px 10px 5px`—or use a single value for all four sides—for example, `border width: 15px`.

To set the width, use either an absolute value such as `5px` for a border that's 5 pixels wide, or `thin`, `medium`, or `thick`.

The border style has five similar properties:

- `border-top-style` specifies the top border's style.

- `border-right-style` specifies the right border's style.

Page Pitfall

For borders to work properly, be sure you set at least the border style.

- `border-bottom-style` specifies the style of the bottom border.

- `border-left-style` specifies the style of the left border.

- `border-style` specifies the style of all the borders, in this order: `border-top-style`, `border-right-style`, `border-bottom-style`, and `border-left-style`. Separate each property with a space, or use a single value for all four sides.

Table 2.1 outlines the various values you can use for each border style property.

Table 2.1   Values for the Various Border Style Properties

Enter ...	To Get a Border That Uses ...
double	A double line
groove	A V-shape line that appears to be etched into the page
inset	A line that appears to be sunken into the page
none	No line (that is, no border is displayed)
outset	A line that appears to be raised from the page
ridge	A V-shape line that appears to be coming out of the page
solid	A solid line

For the border color, you can probably guess which five properties you can use:

- `border-top-color` specifies the color of the top border.

- `border-right-color` specifies the color of the right border.

- `border-bottom-color` specifies the color of the bottom border.

- `border-left-color` specifies the color of the left border.

- `border-color` specifies the color of all the borders, in this order: `border-top-color`, `border-right-color`, `border-bottom-color`, and `border-left-color`. Separate each property with a space, or use a single value for all four sides.

You can set each border color property to one of the usual color values (see Chapter 1).

The following page (it's borders.htm on the CD) demonstrates some of the border-width and border-style values. (See Chapter 5 to learn about the `<style>` tag.) Figure 2.2 shows how they look in the browser.

```
<html>
<head>
<title>Better Borders: Using Border Styles</title>

<style type="text/css">
<!--
table {margin-bottom: 10px}
-->
</style>
</head>
<body>

<table style="border-width: thin; border-style: solid">
<tr><td>
This table uses a thin border with a solid style.
</td></tr>
</table>

<table style="border-width: medium; border-style: groove">
<tr><td>
This table uses a medium border with a groove style.
</td></tr>
</table>

<table style="border-width: thick; border-style: outset">
<tr><td>
```

```
This table uses a thick border with an outset style.
</td></tr>
</table>

<table style="border-width: 1cm; border-style: inset">
<tr><td>
This table uses a 1-centimeter border with an inset style.
</td></tr>
</table>

<table style="border-width: 10px; border-style: ridge">
<tr><td>
This table uses a 10-pixel border with a ridge style.
</td></tr>
</table>

</body>
</html>
```

Figure 2.2

Firefox trying some border styles on for size.

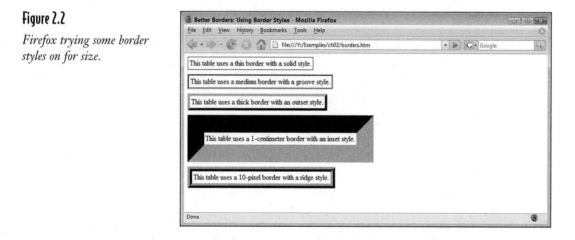

Webmaster Wisdom

If you want to format all the borders at once, use this shorthand notation:

```
{border: border-width border-style border-color}
```

Here, replace *border-width*, *border-style*, and *border-color* with values for each of those properties, as in this example:

```
{border: thin solid Gray}
```

Aligning Text Inside Cells

The standard-issue alignment for table cells is left-aligned for data (`<td>`) cells and centered for header (`<th>`) cells. Not good enough? No sweat. Just plop the `style` attribute and `text-align` property inside the `<td>` or `<th>` tag, and you can specify the text to be left-aligned, centered, right-aligned, or justified. Here's how it works:

```
<td style="text-align: alignment">
<th style="text-align: alignment">
```

In both cases, `alignment` can be `left`, `center`, `right`, or `justify`. Here's an example (look for table-align1.htm on the CD):

```
<html>
<head>
<title>Aligning Text Inside the Cells - Horizontal</title>
</head>
<body>

<table border="1">
<tr>
<th width="150">
Left-aligned text
</th>
<th width="150">
Centered text
</th>
<th width="150">
Right-aligned text
</th>
<th width="150">
Justified text
</th>
</tr>
<tr>
<td style="text-align: left; width: 25%">
Puns are little plays on words that a certain breed of person loves to
spring on you and then look at you in a certain
</td>
<td style="text-align: center; width: 25%">
self-satisfied way to indicate that he thinks that you must think that
he is by far the cleverest person on Earth now
</td>
```

```
<td style="text-align: right; width: 25%">
that Benjamin Franklin is dead, when in fact what you are thinking is
that if this person ever ends up in a lifeboat,
</td>
<td style="text-align: justify; width: 25%">
the other passengers will hurl him overboard by the end of the first
day
even if they have plenty of food and water. &mdash;Dave Barry
</td>
</tr>
</table>

</body>
</html>
```

Figure 2.3 shows what happens in the browser.

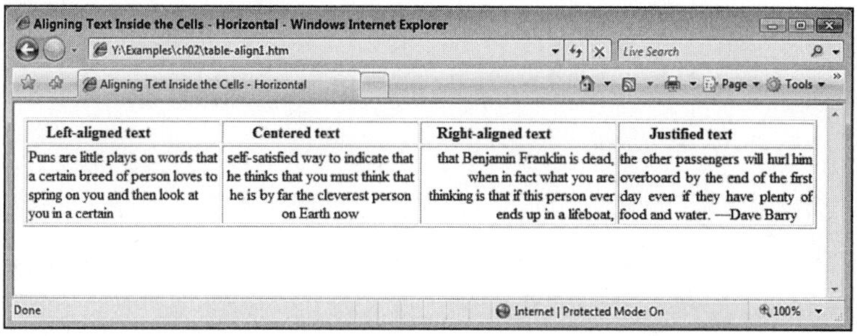

Figure 2.3

Some text niftily aligned within the table cells.

That's not bad, but there's even more alignment fun to be had. You can also align your text vertically within a cell. This comes in handy if one cell is quite large (because it contains either a truckload of text or a relatively large image), and you'd like to adjust the vertical position of the other cells in the same row. In this case, you add the `vertical-align` property to the `style` attribute inside `<td>` or `<th>`:

```
<td style="vertical-align: vertical">
<th style="vertical-align: vertical">
```

Here, *vertical* can be `top`, `middle`, `bottom`, or `baseline`. Here's an example (table-align2.htm on the CD) that demonstrates each of these alignment options:

```
<html>
<head>
<title>Aligning Text Inside the Cells - Vertical</title>
```

```
</head>
<body>

<table border="1">
<tr>
<td><img src="i.gif" />Unaligned</td>
</tr>
<tr>
<td><img src="i.gif" style="vertical-align: top" />top</td>
</tr>
<tr>
<td><img src="i.gif" style="vertical-align: bottom" />bottom</td>
</tr>
<tr>
<td><img src="i.gif" style="vertical-align: baseline" />baseline</td>
</tr>
<tr>
<td><img src="i.gif" style="vertical-align: middle" />middle</td>
</tr>
</table>

</body>
</html>
```

Figure 2.4 shows how the table looks in the browser.

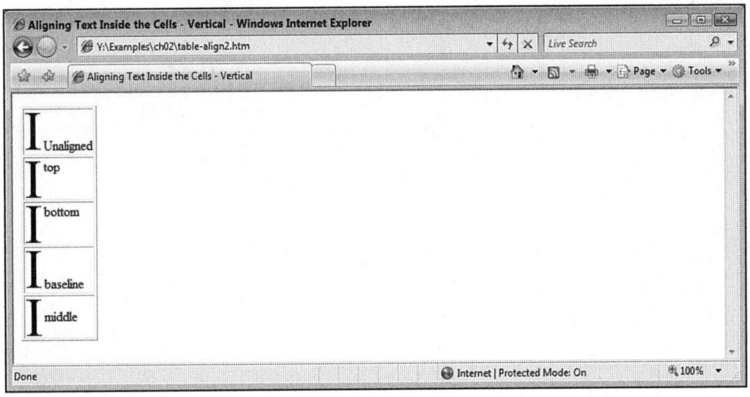

Figure 2.4

Text aligned vertically within the table cells.

Spanning Text Across Rows or Columns

The data we've entered into our table cells so far has been decidedly monogamous. That is, each hunk of data has shacked up with only one cell. But it's possible (and perfectly legal) for data to be bigamous (take up two cells) or even polygamous (take up three or more cells). Such cells are said to *span* multiple rows or columns, which can come in quite handy for headers and graphics.

Let's start with spanning multiple columns. To do this, you need to interpose the `colspan` (column span) attribute into the `<td>` or `<th>` tag:

```
<td colspan="cols">
<th colspan="cols">
```

 In this case, `cols` is the number of columns you want the cell to span. Here's a simple example (span1.htm on the CD) that shows a cell spanning two columns:

```
<html>
<head>
<title>Spanning Text Across Multiple Columns</title>
</head>
<body>
<table border="1">
<caption><b>The Spanning Thing &mdash; Example #1 (colspan)</b>
</caption>

<tr>
<td colspan="2">This item spans two columns</td>
<td>This one doesn't</td>
</tr>

<tr>
<td>The 1st Column</td>
<td>The 2nd Column</td>
<td>The 3rd Column</td>
</tr>

</table>
</body>
</html>
```

Figure 2.5 shows how the table looks in Internet Explorer.

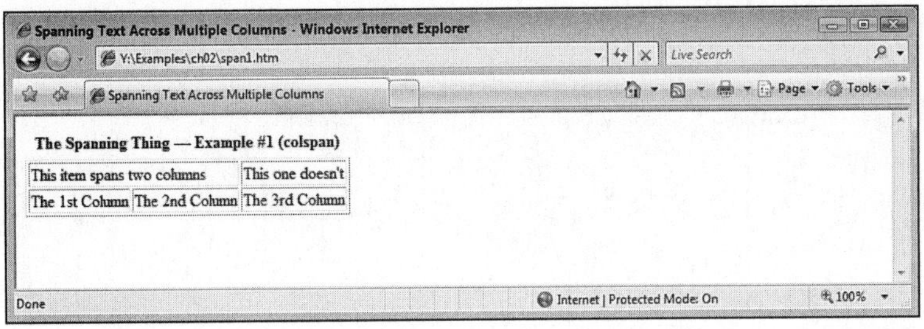

Figure 2.5

Use the `colspan` *attribute to configure a cell to miraculously span two or more columns.*

Spanning multiple rows is similar, except you substitute `rowspan` for `colspan` in `<td>` or `<th>`:

```
<td rowspan="rows">
<th rowspan="rows">
```

The *rows* value is the number of rows you want the cell to span. Here's an example (span2.htm on the CD) that shows a cell spanning two rows:

```
<html>
<head>
<title>Spanning Text Across Multiple Rows</title>
</head>
<body>
<table border="1">
<caption><b>The Spanning Thing &mdash; Example #2 (rowspan)</b>
</caption>

<tr>
<td rowspan="2">This here item spans two whole rows</td>
<td>The 1st row</td>
</tr>

<tr>
<td>The 2nd row</td>
</tr>

<tr>
<td>This one doesn't</td>
<td>The 3rd row</td>
</tr>

</table>
</body>
</html>
```

Figure 2.6 shows the result.

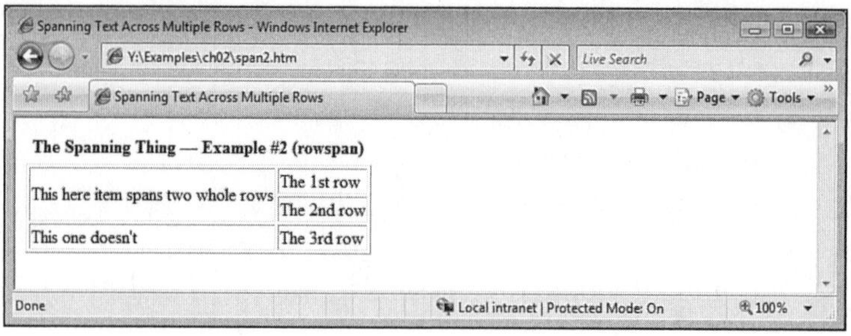

Figure 2.6

Use the `rowspan` *attribute to talk a cell into spanning two or more rows.*

More Table Tidbits

Okay, you're almost ready to start using tables to create interesting and useful site designs and layouts. Before we get to that, you need to know a few other table tricks:

Changing the background color. You learned in Chapter 1 that you can adjust the background color of your entire web page. However, you can also assign a custom color to just the background of a table or even an individual cell. To do this, you modify the `<table>` tag, the `<tr>` tag, the `<th>` tag, or the `<td>` tag to add the `style` attribute and its `background-color` property, which you set to either a color name or to one of those strange RGB values. For example, the following tag gives your table a light gray background:

```
<table style="background-color: #cccccc">
```

A background image. Another thing you can do is set a background image instead of just a background color for a table or cell. This is just like setting a background image for a web page. In this case, you toss the `background` attribute inside the `<table>` or `<td>` tag and set the attribute equal to the name of the image file you want to use, as in this example:

```
<table background="tablebg.gif">
```

The width of the table. The browser usually does a pretty good job of adjusting the width of a table to accommodate the current window size. If you need your table to be a particular width, however, customize the `<table>` tag with the `style` attribute and its `width` property. You can either specify a value in pixels or, more likely, a percentage of the available window width. For example, to be sure your table always usurps 75 percent of the window width, you use this version of the `<table>` tag:

```
<table style="width: 75%">
```

The width of a cell. You can also specify the width of an individual cell by adding the `width` property to a `<td>` or `<th>` tag. Again, you can either specify a value in pixels or a percentage of the entire table. (Note that all the cells in the column will adopt the same width.) In this example, the cell takes up 50 percent of the table's width:

```
<td style="width: 50%">
```

The amount of space between cells. By default, browsers allow just 2 pixels of space between each cell (vertically and horizontally). To bump that up, use the `style` attribute and the `border-spacing` property on the `<table>` tag. Here's an example that increases the cell spacing to 10 pixels:

```
<table style="border-spacing: 10px">
```

The amount of space between a cell's contents and its border. Browsers like to cram data into a cell as tightly as possible. To that end, they leave a mere 1 pixel of space between the contents of the cell and the cell border. (This space is called the *cell padding*.) To give your table data more room to breathe, use the `style` attribute and the `padding` property on the `<td>` tag. For example, the following line tells the browser to reserve a full 10 pixels of padding above, below, left, and right of the content in the cell:

```
<td style="padding: 10px">
```

> ### Webmaster Wisdom
>
> You can also use the `height` property to set the overall height of the table, although this is rarely done. The most common use is to set `height` to 100% so the table always spans the height of the browser window:
>
> ```
> <table style="height:
> 100%">
> ```

> ### Webmaster Wisdom
>
> The `border-spacing` property doesn't work in Internet Explorer, unfortunately. To handle Internet Explorer visitors, use the old `cellspacing` attribute:
>
> ```
> <table cellspacing="10">
> ```

Designing With Tables: The Big Table Picture

Now that you're something of an expert on HTML tables, let's put them to work enhancing your site design. Up to now, you've seen tables that were used as smaller pieces of the overall page puzzle. In other words, this type of table is really a third type of content you can add to your page (text and images being the other two).

However, in the spirit of "go big or go home," it's time to break away from these humble little tables and start thinking on a larger scale. Specifically, I want you to start thinking about using one giant table to hold *all* your page content. That sounds crazy,

I know, but remember that you can put *anything* in a table cell, and you can put *any* amount of content in a table cell. So by adjusting the layout of this giant table, you automatically add structure to your page, which enables you to create separate sections, columns, headers—you name it.

This may seem a bit fuzzy right now, but not to worry. The next three sections show you how to use these giant tables to create various useful site designs.

Creating a Site with a Margin

Many websites set up their pages with a "margin" down the left side. This margin can be an image or, more likely, a color that's different from the page background color. These margins can be either purely decorative, or they can contain links and other info. It's easy to create such a margin by using a table that has the following characteristics:

- The table's height and width are set to 100 percent using the <table> tag's height and width properties. This ensures that the table takes up the entire page.

- The table is populated with a single row and two columns.

- The first column is set up as the margin. In most cases, you use the background-color property to define the color you want to differentiate the margin from the rest of the page. Also, set the width property equal to the width of the margin you want.

- The second column is where you put all your regular web page text and graphics.

Here's the basic layout for the web page (see margin1.htm on the CD):

```
<html>
<head>
<title>
Designing with Tables 101: Creating a Site with a Margin - Skeleton
</title>
</head>
<body style="margin: 0px; padding: 0px">

<table style="height: 100%;
            width: 100%;
            border-spacing: 0px"
```

```
                cellspacing="0">
<tr>

<td style="background-color: Orange; width: 200px; vertical-align:
top">
All the text, links, and images that you want to appear in the margin
go here.
</td>

<td style="vertical-align: top">
All the rest of your web page stuff goes over here.
</td>

</tr>
</table>

</body>
</html>
```

A few of the things you should zero in on when studying this code:

Notice how the <body> tag includes a style attribute that sets both the margin and padding properties to 0 pixels. This ensures that you don't end up with any extra space around the main table.

In the <table> tag, note that I added border-spacing: 0px and cellspacing="0". This gets rids of the table borders, which makes everything fit together neatly.

In the first <td> tag, I set the background-color to Orange to set off the margin from the rest of the page (which uses the default white background).

Also in the first <td> tag, I set the width to 200 pixels, which is a decent size for the margin. Most people surf with screens that are set to either 800 pixels wide or 1,024 pixels wide (assuming their browser windows are maximized), so that still leaves plenty of room to display the rest of your content.

In both <td> tags, I added the vertical-align property and set it to top. By default, the browser displays the content in the middle of the column (vertically speaking), which would look dumb. By setting vertical-align to top, you ensure that the content within each column appears at the top, as it sensibly should.

Figure 2.7 shows the page in the browser. As you can see, the left side of the page displays a margin that was created by the left column of the table.

Figure 2.7

Margin call: this page features a margin down the side.

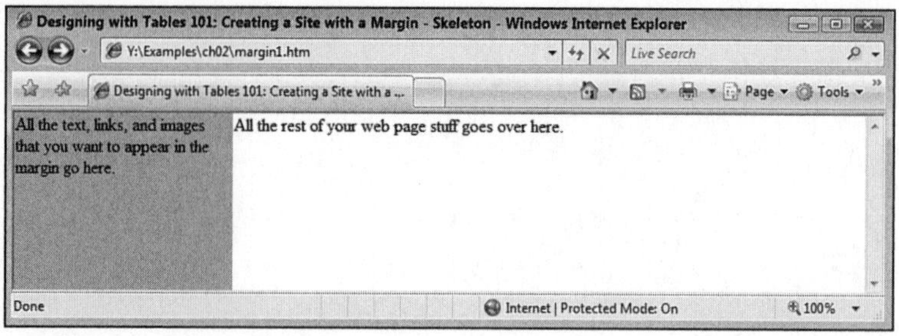

The page shown in Figure 2.7 gives you a rather skeletal look at a page with a margin. However, you'll use the margin to insert text, links, images, and other stuff. Here's some sample code that does this (see margin2.htm on the CD):

```
<html>
<head>
<title>
Designing with Tables 101: Creating a Site with a Margin - Example
</title>
</head>
<body style="font-family: Verdana, Tahoma, Arial, sans-serif">

<table style="height: 100%; width: 100%">
<tr>

<!--The left column creates the margin -->
<td style="width: 200px;
          vertical-align: top;
          padding: 5px;
          border-right-style: solid;
          border-right-color: DarkOrange;
          border-right-width: medium">
<span style="font-size: 16pt">
<p>
<b>The Complete Idiot's Guide to Creating a Website</b>
</p>
</span>
<span style="font-size: 12pt">
<p>
For your surfing pleasure, here are some links to the examples files
from Chapter 2:
</p>
```

```
<p>
<a href="borders.htm">borders.htm</a><br />
<a href="margin1.htm">margin1.htm</a><br />
<a href="margin2.htm">margin2.htm</a><br />
<a href="nicknames.htm">nicknames.htm</a><br />
<a href="span1.htm">span1.htm</a><br />
<a href="span2.htm">span2.htm</a><br />
<a href="table-align1.htm">table-align1.htm</a><br />
<a href="table-align2.htm">table-align2.htm</a><br />
</p>
</span>
</td>

<!-- The right column creates the rest of the page -->
<td style="vertical-align: top; padding: 10px">
<span style="font-size: 20pt">
<p>
<b>Chapter 2&mdash;Designing Your Site with Tables</b>
</p>
</span>
<span style="font-size: 12pt">
<p>
```

If you trudged through the examples in Chapter 1, "Building Blocks: Learning the Basic Tags," you may have noticed something peculiar about cobbling together a web page: You don't have much control over where things go! Yes, the tall-forehead types who invented HTML threw you a bone or two by enabling you to align text and images, but that's hardly much better than those fake wheels little kids use to "steer" the car while driving with mom or dad. For the most part, when you add text and the tags from Chapter 1, your content just tumbles down the page, one thing after another. You can't put things side-by-side; you can't put things in columns like a newspaper; you can't divide your page into separate areas for different types of content.

```
</p>
<p>
```

Why can't you do any of this? The short answer is that your page lacks the underlying structure to do these things. That's the bad news. The good news is all is not lost because it's possible to add just about any structure you want to your pages. The secret to taking your pages to this higher level is a single HTML tag that creates what's known in the website game as a table. When built a certain way using the HTML equivalents of a hammer and saw, a table adds structure to a page by

```
dividing the page into different rectangular sections, and you can plop
whatever content you need into each section. Suddenly, you have the
power to lay out your pages exactly the way you want. Tables are one of
the most powerful tools for creating a great site design, and you learn
all about them in this chapter. You also learn how to use tables to
create three very useful and very common page structures.
</p>
</span>

</td>

</tr>
</table>

</body>
</html>
```

Some notes to mull over for this design:

The first `<td>` tag creates a slightly different kind of margin. Instead of setting the column's background color, the tag uses the `border-right-style`, `border-right-color`, and `border-right-width` properties to add a vertical line along the right side of the column.

You generally don't want your text rubbing up against the sides of the columns because it makes the text harder to read. To avoid this, I added the `padding` property to both `<td>` tags and set it to 5 pixels for the margin column and 10 pixels for the second column. Figure 2.8 shows the results.

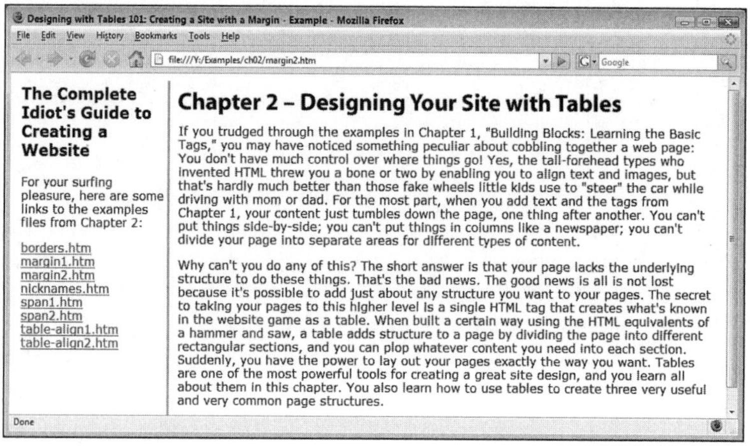

Figure 2.8

Another margin style, this time with some text and links added.

Creating a Site with a Header and Footer

The margin design in the previous section is one of the most commonly used site designs on the web these days. However, it's not the only design out there, which is good news if a margin isn't exactly what you're looking for. Another common design is one that implements a *header* and a *footer*.

def•i•ni•tion

A **header** is an area at the top of each page that you use for stuff like your site's title and icon, links to the main areas of your site, and perhaps some ads (see Chapter 15). A **footer** is an area at the bottom of each page that you use for things like your copyright notice, contact information, and less important links that you want to appear on each page.

This is a bit more complex than the margin page, but not by much. Once again, you configure a table. Set the table's height and width to 100 percent using the `<table>` tag's `height` and `width` properties. This ensures that the table takes up the entire page.

The table is populated with a single column and three rows. The first row is the header. You can use the `background-color` property to define the color you want to use to differentiate the header from the main part of the page. Also, set the `height` property equal to the height of the header you want.

The second row is where you place your main page content.

The third row is the footer. Again, you can use the `background-color` property to define the footer background, and the `height` property to define the height of the footer you want.

Here's the basic layout for the web page (see header-footer1.htm on the CD):

```
<html>
<head>
<title>
Designing with Tables 201: Creating a Site with a Header and Footer -
Skeleton
</title>
</head>
```

```
<body style="margin: 0px; padding: 0px">

<table style="height: 100%;
              width: 100%;
              border-spacing: 0px"
              cellspacing="0">
<tr>
<td style="background-color: Tomato;
           height: 100px;
           text-align: center;
           vertical-align: top">
Put your header text, images, and links here.
</td>
</tr>

<tr>
<td style="vertical-align: top">
Put your main page content here.
</td>
</tr>

<tr>
<td style="background-color: PeachPuff;
           height: 50px;
           vertical-align: top">
Put your footer text, images, and links here.
</td>
</tr>

</table>

</body>
</html>
```

Here are some sights to see as you traverse this code:

Once again, the `<body>` tag includes a `style` attribute that sets both the `margin` and `padding` properties to 0 pixels.

As before, in the `<table>` tag I added `border-spacing: 0px` and `cellspacing="0"` to get rid of the table borders.

In the first row's `<td>` tag, I set the `background-color` to `Tomato` to set off the header from the main content section (which uses the default white background).

In the first row's `<td>` tag, I set the `height` to 100 pixels. Adjust as necessary to fit your header content.

In the third row's `<td>` tag, I set the `height` to 50 pixels, which you can tweak as needed, depending on your footer content.

In all three `<td>` tags, I added the `vertical-align` property and set it to `top`.

Figure 2.9 shows the page in a browser.

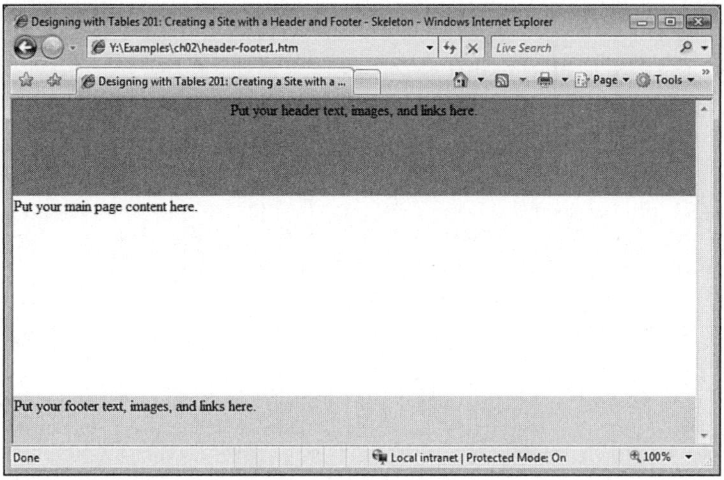

Figure 2.9

A basic web page with a header and footer.

Want an example that's more real-worldish? You got it (see header-footer2.htm on the CD):

```
<html>
<head>
<title>
Designing with Tables 201: Creating a Site with a Header and Footer -
Skeleton
</title>
</head>
<body style="background-color: Black;
             font-family: Verdana, Tahoma, Arial, sans-serif;
             margin-left: 150px;
             margin-right: 150px;
             margin-top: 0px;
             margin-bottom: 0px">
```

```
<table style="height: 100%;
              width: 100%;
              border-spacing: 0px;
              background-color: White"
              cellspacing="0">

<tr>
<td style="height: 100px;
           vertical-align: top;
           border-bottom-style: ridge;
           border-bottom-color: DarkGray;
           border-bottom-width: medium">
<img src="news.jpg" align="left">
<span style="font-size: 24pt"><b>News of the Word</b></span><br>
<span style="font-size: 16pt"><i>All the news that's fit to make up!
</i></span><br>
<span style="font-size: 10pt; margin-top: 5px">
<a href="header-footer2.htm">Archives</a> &bull;
<a href="header-footer2.htm">Blog</a> &bull;
<a href="header-footer2.htm">Forums</a> &bull;
<a href="header-footer2.htm">Give Us Money</a> &bull;
<a href="header-footer2.htm">No, Really, Give Us Money</a>
</span>

</td>
</tr>

<tr>
<td style="vertical-align: top;
           padding: 10px">
<p>
AIEA, Hawaii&mdash;Former United Nations Secretary General Boutros-
Boutros Ghali and current United Nations Undersecretary for Alphabet
Mobilization Yada-Yada Yada announced today the formation of the United
Nations International Vowel Assistance Committee. UNIVAC's mandate is
&quot;to help the vowel-deprived wherever they may live and to fund
vowel relief efforts in the hardest hit areas.&quot;
</p><p>
&quot;We have a good stockpile of a's, e's, and o's,&quot; said Ng Ng,
UNIVAC's Letter Distribution Officer. &quot;We hope to have an adequate
supply of i's and u's over the next six months. In the meantime, we can
use our extra y's in a pinch.&quot;
```

```
</p><p>
&quot;Vowels of every description are badly needed,&quot; said Cwm
Pffft, an activist with the group Consonant Watch. &quot;The people in
places such as Srpska Crnja and Hwlffordd are suffering horribly.&quot;
</p><p>
When asked to comment on the news, writer and animated film voice
specialist Sarah Vowell said, &quot;I haven't the faintest idea what
you're talking about. Leave me alone.&quot;
</p>
</td>
</tr>

<tr>
<td style="height: 50px;
        vertical-align: top;
        text-align: center;
        border-top-style: ridge;
        border-top-color: DarkGray;
        border-top-width: medium">
Copyright &copy; 2007 News of the Word and Logophilia Limited<br>
<span style="font-size: 10pt; margin-top: 5px">
<a href="header-footer2.htm">About Us</a> &bull;
<a href="header-footer2.htm">Privacy Policy</a> &bull;
<a href="header-footer2.htm">Contact Us</a> &bull;
<a href="header-footer2.htm">Okay, One Last Time: Give Us Money</a>
</span>
</td>
</tr>

</table>

</body>
</html>
```

Here are some things to get excited about in this example:

To focus the reader on the content, I changed the page background color (by setting the `<body>` tag's `background-color` property to `Black`) and then used the `<body>` tag's `margin-left` and `margin-right` properties to set 150-pixel margins.

I set the `<table>` tag's `background-color` property to `White`.

In the first `<td>` tag, which holds the header, I used various `border-bottom` styles to create a border running along the bottom. In the third `<td>` tag, which holds the footer, I used various `border-top` styles to create a border running along the top.

Figure 2.10 shows how things look.

Figure 2.10

A more elaborate page with a header and footer.

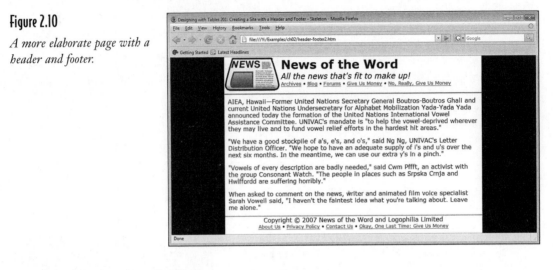

Creating a Three-Column Site

For our final table design trick, I will show you a more elaborate site design that builds on the previous two designs to create a three-column site with a header area above the columns. And it's all done with tables.

As usual, the table's height and width are set to 100 percent using the `<table>` tag's `height` and `width` properties. This ensures that the table takes up the entire page.

The table is populated with two rows and three columns. The first row is the header, and it spans all three columns. As before, you can use the `background-color` property to define the color you want to use to differentiate the header from the main part of the page. Also, set the height property equal to the height of the header you want.

The second row contains the three columns. In most cases, you use the `background-color` property to define the color you want to differentiate the left and right columns the rest of the page. Also, set the `width` property equal to the width you want for the left and right columns.

The middle column is where you put your regular web page text and graphics.

 Here's the basic layout for the web page (see three-column1.htm on the CD):

```
<html>
<head>
<title>
```

```
Designing with Tables 301: Creating a Three-Column Site - Skeleton
</title>
</head>
<body style="margin: 0px; padding: 0px">

<table style="height: 100%;
              width: 100%;
              border-spacing: 0px"
              cellspacing="0">

<tr>
<td style="background-color: LimeGreen;
           height: 100px;
           vertical-align: top"
           colspan="3">
Put your header text, images, and links here.
</td>
</tr>

<tr>
<td style="background-color: PaleGreen;
           width: 200px;
           vertical-align: top">
Put your left column text, links, and images here.
</td>

<td style="vertical-align: top">
Put your main page content (middle column) here.
</td>

<td style="background-color: PaleGreen;
           width: 200px;
           vertical-align: top">
Put your right column text, links, and images here.
</td>
</tr>
</table>

</body>
</html>
```

Figure 2.11 shows what happens when you load this into a browser.

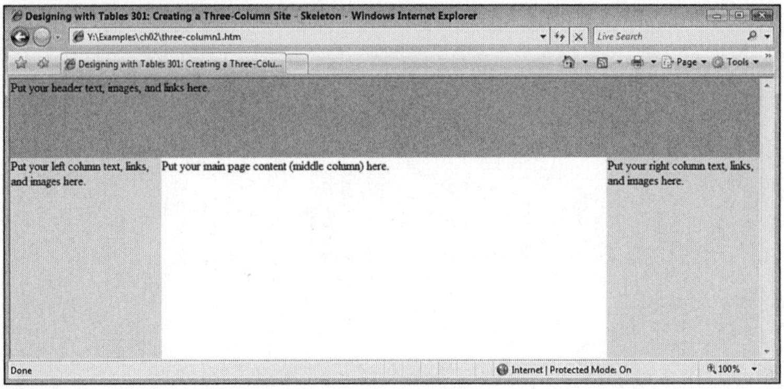

Figure 2.11

A web page with a header and three columns for content.

The Least You Need to Know

♦ The `<table>` tag defines the table as a whole. Use the `width` and `height` properties to define the size of the table, use the border styles to define the table border, and use the `background-color` property to set a background color.

♦ The `<tr>` tag defines a row inside the table.

♦ The `<td>` tag defines a column in the table (or, more precisely, it defines a cell inside the current row). Use the `text-align` property to align the cell data horizontally; use the `vertical-align` property to align the cell data vertically.

♦ To create a page with a margin, set up a table with two columns: the left column is the margin (with a background color or right border) and the right column contains the regular page data.

♦ To set up a page with a header and a footer, create a three-row table: the first row holds the header, the second row holds the main page content, and the third row holds the footer.

♦ To configure a three-column page with a header, create a table with two rows and three columns. The header is the first row, spanned across all three columns. Use the second row to add links and other sidebar content to the left and right column, and your main page content to the middle column.

Chapter 3

Accessorizing Your Site

In This Chapter

- Creating numbered and bulleted lists
- Cobbling together a definition list
- Adding news feeds, weather info, and other free content
- Trinkets, tchotchkes, and other bric-a-brac to make your site look its best

Any snappy dresser will tell you that although you need to start with a good suit or skirt or whatever, if you want to get on someone's Best Dressed list, you need to accessorize. It's the same with your website. Sure, you need to start with good content that's well presented with the right fonts and colors (as seen in Chapter 1) and is organized in a suitable table-based layout (per Chapter 2). But if you want folks to do a double-take when they see your site, you need to accessorize.

As you learn in this chapter, the web equivalent of scarves, brooches, and rings are special HTML features such as bulleted and numbered lists, and third-party content such as news feeds, local weather data, and more. You also learn how to create a special icon just for your site.

Making Lists and Checking Them Twice (Optional)

For some reason, people love lists: Best (and Worst) Dressed lists, Top Ten lists, My All-Time Favorite *X* lists, where *X* is whatever you want it to be: movies, songs, books, *I Love Lucy* episodes—you name it. People like lists, for whatever reasons.

Now, let's make some lists. *Geez Louise, Author Boy, how hard can* that *be? It's just a list, right?* Well, sure, any website jockey can just plop a Best Tootsie Roll Flavors Ever list on a page by typing each item, one after the other. Perhaps our list maker even gets a bit clever and inserts the
 (line break) tag between each item, which displays them on separate lines. Ooooh.

Yes, you can make a list that way, and it works well enough, I suppose, but there's a better way. HTML has a few tags that are specially designed to give you much more control over your list-building chores. For example, you can create a bulleted list that actually has those little bullets out front of each item. Nice! In fact, HTML offers no fewer than three different list styles: bulleted list, numbered lists, and definition lists. The next few sections take you through the basics of each list type and provide you with plenty of examples.

Making Your Point with Bulleted Lists

A no-frills,
-separated list isn't very useful or readable because it doesn't come with any type of eye candy that helps differentiate one item from the next. A bulleted list solves that problem by leading off each item with a bullet—a cute little black dot.

Bulleted lists use two types of tags. The entire list is surrounded by the <ul> and </ul> tags. Why "ul"? Well, what the rest of the world calls a bulleted list, the HTML powers-that-be call an *unordered list*. Each item in the list is preceded by the <li> (list item) tag and is closed with the </li> end tag. The general setup looks like this:

```
<ul>
<li>First bullet point.</li>
<li>Fifty-seventh bullet point.</li>
<li>Sixteenth bullet point.</li>
<li>Hey, whaddya want--it's an unordered list!</li>
</ul>
```

Here's an HTML document (look for bulleted.htm on the CD) that demonstrates how to use the bulleted list tags:

```
<html>
<head>
<title>Making Your Point with Bulleted Lists</title>
</head>
<body>
<h3>My All-Time Favorite Oxymorons</h3>
<ul>
<li>pretty ugly</li>
<li>military intelligence</li>
<li>jumbo shrimp</li>
<li>original copy</li>
<li>random order</li>
<li>act naturally</li>
<li>tight slacks</li>
<li>freezer burn</li>
<li>sight unseen</li>
<li>Microsoft Works</li>
</ul>
</body>
</html>
```

Figure 3.1 shows how the Internet Explorer browser renders this file, little bullets and all.

Figure 3.1

A typical bulleted list.

Customizing the Bullet Style

The basic bulleted list bullet is a small, black circle. However, you can customize the bullet in a couple different ways. The simplest way is to add the `style` attribute to the `<ul>` tag and plop in the `list-style-type` property, like so:

```
<ul style="list-style-type: type">
```

In this case, *type* can be `disc` (the standard bullet), `circle`, or `square`. Here's a for instance (look for bullet-style.htm on the CD):

```html
<html>
<head>
<title>Customizing the Bullet Style</title>
</head>
<body>
<h3>Messing Around with the <tt>list-style-type</tt> Property</h3>
<hr>
<ul style="list-style-type: disc">
<li>Disco</li>
<li>Disc jockey</li>
<li>Disc brake</li>
</ul>
<ul style="list-style-type: circle">
<li>Circle the wagons!</li>
<li>Circle all that apply</li>
<li>Circle the block</li>
</ul>
<ul style="list-style-type: square">
<li>Square root</li>
<li>Square meal</li>
<li>Square peg</li>
</ul>
</body>
</html>
```

Figure 3.2 shows how it looks from Safari's point of view.

Figure 3.2

Add the `list-style-type` property to the `<ul>` tag to choose from any of three different bullet styles.

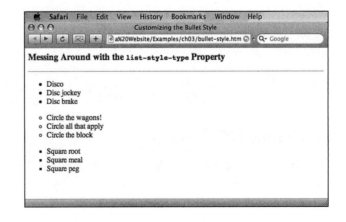

The other way you can tweak the bullet is to specify your own bullet image. That's right, instead of a dinky little disc, circle, or square, you can plunk down your very own image to use as a list's bullets. You do this by adding the `style` attribute to the `<ul>` tag, but this time you add the `list-style-image` property, like this:

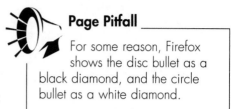

```
<ul style="list-style-image: url(image)">
```

Simply replace *image* with the name of the image you want to use. Here's an example:

```
<ul style="list-style-image: url(my-bullet.gif)">
```

If the image resides in another directory, you need to specify the folder, too (see Chapter 6 to learn more about using directories with your website):

```
<ul style="list-style-image: url(/graphics/pointing-finger.jpg)">
```

Here's an example (check out bullet-image.htm on the CD):

```
<html>
<head>
<title>Customizing the Bullet Image</title>
</head>
<body>
<h3>Giving the <tt>list-style-image</tt> Property a Whirl</h3>
<hr>
<b>Ad Creep</b>: More signs that an advertising-induced apocalypse is
almost upon us:
<ul style="list-style-image: url(eyesright.gif)">
<li>A Danish outdoor-media company called Nytmedie offers new parents a
free baby carriage. The catch? The carriage has a corporate sponsor's
logo on the side.</li>
<li>Acclaim Entertainment offers $10,000 in U.S. savings bonds to the
first family that names its child after Acclaim's new video game,
Turok.</li>
<li>On December 20, 1999, city councilors of Halfway, Oregon
unanimously agree to rename the town to half.com, after an Internet
e-commerce site.</li>
<li>The History Channel sticks hundreds of ad decals on sidewalks all
over New York City. The decals illegally deface public property, but
the agency responsible calls them "whimsical, witty, and fun."</li>
```

```
<li>In 1999, Pizza Hut pays the Russian Aerospace Agency $2.4 million
(U.S.) to place a 30-foot tall logo on a rocket that launched part
of the International Space Station. Pizza Hut once considered using
a laser to display its logo on the moon, but abandoned the idea as
"impractical."</li>
</ul>
</body>
</html>
```

Figure 3.3 shows how it looks in Firefox.

Figure 3.3

Add the `list-style-image` *property to the* `<ul>` *tag to specify your own image to use as a bullet.*

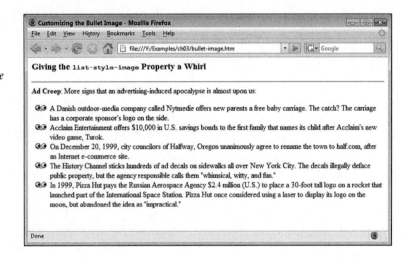

Numbered Lists: Easy as One, Two, Three

If you want to include a numbered list of items—it could be a Top Ten list, bowling league standings, or any kind of ranking—don't bother adding in the numbers yourself. Instead, you can use an *ordered list* to make the web browser generate the numbers for you.

As with a bulleted, er, I mean *unordered* list, ordered lists use two types of tags. The entire list is surrounded by the `<ol>` (ordered list) and `</ol>` tags. And then each item in the list is surrounded by `<li>` and `</li>`. Here's the general structure to use:

```
<ol>
<li>First item.</li>
<li>Second item.</li>
<li>Third item.</li>
<li>You get the idea.</li>
</ol>
```

Here's an example (see numbered.htm on the CD):

```html
<html>
<head>
<title>Numbered Lists - Example #1</title>
</head>
<body>
<h3>My Ten Favorite U.S. College Nicknames</h3>
<ol>
<li>California-Santa Cruz Banana Slugs</li>
<li>Delaware Fightin' Blue Hens</li>
<li>Texas Christian Horned Frogs</li>
<li>Coastal Carolina Chanticleers</li>
<li>Kent State Golden Flashes</li>
<li>Marshall Thundering Herd</li>
<li>Idaho Vandals</li>
<li>Purdue Boilermakers</li>
<li>South Carolina Fighting Gamecocks</li>
<li>Wake Forest Demon Deacons</li>
</ol>
</body>
</html>
```

Notice that I didn't include any numbers before each list item. However, when I display this document in a browser (see Figure 3.4), the numbers are automatically inserted. Pretty slick, huh?

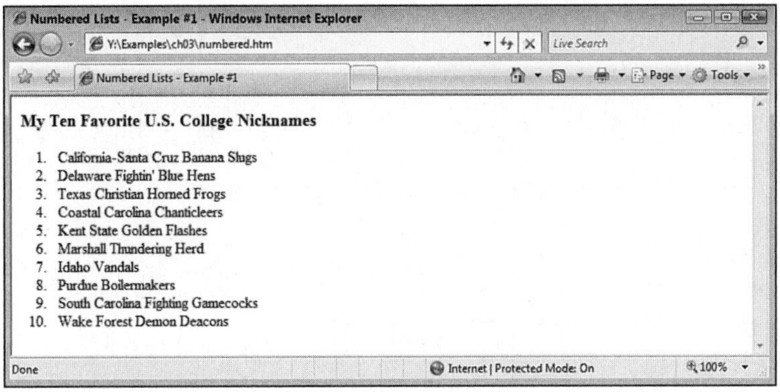

Figure 3.4

How the numbered list appears in Internet Explorer.

Webmaster Wisdom

Your list items don't have to be just plain text, so you're free to insert other HTML tags. For example, you could use `<b>` and `</b>` to boldface a word or two in the item, you could use the `<span>` tag and styles to change the font size or typeface of the item, or you could make an item a link to another web page. Just be sure to start each line with the `<li>` tag and end it with the `</li>` tag.

 The items you toss into your numbered lists don't have to be short words and phrases. For example, if you're explaining how to perform a certain task, a numbered list is the perfect way to take your readers through each step. Here's a more involved example (it's juggling.htm on the CD) that uses a numbered list to explain how to juggle:

```
<html>
<head>
<title>Numbered Lists - Example #2</title>
</head>
<body>
<h3>The Complete Idiot's Guide to Juggling</h3>
<hr />
<p>
Here are the basic steps for the most fundamental of juggling
moves&mdash;the three-ball cascade:
</p>
<ol>
<li>Place two balls in your dominant hand, one in front of the other,
and hold the third ball in your other hand. Let your arms dangle
naturally and bring your forearms parallel to the ground (as though
you were holding a tray).</li>
<li>Of the two balls in your dominant hand, toss the front one toward
your left hand in a smooth arc. Make sure the ball doesn't spin too
much and that it goes no higher than about eye level.</li>
<li>Once the first ball has reached the top of its arc, you need to
release the ball in your other hand. Throw it toward your dominant
hand, making sure it flies <i>under</i> the first ball. Again, watch
that the ball doesn't spin or go higher than eye level.</li>
<li>Now things get a little tricky (!). Soon after you release the
second ball, the first ball will approach your other hand (gravity
never fails). Go ahead and catch the first ball.</li>
<li>When the second ball reaches its apex, throw the third ball (the
remaining ball in your dominant hand) under it.</li>
<li>At this point, it just becomes a game of catch-and-throw-under,
catch-and-throw-under. Keep repeating steps 1&ndash;5 and, before you know
it, you'll be a juggling fool. (However, I'd recommend holding off on
the flaming clubs until you've practiced a little.)</li>
```

```
    </ol>
    </body>
    </html>
```

As you can see, most of the items are quite long, and it's kind of hard to tell where each `<li>` item begins and ends. However, as shown in the Figure 3.5, the list looks pretty good when viewed in a web browser.

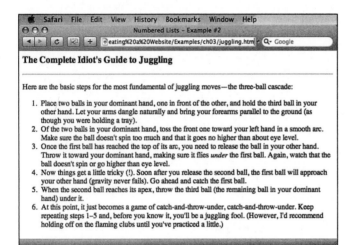

Figure 3.5

Numbered lists are perfect for outlining the steps in a procedure.

Using a Different Numbering Style

You saw earlier that the `<ul>` tag offers a `list-style-type` property for changing the bullet style. Not to be outdone, the `<ol>` accepts the same property, only this time you use it to change the numbering scheme. Here's how it works:

```
<ol style="list-style-type: type">
```

Here, *type* is one of the values shown in Table 3.1.

Table 3.1 The `<ol>` Tag's `list-style-type` Property Values

Value	Numbering Scheme	Example
decimal	standard numbers	1, 2, 3
lower-alpha	lowercase letters	a, b, c
upper-alpha	uppercase letters	A, B, C
lower-roman	small Roman numerals	i, ii, iii
upper-roman	large Roman numerals	I, II, III

An `<ol>` tag attribute that's often useful is `start`, which lets you to define the starting point of the list numbers. For example, if you use `<ol start="100">`, the first item in your numbered list will be 100, the second will be 101, and so on.

Here's an example of some lists you can make (see number-style.htm on the CD):

```
<html>
<head>
<title>Nicer Numbers: Using a Different Numbering Style</title>
</head>
<body>
<p>
<b>list-style-type: lower-alpha</b>
</p>
<ol style="list-style-type: lower-alpha">
<li>First</li>
<li>Second</li>
<li>Third</li>
</ol>
<p>
<b>list-style-type: upper-alpha</b>
</p>
<ol style="list-style-type: upper-alpha">
<li>Win</li>
<li>Place</li>
<li>Show</li>
</ol>
<p>
<b>list-style-type: lower-roman</b>
</p>
<ol style="list-style-type: lower-roman">
<li>Gold</li>
<li>Silver</li>
<li>Bronze</li>
</ol>
<p>
<b>list-style-type: upper-roman</b>
</p>
<ol style="list-style-type: upper-roman">
<li>Miss America</li>
<li>First runner-up</li>
<li>Second runner-up</li>
</ol>
</body>
</html>
```

Figure 3.6 shows how Internet Explorer handles the various types of lists.

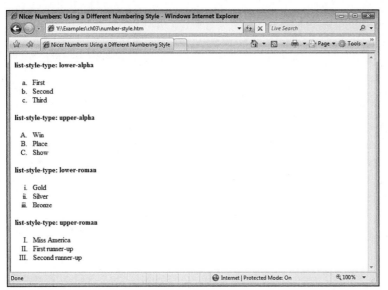

Figure 3.6

The <ol> *tag's list-style-type property in action.*

Defining Definition Lists

The final type of list is called a *definition list*. Originally, people used it for dictionary-style lists where each entry had two parts: a term and the definition of the term. As you'll see, though, definition lists are useful for more than just definitions.

To mark the two different parts of each entry in these lists, you need two different tags. The term is preceded by the <dt> tag, and the definition is preceded by the <dd> tag, like this:

```
<dt>Term</dt><dd>Definition</dd>
```

You can, if you like, put the <dt> part and the <dd> part on separate lines, but I prefer this style. Either way, they end up looking the same in the browser. Then, surround the whole list with the <dl> and </dl> tags to complete your definition list. Here's how the whole thing looks:

```
<dl>
<dt>A Term</dt> <dd>Its Definition</dd>
<dt>Another Term</dt> <dd>Another Definition</dd>
<dt>Yet Another Term</dt> <dd>Yet Another Definition</dd>
<dt>Etc.</dt> <dd>Abbreviation of a Latin phrase that means "and so
forth."</dd>
</dl>
```

Webmaster Wisdom

People often use definition lists for things other than definitions. Some web welders like to use the term (the `<dt>` part) as a section heading and the definition (the `<dd>` part) as the section text. You can also leave out the term and just use the `<dd>` tag by itself. This is handy for those times when you need indented text (say, if you're quoting someone at length).

 Let's look at an example. The HTML document shown next (it's on the CD in the file named definition.htm) uses a definition list to outline a few words and phrases and their definitions. (Notice that I've made all the terms bold. This helps them stand out more when the browser displays them.)

```
<html>
<head>
<title>Defining Definition Lists</title>
</head>
<body>
<h3>Some Relationship-Related Words Coined on <i>Seinfeld</i></h3>
<dl>
<dt><b>bad-breaker-upper</b></dt> <dd>A person who breaks up with other
people in a mean or messy way.</dd>
<dt><b>face-to-face breakup</b></dt> <dd>A breakup that occurs in
person.</dd>
<dt><b>get-out-of-relationship-free card</b></dt> <dd>Something that
enables a person to easily end a relationship.</dd>
<dt><b>pre-emptive breakup</b></dt> <dd>A breakup performed before the
other person can break up with you.</dd>
<dt><b>relationship killer</b></dt> <dd>A mistake or action that dooms
a relationship.</dd>
<dt><b>separat&eacute;e</b></dt> <dd>A person who is separated (cf.
divorc&eacute;e).</dd>
</dl>
</body>
</html>
```

Figure 3.7 shows how the definition list appears in the Firefox scheme of things. (As an aside note, the entity code é gives you the letter *e* with an acute accent: é.)

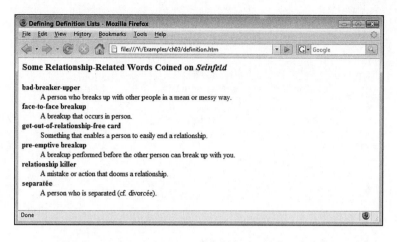

Figure 3.7

A few definitions arrayed, appropriately enough, in a definition list.

These three types of HTML lists should serve you well for most of your website productions. However, you're free to mix and match various list types to suit the occasion. Specifically, it's perfectly legal to plop one type of list inside another (this is called *nesting lists*). For example, suppose you have a numbered list that outlines the steps involved in some procedure. If you need to augment one of the steps with a few bullet points, you can insert a bulleted list after the appropriate numbered list item.

Feeding Your Site: Adding a News Feed

In Chapter 11, you learn how to create an RSS (real simple syndication) feed that lets other people keep up with new content added to your site (see the "Syndicating Your Site" section in that chapter). Here, you learn a few ways to do the opposite, sort of: displaying another site's RSS feed on your own site. This is a fast and easy way to add stuff that complements your own content.

For example, if your site is mostly about technology, you could add headlines from the Technology section of *The New York Times*. This kind of thing is particularly suited to sites that use margins or multiple columns (as described in Chapter 2), because you can have your own content in the main part of each page and then feed headlines off to the side.

The most straightforward way to go about this is to surf to the site that has the content you want to use on your site, and see if they offer some sort of service for providing headlines or feeds. Figure 3.8 shows the page where you can get started with headlines from *The New York Times* (see www.nytimes.com/gst/nytheadlines.html). In most cases, you run through a series of forms where you select the content you want, format it in some way (fonts, colors, and so on), and end up with some code that you insert on your page.

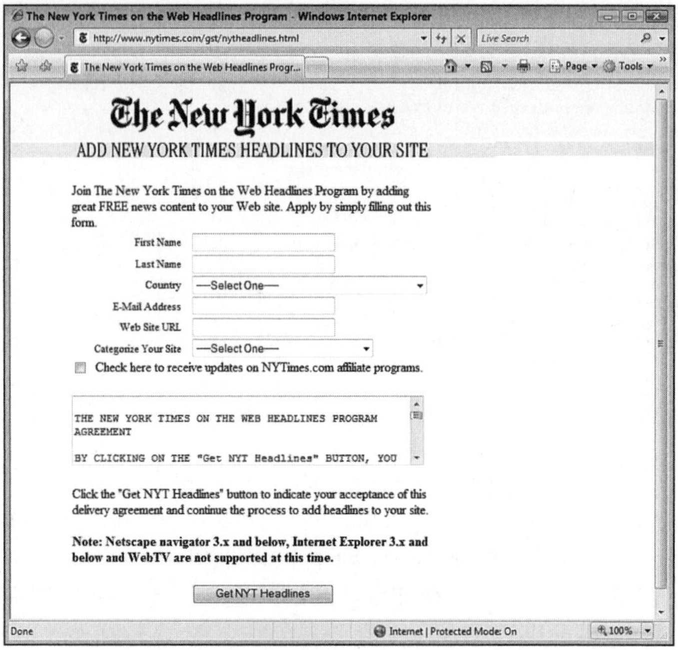

Figure 3.8

Many websites offer headlines and other feeds you can add to your site.

If you can't find a service that provides headlines or feeds, some third-party sites will convert any RSS feed into code that you can plunk onto your site. Here are a few to check out:

- Feed2JS (feed2js.org)
- Feedroll RSS Viewer (www.feedroll.com/rssviewer)
- RSS2HTML (www.rss2html.com)

Figure 3.9 shows Feedroll's RSS Viewer service, where you select from dozens of feeds, add design flourishes, and copy the code that appears at the bottom of the page.

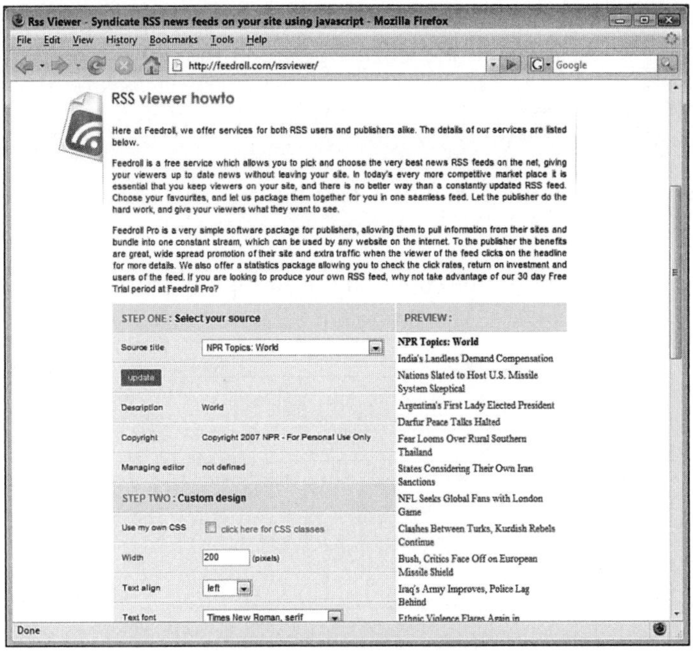

Figure 3.9

Feedroll's RSS Viewer let you display feed headlines from dozens of publishers, including Amazon.com, the BBC, Boing Boing, The New York Times, *and Yahoo!*

If the feed you want to add to your site is already part of your NewsGator or FeedBurner account, those services offer ways to generate the necessary code for displaying the feed. The next two sections take you through the details.

Generating Feed Headlines Using NewsGator

If you have a NewsGator account (you can get one free at www.newsgator.com), you can generate feed headlines for your site using just a single feed, or you can pig out and create headlines from a bunch of related feeds. Here are the steps to follow to generate the code:

1. Surf to NewsGator (www.newsgator.com), and sign in to your account.

2. Click **Settings** to open the My Settings window.

3. Click the **Edit Locations** tab.

4. Scroll to the bottom of the window, type a name (such as **Headlines**) in the **Create location** text box, and click **Add.** NewsGator adds the new location to the Edit Location tab.

5. Find your new location in the tab, and click **Feeds.** NewsGator displays a list of the feeds in the location. (You'll see all your NewsGator feeds at first.)

6. Click **uncheck all** and then click the check box beside each feed you want to use for your site headlines. When you're done, click **Update** at the bottom of the window.

7. Find your new location again, and click **Headlines.**

8. Activate the **Check here to enable Headlines settings for this location** check box.

9. Copy the tags shown in the window (and pointed out in Figure 3.10). This is the code you'll insert in your own page to display the headlines.

Figure 3.10

NewsGator enables you to display headlines from some or all of your RSS feeds.

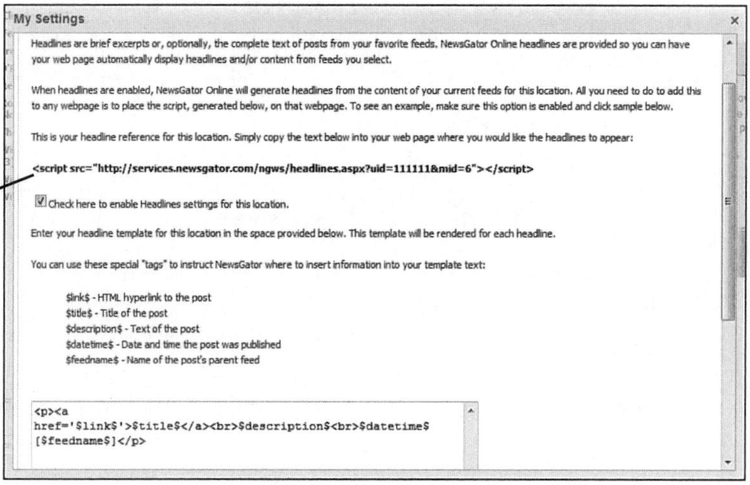

Copy this code
to use on your
website.

10. Adjust the headline template as you see fit (more on this in a sec).

11. Use the **Enter the number of posts to be displayed by the headline script** text box to set the number of posts you want to show on your site.

12. Click **Save Changes.**

The default headline template looks like this:

```
<p>
<a href='$link$'>$title$</a><br>
$description$<br>
$datetime$ [$feedname$]
</p>
```

Those weird codes you see are special NewsGator "tags" that represent feed data:

- $link$ is the address of the post, which is used to generate a link to the original post.

- $title$ is the title of the post.

- $description$ represents the post text.

- $datetime$ is the date and time the post was published.

- $feedname$ is the name of the blog (or whatever) that generated the post.

When you want to just display headlines, you probably want to drop the post text. Here's a revised headline template that does this:

```
<p>
<a href='$link$'>$title$</a><br>
$datetime$ [$feedname$]
</p>
```

Figure 3.11 shows a simple page that implements NewsGator headlines using the following code (see Chapter 12 to learn about the <script> tag):

```
<h3>NewsGator Headline Test</h3>
<script src="http://services.newsgator.com/ngws/headlines.
aspx?uid=111111&mid=6">
</script>
```

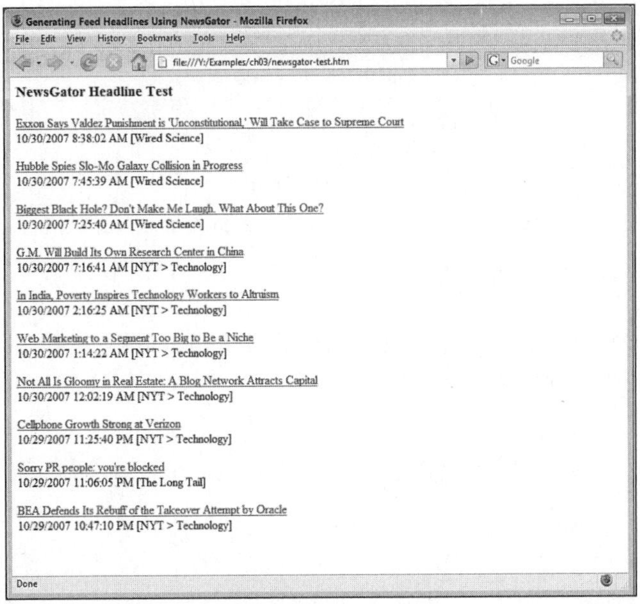

Figure 3.11

Some NewsGator headlines displayed on a web page.

Generating Feed Code Using FeedBurner

If you use FeedBurner as your news aggregator (if not, you can get a free account at www.feedburner.com), you can use it to generate code to display feed headlines on your website. Here are the steps to follow:

1. Surf to FeedBurner (www.feedburner.com), and sign in to your account.

2. Click the feed you want to work with.

3. Click the **Publicize** tab.

4. Click **BuzzBoost.** FeedBurner displays the BuzzBoost page, shown in Figure 3.12.

Figure 3.12

Use FeedBurner's BuzzBoost service to generate code to display a feed on your website.

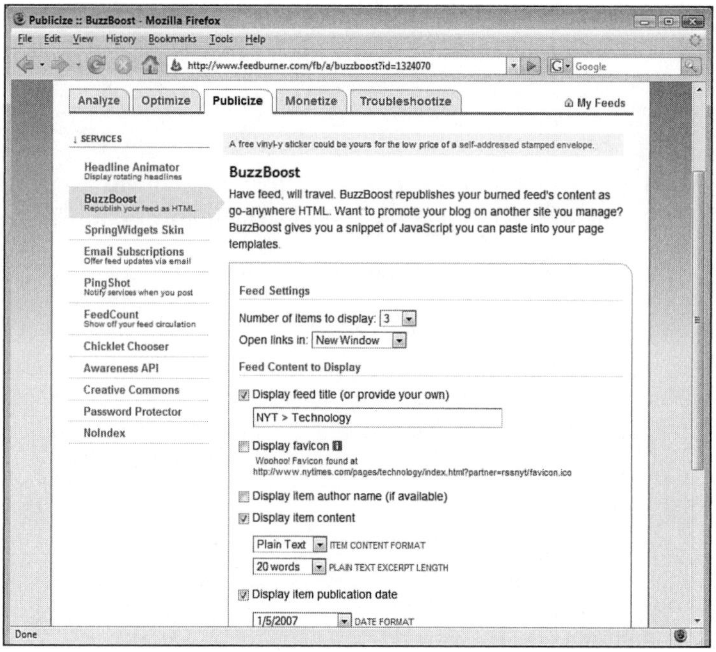

5. Configure the various feed settings to suit your needs.

6. Click **Activate.** FeedBurner activates BuzzBoost and then displays the script code you need to add to your page.

7. Copy the script code, and insert it on your page.

Adding a Weather Module to Your Site

If you want your site visitors to know a bit more about where you live, one easy way to do that is to add some local weather info for your city. Happily, The Weather Channel has a special *weather module* you can add just by generating and copying a bit of custom code. Here are the steps to follow:

1. Go to The Weather Channel site (www.weather.com).

2. At the bottom of the page, click the **Weather on Your Website** link.

3. Click **Get It Today.**

4. Sign in using your weather.com member details. (If you're not yet a member, click **Sign up!** instead.)

5. Fill in your user profile data and your settings data.

6. Click **Save and Continue.** The Weather On Your Website Builder appears.

7. Click **Customize.**

8. Use the Basics, Background, @weather.com Links, and Weather Info tabs (see Figure 3.13) to customize various aspects of the weather module.

Figure 3.13

Use The Weather Channel's Weather On Your Website feature to add your local weather to your website.

9. Click **Finish & Generate Code.** A new page appears, and the code you need appears in a text box.

10. Click **Highlight All Code,** and press **Ctrl+C** (or ⌘+C on your Mac) to copy it.

11. Paste the code into your web page.

Stuffing Your Site with More Free Content

News feeds and the weather are a good start, but you can clutter up your site with billions of other free things. These include regularly updated cartoons and jokes, games, horoscopes, photographs, maps, articles, and so much more. Here are a few sites to check out for free stuff:

◆ FreeSticky (www.freesticky.com)

◆ Free Dictionary (www.thefreedictionary.com)

◆ Fresh Content (www.freshcontent.net)

Personalizing Your Site with a Favicon

No website worth its e-salt would dare show its home page on the web without having a favicon set up. *A favicon? This is English, yes?* Yup, and it's a relatively new word that's short for "favorite icon," which is a way of saying that it's the icon that identifies your site in the browser's address bar and tabs. For example, check out the shot of the Google home page in Figure 3.14. See how the address bar and the tab both show a Google icon? That's Google's favicon.

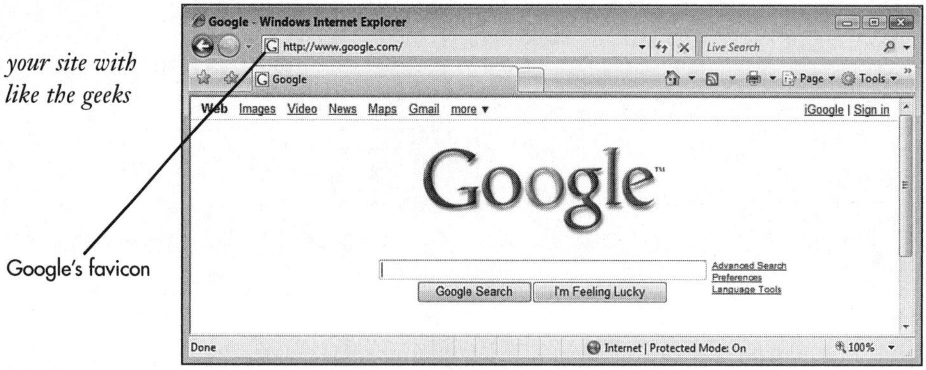

Figure 3.14

You can set up your site with a favicon, just like the geeks at Google.

Google's favicon

Google took the first "G" in the Google logo and used that as the favicon image. For your own site, you can either use part of your logo, if you have one, or some other image representative of who you are or what your site is all about. The favicon must be either 16 pixels wide and 16 pixels high or 32 by 32, so there's not a lot of detail going to go into this thing. Choose something simple with a lot of contrast so your visitors know what they're looking at.

Here are the steps to follow to create a favicon:

1. In your favorite graphics program, create or copy the image you want to use and resize the image so it's 16 pixels wide and 16 pixels high.

2. Save the image as a JPEG or GIF.

3. Start a graphics program that can save graphics files in the Windows Icon (.ico) format. GraphicConverter (www.lemkesoft.com), IconForge (www.cursorarts. com), and IrfanView (www.irfanview.com) are three such programs.

4. Open your 16×16 (or 32×32) image in the program.

5. Select **File, Save As** to open the Save As (or Save Picture As) dialog box.

6. In the **File name** text box, type **favicon.**

7. In the **Save as type** list, select the ICO—Windows Icon format.

8. Click **Save.**

When it's time to upload your file to your website (see Chapter 9), place the favicon.ico file in the main directory. Most web browsers should look for and find the favicon file automatically. To be safe, you can stick the browser's nose in it by adding the following `<link>` tag to your home page's head section:

```
<link rel="shortcut icon" href="/favicon.ico" type="image/x-icon" />
```

 Page Pitfall _____

If the browser doesn't show your new favicon right away, clear your browser's cache (the collection of site files the browser stores on your computer for later use). In Internet Explorer 7, select **Tools, Delete Browsing History,** and then click the **Delete files** button in the **Temporary Internet Files** group. In Firefox, select **Tools, Options,** display the **Advanced** tab, and click **Clear Now.** In Safari, select **Safari, Empty Cache,** and click **Empty.**

The Least You Need to Know

♦ For a bulleted list, use the `<ul>` and `</ul>` tags and surround each list item with `<li>` and `</li>`.

♦ To change the bullet type, add the `style` attribute and the `list-style-type` property to the `<ul>` tag.

♦ For a numbered list, use the `<ol>` and `</ol>` tags and surround each list item with `<li>` and `</li>`.

♦ To change the number type, add the `style` attribute and the `list-style-type` property to the `<ol>` tag.

♦ For a definition list, use the `<dl>` and `</dl>` tags. Surround each term with `<dt>` and `</dt>` and each definition with `<dd>` and `</dd>`.

Making Your Website More Social

In This Chapter

- Adding an e-mail link to your site
- Using a form to get feedback
- Populating your form with buttons, boxes, and other bangles
- Putting up a chat room or bulletin board
- How to make your site more touchy-feely—without *any* touching or feeling!

In 1996, Craig Howe, who was then director of the D'Arcy McNickle Center for American Indian History at Chicago's Newberry Library, wrote that "The Internet is either anti-social or asocial. It promotes the isolation of the individual." In his 1995 book *Silicon Snake Oil*, astronomer Clifford Stoll described the Internet as "a guide of how to be anti-social in that it undercuts our schools, our neighborhoods, and our communities."

Sentiments such as these were easy to find back in the mid-1990s when the Internet's accession to global domination was just revving up. Conservatives, curmudgeons, and schoolteachers with too-tight hair buns all decried what they saw as the Internet's corrosion of the social. Predictions of societal breakdown and individual meltdown were commonplace, but a funny thing happened on the road to ruination: nothing much. Society as a whole remains intact and, a few cases of Internet addiction notwithstanding, online users don't seem any worse off. In fact, it seems that we're in the midst of the opposite phenomenon: the return and revitalization of the social.

So what does all this mean for you and your nascent website? Simply that the more social you can make your site, the more people will show up and the more often they'll come back. Fortunately, making your site more social isn't all that complicated. As you see in this chapter, it's all about communication: letting your visitors communicate with you and with each other.

E-Mail Me!

You learned how to do the link thing in Chapter 1. However, there's no reason a link has to lead to a web page. In fact, all you have to do is alter the link address in a certain way, and you can connect to most other Internet services, including FTP (File Transfer Protocol; see Chapter 9).

In this section, I concentrate on the most common type of nonweb link: e-mail. In this case, someone clicking an e-mail link is presented with a window he or she can use to send a message to your e-mail address. Now that's interactive!

Page Pitfall _____

Setting up an e-mail link may not work properly if the user has a web-based e-mail service such as Hotmail, Gmail, .Mac, or Yahoo! because when the user clicks the e-mail link, the browser attempts to launch the user's e-mail software. But that software isn't used for web e-mail, so the browser has no way of sending the message. To handle such cases, you might want to create a form as well (as discussed a bit later in this chapter), and tell web-based e-mailers to use that instead.

This type of link is called a *mailto link* because you include the word `mailto:` in the `<a>` tag. Here's the general form:

```
<a href="mailto:address">link text</a>
```

Replace `address` with your e-mail address and `link text` with the text you want to reader to click. Here's an example:

```
<a href="mailto:me@here.com">Send me a message!</a>
```

Figure 4.1 shows how it looks in Internet Explorer. Note that when you point at the link with your mouse, the mailto address appears in the browser's status bar.

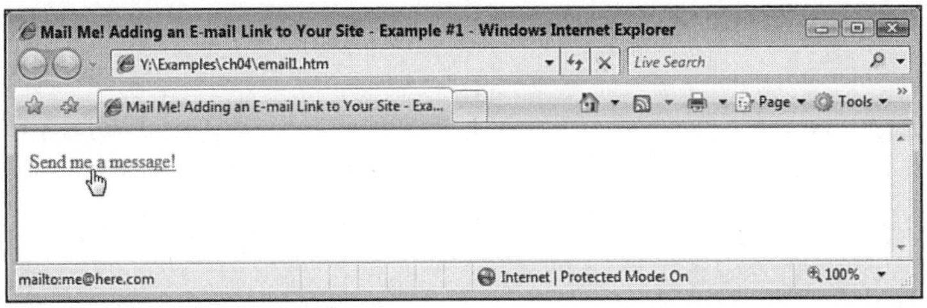

Figure 4.1

A web page with an e-mail link.

Page Pitfall

Putting your (or someone else's) address on a web page can be problematic because spammers have programs that automatically "harvest" such addresses. You can *munge* (as the hackers say) the address by altering it in such a way that will fool the spammer program but not a human. Here are some examples:

```
me@-NOSPAMPLEASE-here.com
president@DELETETHISPARTwhitehouse.gov
```

The reader must delete the extra text—the -NOSPAMPLEASE- or the DELETETHISPART—to get the actual address.

You can make life even easier for your visitors by specifying the message subject line in advance. Do it by cramming the subject property into the <a> tag, like so:

```
<a href="mailto:address?subject=Subject text">link text</a>
```

Just replace Subject text with the subject line you want to use. Here's an example:

```
<a href="mailto:me@here.com?Subject=You are the greatest person ever!">
Send me a message with a subject!</a>
```

Figure 4.2 shows an example of a message window that appears when someone clicks the link. As you can see, the subject line is already filled in. Thanks!

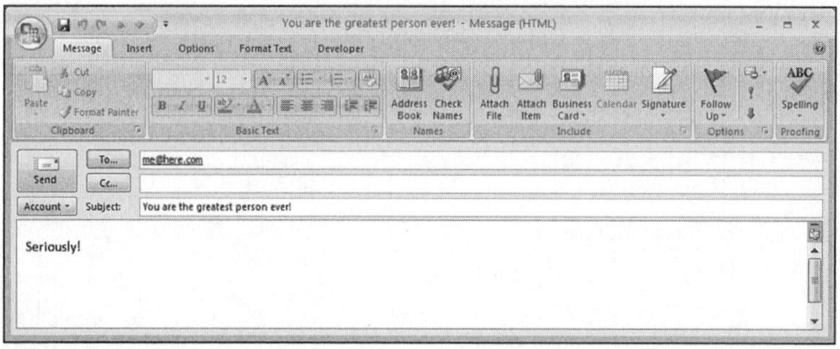

Figure 4.2

You can make it easier for folks to e-mail you by specifying the message subject in advance.

Webmaster Wisdom

Don't go to the trouble of creating an e-mail link and then hide it in some obscure nook of your website. Remember, you *want* people to contact you! On a well-designed website, the e-mail link appears not only on every page, but in the same spot on every page. Good locations for e-mail links are the site's header or footer. (See Chapter 2 to learn how to configure your site with a header or footer.)

What Are You Thinking?: Feedback

Gathering visitor feedback using an e-mail link is easy for you to set up and easy for your readers because they'll all be familiar with how e-mail works. However, it does come with a couple drawbacks. As I mentioned earlier, it won't work if a visitor doesn't have an e-mail program installed. And other than being able to specify the subject line, the rest of the message is out of your hands.

Why is the latter a problem? Because it doesn't give you any way to structure the type of feedback you get. For example, if you're running an opinion poll and you give everyone a few possible answers to a question, you have to rely on each user to type or copy and paste the answer. It would be so much better to set up some option buttons and have the user click the option he or she wants to use.

Sounds like pie-in-the-sky stuff, right? Not at all. In fact, you can do this and many other similar things by creating a form. A form is essentially the web page equivalent of a dialog box. It's a page populated with text boxes, check boxes, option buttons, command buttons, and even drop-down lists, and it's all there so you can get information from the user. For example, Figure 4.3 shows a form from my website. This is a sign-up form people can use to join my site.

Figure 4.3

An example of a web page form.

Of course, there are many possible uses for forms. If you put out a newsletter or magazine, you can use forms to gather information from subscribers. If your website includes pages with restricted access, you can use a form to get a person's user name and password for verification. If you have information in a database, you can use a form to have people specify what type of information they want to access.

Creating a Form

You create a form using special HTML tags, and it's pretty easy to set one up. To get started, add the `<form>` and its corresponding `</form>` end tag. You place all the other form-related tags (which I show you in the rest of this section) between `<form>` and `</form>`.

The `<form>` tag always includes a couple extra goodies that tell the web server how to process the form. Here's the general format:

```
<form action="address"
method="method">
</form>
```

Here, the `action` attribute tells the browser where to send the form's data. This is almost always a program (or *script*, as they're often

Page Pitfall _____

Creating a form is fairly easy, but getting your mitts on the information the reader types into the form is another matter. This requires some programming, so it's well beyond the scope of this book. So what's a programming-challenged web wizard to do? Check out the "Getting the Data Delivered to Your Door" section later in this chapter.

called) that processes the data and then performs some kind of action (hence the name). The *address* is the web address of the script file that contains the program.

The method attribute tells the browser how to send the form's data to the address specified by the action attribute. You have two choices here for method: post and get. The method you use depends on the script, but post is the most common method.

Let's look at an example. You can test your forms by using a special script that I host on my server. Here's how to use it:

```
<form action="http://www.mcfedries.com/scripts/formtest.asp"
method="post">
```

This script returns a page that shows you the data you entered into the form. You can try this out after you build a working form. Speaking of which, the next few sections take you through the basic form elements.

Sending the Form: The Submit Button

Most dialog boxes, as you probably know from hard-won experience, have an OK command button. Clicking this button says, in effect, "All right, dude, I've made my choices. Now go put everything into effect." Forms also have command buttons, which come in two flavors: submit buttons and reset buttons.

A *submit button* (I talk about the reset button in the next section) is the form equivalent of an OK dialog box button. When the reader clicks the submit button, the form data is shipped out to the program specified by the <form> tag's action attribute. Here's the simplest format for the submit button:

```
<input type="submit" />
```

As you'll see, most form elements use some variation on the <input> tag and, as you know, all these tags go between <form> and </form>. In this case, the type="submit" attribute tells the browser to display a command button labeled Submit Query (or Submit or Send on some browsers). Note that each form can have just one submit button.

If the standard Submit Query label is a bit too stuffy for your needs, you can make up your own label:

```
<input type="submit" value="label" />
```

Here, *label* is the label that appears on the button. In the following example (submit.htm on the CD), I've inserted a submit button with the label Make It So!:

```
<html>
<head>
<title>Sending the Form: The Submit Button</title>
</head>
<body>
<h3>An example of a custom label for a submit button:</h3>

<form action="http://www.mcfedries.com/scripts/formtest.asp"
method="post">
<input type="submit" value="Make It So!" />
</form>

</body>
</html>
```

Figure 4.4 shows how it all looks in Firefox.

Figure 4.4

A submit button with a custom label.

Webmaster Wisdom

Rather than using a boring command button to submit a form, you might prefer to have the user click an image. That's no sweat. Just add `type="image"` to the `<input>` tag, and add a `src` attribute that specifies the name of the graphics file (much like you do with the `<img>` tag). Here's an example:

```
<input type="image" src="go.gif" />
```

You should know, too, that when you use an image as a submit button, my form test script returns two extra values—"x" and "y"—that give you the coordinates of the spot on the image that the user clicked. They can be safely ignored.

A Fresh Start: The Reset Button

If you plan on creating fairly large forms, you can do your readers a big favor by including a reset button somewhere on the form. A reset button clears all the data from the form's fields and reenters any default values you specified in the fields. (I explain how to set up default values for each type of field as we go along.) Here's the tag you use to include a reset button:

```
<input type="reset" />
```

This creates a command button labeled Reset. You can create a custom label by tossing the `value` attribute into the `<input>` tag:

```
<input type="reset" value="Start From Scratch" />
```

Harvesting Text with Text Boxes

For simple text entries, such as a person's name or favorite Beatle, use text boxes. These are just rectangles within which readers can type whatever they like. Here's the basic format for a text box:

```
<input type="text" name="field name" />
```

Page Pitfall

It's crucial to remember that every form control (button, text box, and so on) must have a unique name. The only exception to this is that a group of related radio buttons (discussed a bit later) must have the same name.

In this case, *field name* is a name you assign to the field that's unique among the other fields in the form. For example, to create a text box the reader can use to enter his first name (let's call it first), you'd enter the following:

```
<input type="text" name="first" />
```

For clarity, you also want to precede each text box with text that tells the reader what kind of information to type in. For example, the following line precedes a text box with `First Name:` so the reader knows to type in his first name:

```
First Name: <input type="text" name="first" />
```

 Here's some HTML code (textbox.htm on the CD) that utilizes a few text boxes to gather some information from the reader:

```
<html>
<head>
<title>Harvesting Text with Text Boxes</title>
</head>
<body>
<h3>Please tell me about yourself:</h3>

<form action="http://www.mcfedries.com/scripts/formtest.asp"
method="post">
<p>
First Name: <input type="text" name="first" />
</p>
<p>
Last Name: <input type="text" name="last" />
</p>
<p>
Nickname: <input type="text" name="nickname" />
</p>
<p>
Nom de Plume: <input type="text" name="nomdeplume" />
</p>
<p>
Nom de Guerre: <input type="text" name="nomdeguerre" />
</p>
<p>
<input type="submit" value="Just Do It!" />
<input type="reset" value="Just Reset It!" />
</p>
</form>

</body>
</html>
```

Figure 4.5 shows how it looks in Safari.

If you run this form (that is, if you click the Just Do It! button), the data is sent to my test script. Why? Because I included the following line:

```
<form action="http://www.mcfedries.com/scripts/formtest.asp"
method="post">
```

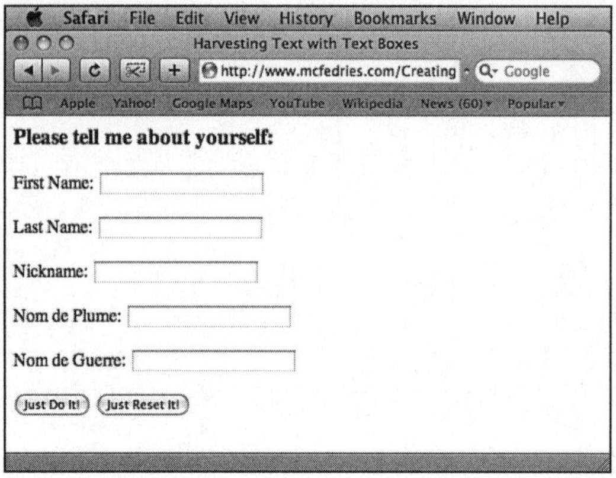

Figure 4.5

A form with a few text boxes.

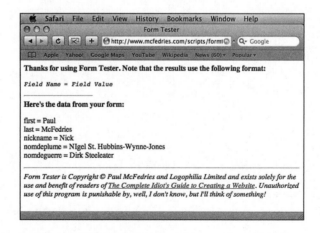

You'd normally replace this `action` attribute with one that points to a script that does something useful to the data. You don't have such a script right now, so it's safe just to use my script for testing purposes. Remember that this script doesn't do much of anything except send your data back to you. If everything comes back okay (that is, there are no error messages), you know your form is working properly. Just so you know what to expect, Figure 4.6 shows an example of the page that gets returned to the browser. Notice how the page shows the names of the fields followed by the value the user entered.

Figure 4.6

An example of the page that's returned when you send the form data to my text script.

Text boxes also come with the following bells and whistles:

Setting the default value. If you'd like to put some prefab text into the field, include the `value` attribute in the `<input>` tag. For example, suppose you want to know the address of the user's home page. To include `http://` in the field (because most addresses begin with this), you'd use the following tag:

```
<input type=text name="url" value="http://" />
```

Setting the size of the box. To determine the length of the text box, use the `size` attribute. (Note that this attribute affects only the size of the box and not the length of the entry; for the latter, see the `maxlength` attribute, discussed next.) For example, the following tag displays a text box that's 40 characters long:

```
<input type=text name="address" size="40" />
```

Limiting the length of the text. In a standard text box, the reader can type away until her fingers are numb. If you'd prefer to restrict the length of the entry, use the `maxlength` attribute. For example, the following text box is used to enter a person's age and sensibly restricts the length of the entry to three characters:

```
<input type=text name="age" maxlength="3" />
```

Harvesting Multiline Text with Text Areas

If you want to give your readers lots of room to type their hearts out, or if you need multiline entries (such as an address), you're better off using a *text area* than a text box. A text area is also a rectangle that accepts text input, but text areas can display two or more lines at once. Here's how they work:

```
<textarea name="field name" rows="total rows" cols="total columns"
wrap>
</textarea>
```

Here, *field name* is a unique name for the field, *total rows* specifies the total number of lines displayed, and *total columns* specifies the total number of columns displayed. The optional `wrap` attribute tells the browser to wrap the text onto the next line whenever the user's typing hits the right edge of the text area.

Note, too, that the `<textarea>` tag requires the `</textarea>` end tag. If you want to include default values in the text area, just enter them—on separate lines, if necessary—between `<textarea>` and `</textarea>`.

The following HTML tags (textarea.htm on the CD) show a text area in action, and Figure 4.7 shows how it looks in a browser.

```
<html>
<head>
<title>Harvesting Multiline Text with Text Areas</title>
</head>
<body>
```

```
<h3>Today's Burning Question</h3>

<form action="http://www.mcfedries.com/scripts/formtest.asp"
method="post">
<p>
First Name: <input type="text" name="first" />
</p>
<p>
Last Name: <input type="text" name="last" />
</p>
<p>
Today's <i>Burning Question</i>: <b>How did the fool and his money get
together in the first place?</b>
</p>
<p>
Please enter your answer in the text area below:
<br>
<textarea name="answer" rows="10" cols="60" wrap>
</textarea>
</p>
<p>
<input type="submit" value="I Know!" />
<input type="reset" />
</p>
</form>

</body>
</html>
```

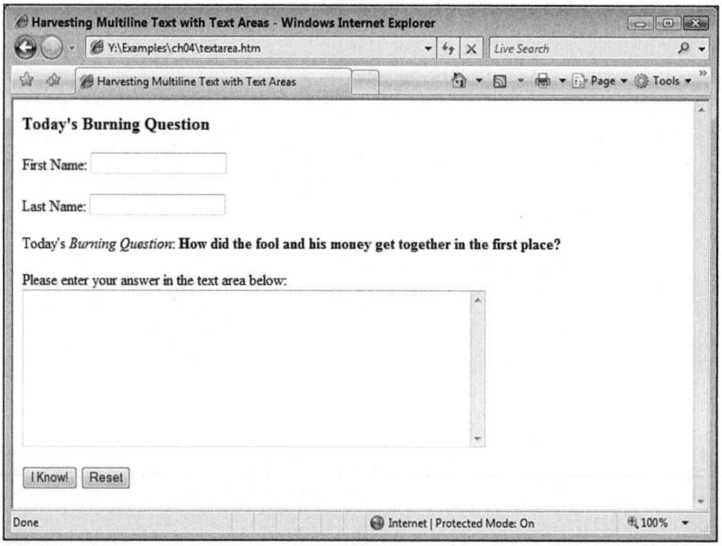

Figure 4.7

An example of a text area.

Yes or No? Using Check Boxes

If you want to elicit yes/no or true/false information from your readers, use check boxes. After all, it's a lot easier to check a box than it is to type in the required data. Here's the general format for an HTML check box:

```
<input type="checkbox" name="field name" />
```

As usual, `field name` is a unique name for the field. You can also add the `checked` attribute to the `<input>` tag, which tells the browser to display the check box "pre-checked." Here's an example:

```
<input type="checkbox" name="species" checked />Human
```

Notice in the preceding example that I placed some text beside the `<input>` tag. This text is used as a label that tells the reader what the check box represents. Here's a longer example (checkbox.htm on the CD) that uses several check boxes:

```
<html>
<head>
<title>Yes or No? Using Check Boxes</title>
</head>
<body>
<h3>Welcome to Hooked On Phobics!</h3>
<hr />

<form action="http://www.mcfedries.com/scripts/formtest.asp"
method="post">
<p>
What's <i>your</i> phobia? (Please check all that apply):
</p>
<p>
<input type="checkbox" name="ants" />Myrmecophobia (Fear of ants)<br />
<input type="checkbox" name="bald" />Peladophobia (Fear of becoming
bald)<br />
<input type="checkbox" name="beards" checked />Pogonophobia (Fear of
beards)<br />
<input type="checkbox" name="bed" />Clinophobia (Fear of going to
bed)<br />
<input type="checkbox" name="chins" checked />Geniophobia (Fear of
chins)<br />
<input type="checkbox" name="flowers" />Anthophobia (Fear of
flowers)<br />
<input type="checkbox" name="flying" />Aviatophobia (Fear of flying)<br
/>
```

```
<input type="checkbox" name="purple" />Porphyrophobia (Fear of
purple)<br />
<input type="checkbox" name="teeth" checked />Odontophobia (Fear of
teeth)<br />
<input type="checkbox" name="thinking" />Phronemophobia (Fear of
thinking)<br />
<input type="checkbox" name="vegetables" />Lachanophobia (Fear of
vegetables)<br />
<input type="checkbox" name="fear" checked />Phobophobia (Fear of
fear)<br />
<input type="checkbox" name="everything" />Pantophobia (Fear of
everything)<br />
</p>
<p>
<input type="submit" value="Submit">
<input type="reset">
</p>
</form>
</body>
</html>
```

Figure 4.8 shows how it looks (I've checked a few of the boxes so you can see how they appear).

Figure 4.8

Some check box examples.

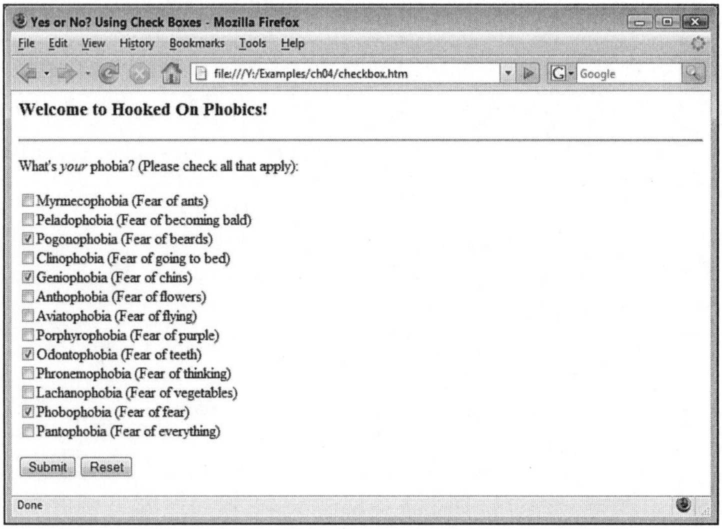

Webmaster Wisdom

When you submit a form with a check box, the data returned by the test script is a bit different from the data returned by the other controls. For one thing, the script returns only the values for check boxes that were activated; for another, the value returned for these checked check boxes is "on." For example, in the checkbox.htm file, if the check box named "beards" is activated when the form is submitted, the following line appears in the results:

```
beards = on
```

Pick One: Using Radio Buttons

Instead of yes/no choices, you might want your readers to have a choice between three or four options. In this case, *radio buttons* are your best bet. With radio buttons, users get (usually) three or more options, but they can pick only one of them.

Here's the general format:

```
<input type="radio" name="field name" value="value" />
```

Again, `field name` is the unique field name, except in this case you supply the same name to *all* the radio buttons you want grouped together. (More on this in a sec.) The `value` is a unique text string that specifies the value of the option when it's selected. In addition, you can also add `checked` to one of the buttons to have the browser activate the option by default. The following HTML document (radiobutton.htm on the CD) puts a few radio buttons through their paces.

```
<html>
<head>
<title>Pick One: Using Radio Buttons</title>
</head>
<body>
<h3>Survey</h3>

<form action="http://www.mcfedries.com/scripts/formtest.asp"
method="post">
<p>
Which of the following best describes your current salary level:
</p>
<dl><dd>
<input type="radio" name="salary" value="poverty" checked />Below the
poverty line<br />
```

```
<input type="radio" name="salary" value="living" />Living wage<br />
<input type="radio" name="salary" value="comfy" />Comfy<br />
<input type="radio" name="salary" value="dink" />DINK (Double Income,
No Kids)<br />
<input type="radio" name="salary" value="rockefellerish"
/>Rockefellerish
</dd></dl>
<p>
Which of the following best describes your political leanings:
</p>
<dl><dd>
<input type="radio" name="politics" value="way left" checked />So far
left, I'm right<br />
<input type="radio" name="politics" value="yellow dog" />Yellow Dog
Democrat<br />
<input type="radio" name="politics" value="middle" />Right down the
middle<br />
<input type="radio" name="politics" value="republican" />Country Club
Republican<br />
<input type="radio" name="politics" value="way right" />So far right,
I'm left
</dd></dl>
<p>
<input type="submit" value="Submit" />
<input type="reset" />
</p>
</form>

</body>
</html>
```

Webmaster Wisdom

In a rare burst of nerd whimsy, the HTML powers-that-be named radio buttons after the old car radio buttons you had to push to select a station.

Notice that the first five radio buttons all use the name `salary` and the next five all use the name `politics`. This tells the browser that it's dealing with two separate groups of buttons. This way, the user can select one (and only one) button in the `salary` group and one (and only one) button in the `politics` group, as shown in Figure 4.9.

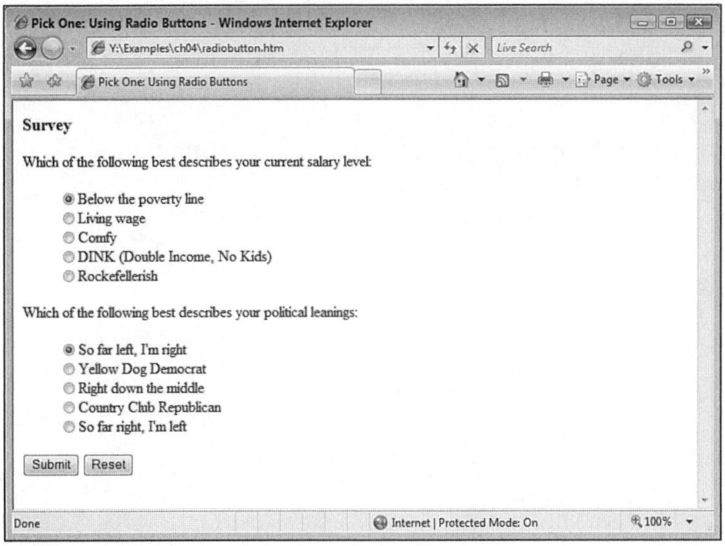

Figure 4.9

A form that uses radio buttons for multiple-choice input.

Selecting Data from Lists

Radio buttons are a great way to give your readers multiple choices, but they get unwieldy if you have more than about five or six options. For longer sets of options, you're better off using lists, or *selection lists* as they're called in the HTML world. Selection lists are a bit more complex than the other form tags we've looked at, but not by much. Here's the general format:

```
<select name="field name" size="items">
<option>First item text</option>
<option>Second item text</option>
<option>And so on...</option>
</select>
```

As I'm sure you've guessed by now, `field name` is the unique name for the list. For the `size` attribute, `items` is the number of items you want the browser to display. If you omit `size`, the list becomes a drop-down list. If `size` is two or more, the list becomes a rectangle with scroll bars for navigating the choices. Also, you can insert the `multiple` attribute into the `<select>` tag. This tells the browser to enable the user to select multiple items from the list.

> ### Webmaster Wisdom
>
> To select multiple list items in Windows, hold down the Control key and click each item. To do this on a Mac, hold down the ⌘ key and click each item.

Between the `<select>` and `</select>` tags are the `<option></option>` tags; these define the list items. If you add the selected attribute to one of the items, the browser selects that item by default.

 To get some examples on the table, the following document (lists.htm on the CD) defines no less than three selection lists:

```
<html>
<head>
<title>Selecting Data from Lists</title>
</head>
<body>
<h3>Putting On Hairs: Reader Survey</h3>

<form action="http://www.mcfedries.com/scripts/formtest.asp"
method="post">
<p>
Select your hair color:<br />
<select name="color">
<option>Black</option>
<option>Blonde</option>
<option selected>Brunette</option>
<option>Red</option>
<option>Something neon</option>
<option>None</option>
</select>
</p>
<p>
Select your hair style:<br />
<select name="style" size="4">
<option>Bouffant</option>
<option>Mohawk</option>
<option>Page Boy</option>
<option>Permed</option>
<option>Shag</option>
<option selected>Straight</option>
<option>Style? What style?</option>
</select>
</p>
<p>
Hair products used in the last year:<br />
<select name="products" size="5" multiple>
<option>Gel</option>
<option>Grecian Formula</option>
```

```
<option>Mousse</option>
<option>Peroxide</option>
<option>Shoe black</option>
</select>
</p>
<p>
<input type="submit" value="Hair Mail It!" />
<input type="reset" />
</p>
</form>

</body>
</html>
```

Figure 4.10 shows what the Firefox browser does with them.

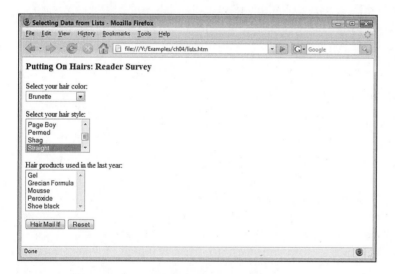

Figure 4.10

A form with a few selection list examples.

Getting the Data Delivered to Your Door

All this form folderol is fine, but what good is a form if it doesn't really do much of anything? That is, why bother building a fancy form if you have no way to get the data? Unfortunately, as I mentioned earlier, grabbing form data and manipulating it is a programmer's job. Specifically, you usually have to use something called the *Common Gateway Interface*, or CGI for short. CGI is a method of transferring form data in a manner that makes it relatively easy to incorporate into a program and then massage it all you need. Easy, that is, if you have the requisite nerd skills.

Well, I might not have the pages to teach you how to program forms, and you might not have the inclination in any case, but that doesn't mean you're totally stuck. You do have some options for getting your forms to do something useful:

Ask your provider. Many people want to add simple guest books and feedback mechanisms to their sites, but they don't want to have to bother with the programming aspect. So in response to their customers' needs, most web hosting providers make some simple CGI scripts (programs) available to their customers. For example, one common type of script grabs form data, extracts the field names and values, and sends them to an e-mail address you specify (like my MailForm program). Check with the provider's administrator or webmaster to see if it has any CGI scripts you can use. And if you haven't settled on a provider yet, ask in advance if it has CGI programs available.

Get another site to do the dirty work. Some sites out there process your forms for you, and some of them even do it for free! These sites usually offer some kind of wizard that helps you build your form, and you then copy the resulting code to your website. Here are three to check out:

- FormBuddy (www.formbuddy.com)

- Responders.com (www.responders.com)

- Response-o-matic (www.response-o-matic.com)

A service exclusively for readers. The easy solution to this CGI stuff is to have a helpful author write a program you can use for submitting your form data. And that's exactly what I've done. I've created a program called MailForm that takes form data and e-mails it to an address you specify. To use MailForm, you have to register on my website: www.mcfedries.com/mailform/register.asp. After you register, you'll receive instructions that tell you how to set up your form to take advantage of what MailForm has to offer.

Take the CGI-Joe route. A more expensive alternative is to hire the services of a CGI wizard (also known as a *CGI-Joe* in web programming circles) to create a custom program for you. Most web hosting providers are only too happy to put together a nice little program tailored to your needs. There's also no shortage of hired guns on the web who create programs to your specifications. As a starting point, check out some of the resources mentioned next.

Check out the web's CGI resources. If your service provider or web hosting provider doesn't have ready-to-run CGI programs you can use, there's no shortage of sites on the Net willing and able to either teach you CGI or supply you with programs. Here are some of these sites (see cgisites.htm on the CD):

- *Bravenet* (www.bravenet.com) offers lots of free scripts and other webmaster goodies.

- *CGI 101* (www.cgi101.com), as its name implies, offers beginner-level training and tutorials for CGI wannabe programmers. It also offers CGI hosting, links to other CGI sites, and much more.

- *The CGI Directory* (www.cgidir.com) is bursting at the seams with great CGI info, including tutorials, book reviews, FAQ, links to other CGI sites, and hundreds of scripts.

- *CGIexpo.com* (www.cgiexpo.com) is a nice site with lots of links to scripts, tutorials, mailing lists, books, and much more.

- *The CGI Resource Index* (www.cgi-resources.com) has thousands of links to scripts, tutorials, articles, programmers for hire, and much more. If there's a good CGI resource on the web, this site knows about it.

- *eXtropia* (www.extropia.com/applications.html) is the brainchild of Selena Sol and Gunther Birznieks, and it's one of the best CGI resources on the web.

- *Matt's Script Archive* (www.scriptarchive.com), by Matt Wright, offers tons of CGI scripts free to the web community. Matt has scripts for a guest book, random link generator, animation, and lots more. It's a great site and a must for would-be CGI mavens.

- *NCSA—The Common Gateway Interface* (hoohoo.ncsa.uiuc.edu/cgi) is *the* place on the web for CGI info. NCSA (the same folks who made the original Mosaic browser) has put together a great collection of tutorials, tips, and sample programs.

- *ScriptSearch* (www.scriptsearch.com) bills itself as "the world's largest CGI library," and with thousands of scripts in dozens of categories, I can believe it.

- *comp.infosystems.www.authoring.cgi* (http://news-reader.org) newsgroup is a useful spot for CGI tips and tricks, and it's just a good place to hang around with fellow web programmers.

- *Yahoo's CGI Index* (dir.yahoo.com/Computers_and_Internet/Software/Internet/ World_Wide_Web/Servers/Server_Side_Scripting/Common_Gateway_ Interface__CGI_/) is a long list of CGI-related resources. Many of the links have either CGI how-to info or actual programs you can use.

Talk Amongst Yourselves: Adding a Chat Room

On your site, visitors can "talk" to you if you include a mailto link on your pages or if you set up a feedback form. But what if you want your visitors to be able to talk to each other? That may sound strange at first glance, but it's a great way to set up a kind of "community" on your site and to ensure that people keep popping by.

Chat rooms come in many different flavors, of which three are the most popular: Java applets, JavaScript/AJAX (both are hosted on the remote server), and CGI scripts (which is usually installed on your own host). Here are some sites that offer chat rooms:

+ *Bravenet* (www.bravenet.com/webtools/chat) offers free Java-based chat rooms.

+ *Chat-Forum* (chat-forum.com) offers both free and commercial Java-based chat services. On the free service, you'll see banner ads or pop-up ads.

+ *Multicity* (www.multicity.com) offers a chat module that comes in both Java and HTML flavors you can install on your site.

+ *ParaChat* (www.parachat.com) has been around since 1996 and it offers a Java chat server hosted on the ParaChat site. A free service includes ads, or you can get rid of the ads by paying a few dollars a month.

+ *Pliner.Net* (www.pliner.net/chat) offers JavaScript-based chat rooms in both free (with ads) and commercial (no ads) flavors.

+ *QuickChat* (www.quickchat.org) hosts a chat server and gives you a Java applet to place on your site.

Discuss: Implementing Forums

Chatting is fun, even addictive for some, but it does have some drawbacks. For one, you may not always have time to join in or monitor the conversation, and there's rarely a record of the chat, so if something interesting comes up, it's tough to save it for posterity.

A good way to work around these problems while still boosting your site's community cred is to implement a forum or bulletin board. A forum operates a lot like a newsgroup. That is, people post a message, other people reply to that message, still other people reply to the replies, and so on. Visitors can ask or answer questions, you can join in anytime it's convenient for you, and the forum posts are archived for later viewing.

As with chat rooms, there are plenty of forum or bulletin board services available on the web. These are usually either Java applets or PHP/MySQL scripts hosted on the remote server. You can also find forums implemented with CGI scripts, which you usually install on your host. Here are some sites that offer forums or bulletin boards:

◆ *Boards2Go* (www.boards2go.com) is a CGI bulletin board service that offers both a free version with ads, and a paid version without them.

◆ *BoardServer* (boardserver.superstats.com) is a JavaScript-based bulletin board that's hosted on the BoardServer site. It costs (as I write this) $14.95 per month or $99 per year.

◆ *Bravenet* (www.bravenet.com/webtools/forum) offers free Java-based forums.

◆ *Groupee* (www.ubbcentral.com; formerly called Infopop) offers UBB.threads, a PHP/MySQL bulletin board script that you install on your web host.

◆ *MyBB* (www.mybboard.net) is powerful and free bulletin board software you can install on your site.

◆ *Multicity* (www.multicity.com) offers a message-board module that comes in both Java and HTML flavors you can install on your site.

◆ *Pliner.Net* (www.pliner.net/boards) offers JavaScript-based message boards in both free (with ads) and commercial (no ads) flavors.

The Least You Need to Know

◆ E-mail links use the *mailto* form of the `<a>` tag:

```
<a href="mailto:e-mailaddress">Link Text</a>
```

◆ To create a submit button, use `<input type="submit" value="`*label*`" />`.

◆ To create a text box, use `<input type="text" name="`*field name*`" />`.

◆ To create a check box, use `<input type="checkbox" name="`*field name*`" />`. To create a radio button, use `<input type="radio" name="`*field name*`" value="`*value*`" />`.

◆ To create a selection list, use `<select name="`*field name*`" size="`*items*`"> </select>` and `<option>`Item text`</option>`.

◆ Most chat rooms and bulletin boards are hosted on remote servers, and you place either a Java applet or some JavaScripts on your page.

Part 2

Designing Your Website

If you were building your own house, you wouldn't just nail up some dry-wall, pour some concrete, and then break out the bubbly to celebrate your finished home. You've got to slap on some paint, lay down some hardwood, and find just the right spot to hang that picture of the dogs playing poker. Your website is no different. You're at the drywall-and-concrete stage right now, and you need to start working on the website equivalents of paint, hardwood, and poker-playing dogs. You need, in short, to start thinking about the overall design of your web house. Can't design your way out of a paper bag? Not to worry! The chapters in Part 2 tell you everything you need to know.

The Elements of Good Site Design

In This Chapter

- ◆ Understanding style sheets
- ◆ Ideas for organizing your site
- ◆ Getting the hang of server-side includes
- ◆ The do's and don'ts of world-class webcraft

With all you've learned so far, you might be able to dress up your web pages, but can you take them anywhere? That is, you might have a web page for people to read, but is it a readable web page? Will web wanderers take one look at your page, say "Yuck!" and click their browser's Back button to get out of there, or will they stay awhile and check out what you have to say? Is your site a one-night surf, or will people add your page to their list of bookmarks?

My goal in this chapter is to show you there's a fine line between filler and killer—between "Trash it!" and "Smash hit!"—and show you how to end up on the positive side of that equation. To that end, I give you a few site design suggestions that help you put your best web page foot forward.

What Is Good Site Design?

Ask 10 web weavers to define "site design," and you'll almost certainly get 10 wildly diverse answers because it means different things to different people. The design of an artist's site is quite different from a programmer's site, and both won't be designed anything like a company's e-commerce site. However, if people say that these sites all have good site design, it's probably because they all have a few things in common:

Use a non-headache-inducing look. When most people think "design," they think about colors, images, and other visual doodads. These are important, but few of us have an artist's eye, so creating a visually gorgeous site is asking a bit much. Fortunately, your site doesn't have to be stunning looking to qualify as well designed. You just need to avoid the most egregious graphical faults, such as ugly backgrounds that make text hard to read, colors that clash with each other, and excessive use of fonts.

Remember, content is king. Good site design really begins and ends with the design of the content itself. Nobody will give a hoot about any other aspect of your site if they don't find your content compelling or useful. For more on this all-important topic, see the upcoming "Site Design Begins with Good Content" section.

Consistency, consistency, consistency. If you shoot for anything when designing your website, it should be for consistency. Use the same or a similar color scheme on each page, place important elements (such as a link to a contact form) not only on every page, but also in the same spot on every page. See "Using Style Sheets to Design Your Site" and "Use a Consistent Layout," later in this chapter.

Make things easy to find. We've all got too many sites to see, so no one likes to waste time trying to find things on a page. Good site design means making things easy for your visitors to find. See "Organizing Your Site," later in this chapter.

Make your reader feel welcome. If you want people to keep coming back to your website, you've got to lay out a virtual welcome mat and make everyone feel at home in your digital domicile. Having good content and a consistent, easy-to-figure-out layout are all very welcoming, but so are social elements such as feedback forms and bulletin boards. I talked about this in detail in Chapter 4.

Site Design Begins with Good Content

In earlier chapters, I gave you the goods on a number of web page techniques most folks would shelve under "Eye Candy" in the HTML store. These include fonts, colors, images, and free content such as weather maps. In later chapters, you learn about things like mouseovers and scrolling status bar messages. While even the most sober of web page engineers can and should use all these things, never forget one thing: it's the content, silly! This is the central fact of web page publishing, and all the glitz often obscures it.

And unless you're an artist or a musician or some other right-brain type, *content* means *text*. The vast majority of web pages are written documents that rely on words and phrases for impact. It makes sense, then, to put most of your page-production efforts into your writing. Sure, you'll spend lots of time fine-tuning your HTML codes to get things laid out just so, or tweaking your images, or scouring the web for "hot links" to put on your page, but you should direct most of your publishing time toward polishing your prose.

That isn't to say, however, that you need to devote your pages to earth-shattering topics composed with a professional writer's savoir faire. Many of the web's self-styled "style gurus" complain that most pages are too trivial and amateurish. Humbug! These ivory tower, hipper-than-thou types are completely missing the point of publishing on the web. They seem to think the web is just a slightly different form of book and magazine publishing, where only a select few deserve to be in print. *Nothing could be further from the truth!* With the web, anybody (that is, anybody with the patience to muddle through this HTML stuff) can get published and say what he or she wants to the world.

In other words, the web has opened up a whole new world of publishing opportunities, and we're in "anything goes" territory. So when I say, "Content is king," I mean you need to think carefully about what you want to say and make your page a unique experience. If you're putting up a page for a company, the page should reflect the company's philosophies, target audience, and central message. If you're putting up a personal home page, put the emphasis on the personal:

Write about topics that interest you. Heck, if *you* are not interested in what you're writing about, I guarantee your readers won't be interested, either.

Write with passion. If the topic you're scribbling about turns your crank, let everyone know. Shout from the rooftops that you love this stuff—you think it's the greatest thing since they started putting mute buttons on TV remotes.

Write in your own voice. The best home pages act as mirrors that show visitors at least an inkling of the authors' inner workings. Everybody—amateurs and professional scribes alike—has a unique writing voice; find yours and use it unabashedly.

Webmaster Wisdom

One surefire way to make your page a reflection of yourself is to write the way you talk. If you say "gotta" in conversation, go ahead and write "gotta" in your page. If you use contractions such as "I'll" and "you're" when talking to your friends, don't write "I will" and "you are" to your readers.

Tell stories. The enjoyment of a good story is hard-wired into the human brain. There's something about an engaging, well-told narrative that captures the imagination of readers and leaves them looking for more. Telling a tale doesn't mean crafting a Nabokovian short story or a Homeric ode. Rather, it just means narrating a story with some attention to detail, color, and pacing. Even a trip to the Department of Motor Vehicles for a license renewal can turn into a compelling yarn if you take your time and flesh out the characters you saw, the hurdles you had to overcome, the success you finally achieved.

Telling individual tales is wonderful, but you can also spin out lengthier narratives that develop over the course of a week, a month, or even longer.

Be yourself. As the (by now) old joke goes, in cyberspace, no one knows you're a dog. So it may be tempting to use the relative anonymity of the web to try on different personalities and do a little role-playing. There's nothing wrong with that per se, but your website is a lousy place to do it. For one thing, your site is supposed to be a unique expression of who you are, so by definition you should strive for personal honesty. Plus, your readers are savvier than you think and can spot a phony from a mile away. You might think you're being quite clever, but believe me, unless you're a particularly brilliant actor, the rest of us can see right through you.

 Page Pitfall

Each of us has a diverse inner life that allows for many different expressions and ways of being. If, for example, you spend your days being pleasant and polite, but you secretly harbor passionate or even controversial views about, say, politics, it's fair game to give that secret side an outlet in a website. The important thing is that what you write should be a true reflection of who you are. Otherwise, you're just wasting both your time and ours.

Have fun. Finally, always remember that having a website is not meant to be a deadly serious activity. It's true that a certain air of triumph and self-congratulations pervades cyberspace, with its boosters boasting that the web is superior to the "ancient media." This is mere hype, so don't believe it. The web is nothing more or less than a wonderful new medium for the likes of you and me to express ourselves, stretch our writing wings a bit, and commune with people who share our warped view of the world. In my mind, that's a recipe not for frown-causing seriousness or yawn-inducing earnestness, but for the smile-cracking joy and brain-stimulating excitement that are a natural by-product of sharing bits of ourselves within a caring and supportive community. That's a long-winded way of saying a simple thing: have fun out there!

Using Style Sheets to Design Your Site

If you've ever used a word processor such as Microsoft Word or WordPerfect, you've probably stumbled over a *style* or two in your travels. For example, you might have a "Title" style that combines four formatting options: bold, centered, 24-point type size, and an Arial typeface. You can then "apply" this style to any text, and the program dutifully formats the text with all four options. If you change your mind later and decide your titles should use an 18-point font, all you have to do is redefine the Title style. The program automatically trudges through the entire document and updates each bit of text that uses the Title style.

In a web page, a style performs a similar function. That is, it enables you to define a series of formatting options for a given tag, such as `<p>` or `<h1>`. Like word processor styles, page styles offer two main advantages: they save time because you create the definition of the style's formatting once, and the

def•i•ni•tion

In a nutshell, a **style** is one or more formatting options rolled into a nice, neat package.

browser applies that formatting each time you use the tag. And they make your pages easier to modify because all you need to do is edit the style definition and all the places where the style is used within the page are updated automatically.

So far so good, but what's a "style sheet"? The term *style sheet* harkens back to days of yore when word processors enabled you to store your styles in a separate document known as a style sheet. This is equivalent to what we today usually call a template. As you see later, it's possible to define all your HTML styles in a separate file and then tell the browser where that file is located, so it's a bit like those old style sheets (although *style file* might have been a better name). More generally, an HTML style sheet is any collection of styles, whether it exists in a separate file or within the current page.

You've seen quite a few styles already in this book, and you've learned one way to apply a style: add the `style` attribute to a tag (this is called an *inline style*). However, there are a couple other ways to use styles, and these methods can make it much easier to define a consistent and easily modified site design.

Using the `<style>` Tag

The problem with using the `style` attribute is that it applies the style to just a single tag. For example, if you have a page with a half-dozen `<h1>` headings and you want each of them to use, say, 24-point text, you need to add a `style` attribute and the `font-size` property to all six tags. Too much work!

To make your life easier, you can use just a single `<style>` tag instead. To see how this works, let's examine the general way you use this tag:

```
<html>
<head>

<style type="text/css">
<!--
Your style definitions go here
-->
</style>

</head>
<body>
The visible web page stuff goes here
</body>
</html>
```

def•i•ni•tion

A set of styles between the `<style>` and `</style>` tags is called an **embedded style sheet**.

Style sheet mavens call the `<style></style>` method an *embedded style sheet*. Note, too, that I tossed in the HTML comment tags for good measure—`<!--` opens the comment and `-->` closes it. This hides your style definitions from older browsers that don't know a style sheet from a rap sheet.

Between the `<style>` and `</style>` tags, you add one or more style definitions. Here's an example:

```
h1 {font-size: 24pt}
```

The definition usually begins with the HTML tag you want the style to modify, without the usual angle brackets (`<` and `>`).

The rest of the definition is ensconced inside those curly brackets—{ and }—which are known officially as *braces*.

The first thing inside the braces is the name of the property you want to set, followed by a colon (:). In our example, the property is `font-size`. After the colon, type the value you want to assign to the property (`24pt`, in the example, where `pt` is short for points).

As a different example, suppose you want all your `<tt>` text to appear in a gray font. As you learned earlier in the book, font color is governed by the `color` property, so you'd set this style as follows:

```
tt {color: gray}
```

Finally, you can set multiple properties in a single style by separating each property and value with a semicolon (;). In the following example, `<h2>` tags are displayed with purple, 20-point text:

```
h2 {color: purple; font-size: 20pt}
```

Here's an example (see embedded.htm on the CD):

```
<html>
<head>

<style type="text/css">
<!--
h1 {font-size: 24pt}
h2 {color: purple; font-size: 20pt}
-->
</style>

</head>
<body>
<h1>This is an &lt;h1&gt; heading</h1>
<h1>This is yet another &lt;h1&gt; heading</h1>
<h1>And another one</h1>
<h1>Okay, I'll stop now.</h1>
<h2>This is an &lt;h2&gt; heading</h2>
<h2>This, too, is an &lt;h2&gt; heading</h2>
</body>
</html>
```

> **Webmaster Wisdom**
>
> Besides applying multiple styles to a single tag, you can also apply a single style to multiple tags. List the tags you want to affect, separated by commas, before the opening brace ({):
>
> ```
> p, ol, ul, dt, dd {font-size: 10pt}
> ```

Figure 5.1 shows how the page looks in the browser. As you can see, all the `<h1>` headings look exactly the same, as do all the `<h2>` headings.

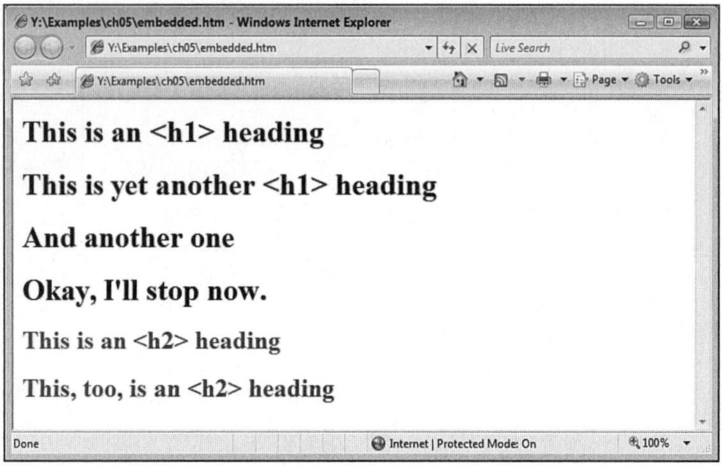

Figure 5.1

Use the `<style>` tag to apply a style to every instance of a particular tag in your page.

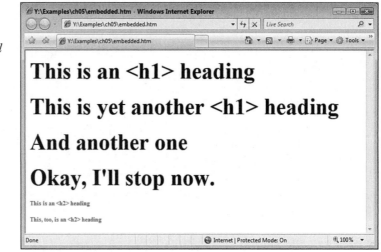

Now watch what happens when I tweak the style definitions:

```
h1 {font-size: 36pt}
h2 {color: green; font-size: 10pt}
```

Figure 5.2 shows the result. As you can see, with just a few simple edits, I completely changed the look of the headings.

Figure 5.2

Change the style definition, and you change the look of all the tags.

Linking to an External Style Sheet

Style sheets get insanely powerful when you use an "external" style sheet, a separate file that contains your style definitions. To use these definitions within any web page, you add a special `<link>` tag inside the page header. This tag specifies the name of the external style sheet file, and the browser then uses that file to grab the style definitions.

Here are the steps you need to set up an external style sheet:

1. Use your favorite text editor to create a shiny new text file.

2. Add your style definitions to this file. You don't need the `<style>` tag or any other HTML tags.

3. Save the file in the same directory as your HTML files, and use a .css extension (for example, "mystyles.css"). This helps you remember down the road that this is a style sheet file. (The "css" stands for cascading style sheet.)

4. For every page in which you want to use the styles, add a `<link>` tag inside the page header. Here's the general format to use (where *filename.css* is the name of your external style sheet file):

```
<link rel="stylesheet" type="text/css" href="filename.css" />
```

For example, suppose you create a style sheet file named mystyles.css and include the following style definitions in that file:

```
h1 {color: red}
tt {font-size: 16pt}
```

You then refer to that file by using the `<link>` tag shown in the following example (see external.htm on the CD):

```
<html>
<head>
<link rel="stylesheet" type="text/css" href="mystyles.css" />
</head>
<body>
<h1>This Heading Will Appear Red</h1>
<tt>This text will be displayed in a 16-point font</tt>
</body>
</html>
```

Why is this so powerful? Because you can add the same `<link>` tag to any number of web pages and they'll all use the same style definitions. This makes it a breeze to create a consistent look and feel for your site. And if you decide that your `<h1>` text should be green instead, all you have to do is edit the style sheet file (mystyles.css). Automatically, every single one of your pages that link to this file will update with the new style!

Webmaster Wisdom

The HREF part of the `<link>` tag doesn't have to be a simple file name. You can use a full URL, if necessary. This is handy if you've set up your site with multiple directories, or if you want to link to an external style sheet file on another site. (I don't recommend the latter, however; it takes your pages a bit longer to load because the browser has to go fetch the file.)

Working With Style Classes

You now know the three most common methods for implementing styles in your site, but I must mention a variation on the theme that can be really handy: the *style class*. The style class was created to solve a common problem: what if you want to apply a specific style to a number of different tags and sections throughout the document?

One solution would be to use inline styles. However, what if you decide to change the style? You would have to go through the entire page and edit all the inline styles. An easier approach is to set up a style class within your main style sheet (that is, either within the `<style>` tag or within an external style sheet file). Here's the basic format to use:

```
.ClassName {style definitions go here}
```

Here, `ClassName` is a unique name (without any spaces) that you use for the class. Here are a couple examples:

```
.TitleText {font-size: 20pt; color: Navy; text-align: center}
.SubtitleText {font-size: 16pt; color: Gray; text-align: center}
```

The `TitleText` class uses a font size of 20 points, navy text, and a center alignment; the `SubtitleText` class uses a font size of 16 points, gray text, and a center alignment.

To use these classes, add a `class` attribute to the tags you want the styles applied to, and set it equal to the class name (without the dot). Here's an example:

```
<div class="TitleText">
This is the Title of the Document
</div>
```

So if you decide to change this style, you need edit only the style class; after that, every tag that uses the class changes automatically.

Here's a page (see class.htm on the CD) that offers up a complete example:

```html
<html>
<head>
<title>Working with Style Classes</title>

<style type="text/css">
<!--
.TitleText {font-size: 20pt; color: navy; text-align: center}
.SubtitleText {font-size: 16pt; color: gray; text-align: center}
-->
</style>

</head>
<body>
<div class="TitleText">This is the Title of the Document</div>
<div class="SubtitleText">This is the Subtitle of the Document</div>
</body>
</html>
```

Figure 5.3 shows how Firefox interprets the classes.

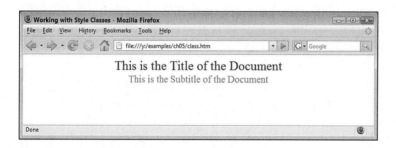

Figure 5.3

Use style classes for even more control over your styles.

Organizing Your Site

Let's now turn our attention to some ideas for getting (and keeping) your website affairs in order. You need to bear in mind, at all times, that the web is all about naviga-tion. Heck, half the fun comes from just surfing page to page via links. Because you've probably been having so much fun with this HTML stuff that you've created multiple pages for your site, you can give the same navigational thrill to your readers. All you need to do is organize your site appropriately and give visitors some way of getting from one page to the next.

What do I mean by organizing your site "appropriately"? Well, look at two things:

- How you split up the topics you talk about
- How many total documents you have

The One-Track Web Page

Although there are no set-in-stone rules about this site organization stuff, most people follow one principle: one topic, one page. That is, cramming a number of disparate topics into a single page is not usually the way to go. For one thing, it's wasteful because a reader might be interested in only one of the topics, but he or she still has to load the entire page. It can also be confusing to read. If you have, say, some insights into metallurgy and some fascinating ideas about Chia Pets, tossing them together in a single page is just silly. (Unless you have a *very* strange hobby!) Make each of your pages stand on its own by dedicating a separate page for each topic. In the long run, your readers will be eternally thankful.

There's an exception to this one page, one topic rule for the terminally verbose: if your topic is a particularly long one, you end up with a correspondingly long page. Why is that a problem? Lengthy web pages have their disadvantages:

- Large files can take forever to load, especially for visitors accessing the web from a slow connection. (This becomes even worse if the page is full of images.) If loading the page takes too long, most people aren't likely to wait around for the cobwebs to start forming; they're more likely to abandon your site and head somewhere else.

- If you have navigation links at the top and bottom of the page (which I talk about later on), they aren't visible most of the time if the page is long.

- Nobody likes scrolling through endless screens of text. Pages with more than three or four screenfuls of text are hard to navigate and tend to be confusing for the reader.

Page Pitfall

Some studies show that many web ramblers don't like to scroll at all! They want to see one screenful and then move on. This is extreme behavior, to be sure, and probably not all that common (for now, anyway). My guess is that many folks make a snap judgment about a page based on their initial impression. If they don't like what they see, they catch the nearest wave and keep surfin'.

To avoid these pitfalls, consider dividing large topics into smaller subtopics and assigning each one a separate page. Be sure you include links in each page that make it easy for the reader to follow the topic sequentially (more on this later).

For example, I have an e-mail primer on my site. It's a long article, so I divided it up into eight separate pages and then added navigation links to help the reader move from section to section. Figure 5.4 shows one of those sections.

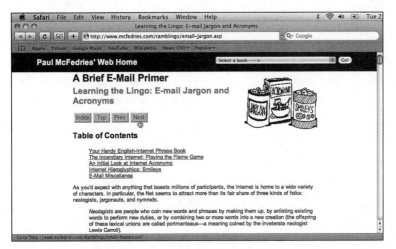

Figure 5.4

Break down long-winded topics into several pages by putting navigation links on each page.

Tie Everything Together with Your Home Page

Most people begin the tour of your pages at your home page. With this in mind, you should turn your home page into a sort of electronic launch pad that gives the surfer easy access to all your stuff. Generally, that means peppering your home page with links to all your topics. For example, check out my Word Spy site's home page shown in Figure 5.5. Through the various types of links, readers can get to any part of the site with just a click or two.

Figure 5.5

Surfers should be able to navigate to almost anywhere on your site from your home page.

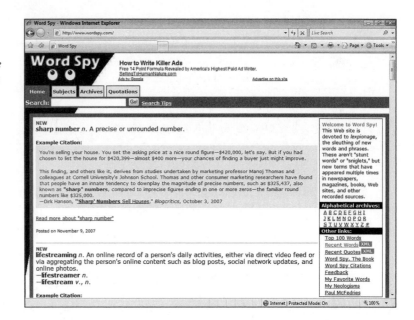

Use a Consistent Layout

Another thing to keep in mind when designing your pages is consistency. When folks are furiously clicking links, they don't often know immediately where they've ended up. If you use a consistent look throughout your site (or throughout a set of related pages), everyone will know that they're still on your home turf.

If you have a logo or other image that identifies your site, plant a copy on each of your pages (and be sure to set up that image as a link back to your home page). Or if you'd prefer to tailor your graphics to each page, at least put the image in the same place on each page. And use the same background color or image on all your pages.

Close your page titles with a consistent phrase. For example, "Why I Love Zima - Jim Bob's Site," or "The BeDazzler Page - Alphonse's CyberHome."

If you use links to help people navigate through your pages, put the links in the same place on each page.

Use consistent sizes for your headings. For example, if your home page uses the `<h1>` tag for the main heading and `<h3>` tags for subsequent headings, use these tags the same way on all your pages.

Figures 5.6 and 5.7 show you what I mean. The first is the home page of my book *The Complete Idiot's Guide to a Smart Vocabulary*, and the second is the home page of my book *The Complete Idiot's Guide to Windows XP*. As you can see, the two pages use an almost identical layout. So if you know how to get around in one site, you have no problem figuring out the other.

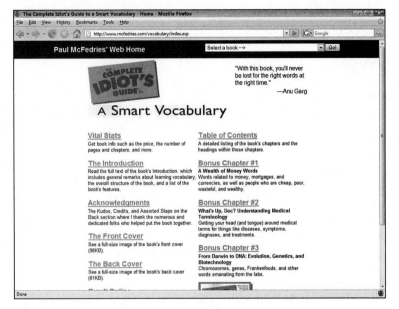

Figure 5.6

The home page of my book The Complete Idiot's Guide to a Smart Vocabulary.

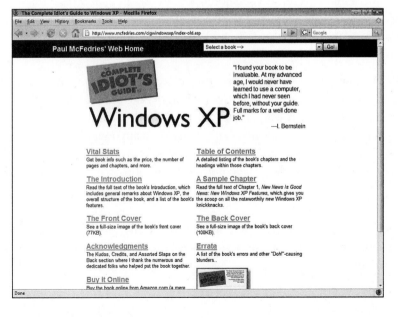

Figure 5.7

The home page of my book The Complete Idiot's Guide to Windows XP. *Note the consistent layout between the two pages.*

Laying Out Your Pages

After you get the forest of your website in reasonable shape, it's time to start thinking about the trees, or the individual pages. The next few sections give you a few pointers for putting together perfect pages.

What to Include in Each Page

For each of your web pages, the overall subject of the page dictates the bulk of the content that appears. If you're talking about Play-Doh, for example, most of your text and images will be Play-Doh related. But there are a few elements you should include in all your pages, no matter what the subject matter.

Give it a title. A site without page titles is like a cocktail party without "Hi! My Name Is ..." tags.

Add a main heading. Nobody wants to scour a large chunk of a page to determine what it's all about. Instead, include a descriptive, large heading (`<h1>` or `<h2>`) at the top of the page to give your readers the instant feedback they need. In some cases, a short, introductory paragraph below the heading is also a good idea.

Add a "signature." If you're going on the web, there's no point in being shy. People appreciate knowing who created a page, so you should always "sign" your work. You don't need anything fancy; just your name and your e-mail address will do. If the page is for a business, also include the company name, address, phone number, and fax number.

List any pertinent copyright info. If the web pages you create are for your company, the company owns the material that appears on the page. Similarly, the contents of personal home pages belong to the person who created them. In both cases, copyright law protects the contents of the pages, and they can't be used by anyone else without permission. To reinforce this, include a copyright notice at the bottom of the page. Here's an example (the `&copy;` code displays the copyright symbol):

```
The content of this site is Copyright &copy; 2008 Millicent Peeved
```

Give the current status of the page. If your page is a preliminary draft, contains unverified data, or is just generally not ready for prime time, let your readers know so they can take that into consideration.

Include a feedback mechanism. Always give your visitors some way to contact you so they can lavish you with compliments or report problems. The usual way to do this is to include a "mailto" link somewhere on the page (as described in Chapter 4).

Link back to your home page. As I mentioned earlier, your home page should be the "launch pad" for your site, with links taking the reader to different areas. To make life easier for the surfers who visit, however, each page should include a link back to the home page.

Most of these suggestions can appear in a separate section at the bottom of each page (this is often called a *footer*). To help differentiate this section from the rest of the page, use an `<hr>` (horizontal rule) tag and an `<address>` tag. On most browsers, the `<address>` tag formats text in italics. Here's an example footer (look for footer.txt on the CD) you can customize:

Page Pitfall

Many webmeisters include some kind of "Under Construction" icon on unfinished pages. This is fine, but don't overdo it. The nature of the web is that most pages are in a state of flux and are constantly being tweaked. (This is, in fact, a sign of a good site.) Scattering cute construction icons everywhere reduces their impact and annoys many readers.

```
<hr>
<address>
This page is Copyright &copy; 200?, your name here<br />
company name here<br />
company address here<br />
Phone: (###) ###-####<br />
Fax: (###) ###-####<br />
Email: <a href="mailto:your-email-address-here">your email address
here</a>.
</address>
<p>
Last revision: date goes here
</p>
<p>
Return to my <a href="home-page-url-goes-here.htm">home page</a>.
</p>
```

Make Your Readers' Lives Easier

When designing your web pages, always assume your readers are in the middle of a busy surfing session and, therefore, won't be in the mood to waste time. It's not that people have short attention spans. (Although I'd bet dollars to doughnuts that the percentage of habitual web surfers with some form of ADD—attention-deficit disorder—is higher than that of the general population.) It's just the old mantra of the perpetually busy: "Things to do, places to go."

So how do you accommodate folks who are in barely-enough-time-to-*see*-the-roses-much-less-stop-and-smell-the-darn-things mode? Here are a few ideas:

◆ Organize your pages so people can find things quickly. Break up your text into reasonable-size chunks and make judicious use of headers to identify each section.

◆ Put all your eye-catching good stuff at the top of the page where people are more likely to see it.

◆ If you have a long document, place anchors (see the next section) at the beginning of each section and include a "table of contents" at the top of the document that includes links to each section.

◆ Add new stuff regularly to keep people coming back for more. This is particularly true of blog pages, where frequent updates are standard. You should also mark your new material with some sort of "new" graphic so regular visitors can easily find the recent additions.

Anchors Aweigh!: Internal Links

When a surfer clicks a standard link, the page loads and the browser displays the top part of the page. However, it's possible to set up a special kind of link that will force the browser to initially display some other part of the page, such as a section in the middle of the page. For these special links, I use the term *internal links*, because they take the reader directly to some inner part of the page.

When would you ever use such a link? Most of your HTML pages will probably be short and sweet, and the web surfers who drop by will have no trouble navigating their way around. But if, like me, you suffer from a bad case of terminal verbosity combined with bouts of extreme long-windedness, you'll end up with lengthy web pages. Rather than force your readers to scroll through your tomelike creations, you can set up links to various sections of the document. For example, you could then assemble these links at the top of the page to form a sort of "hypertable of contents."

Internal links actually link to a special version of the `<a>` tag—called an *anchor*—that you've inserted somewhere in the same page. To understand how anchors work, think of how you might mark a spot in a book you're reading. You might dog-ear the page, attach a note, or place something between the pages, such as a bookmark or your cat's tail. An anchor performs the same function. It "marks" a particular spot in a web page, and you can then use a regular <a> tag to link to that spot.

I think an example is in order. Suppose I want to create a hypertext version of this chapter. To make it easy to navigate, I want to include a table of contents at the top of the page that includes links to all the section headings. My first chore is to add anchor tags to each heading. Here's the general format for an anchor:

```
<a name="Name"></a>
```

As you can see, an anchor tag looks a lot like a regular link tag. The major difference is that the HREF attribute is replaced by name="Name"; Name is the name you want to give the anchor. You can use whatever you like for the name, but most people choose relatively short names to save typing. Notice, too, that you don't need any text between the <a name> tag and the </a> end tag.

Where do you put this tag? The best place is immediately before the start of the section you want to link to. For example, this chapter's first section is titled "What Is Good Site Design?" If I want to give this section the uninspired name Section1, I use the following anchor:

```
<a name="section1"></a>
<h2>What Is Good Site Design?</h2>
```

Now, when I set up my table of contents, I can create a link to this section by using a regular <a> tag (with the usual HREF attribute) that points to the section's name. And just so a web browser doesn't confuse the anchor name with the name of another document, I preface the anchor name with a number sign (#). Here's how it looks:

```
<a href="#section1">What Is Good Site Design?</a>
```

Here's some HTML code (see chapter5.htm on the CD) that sets up this chapter's section titles as headings, and uses anchors on the main (<h2>) headings to set up internal links to those sections:

```
<html>
<head>
<title>Anchors Aweigh!: Internal Links</title>
</head>
<body>
<h1>The Elements of Good Site Design</h1>
<b>Hypertable of Contents:</b>
```

```
<dl>
<dd><a href="#section1">What Is Good Site Design?</a>
<dd><a href="#section2">Site Design Begins with Good Content</a>
<dd><a href="#section3">Using Style Sheets to Design Your Site</a>
<dd><a href="#section4">Organizing Your Site</a>
<dd><a href="#section5">Laying Out Your Pages</a>
<dd><a href="#section6">Inserting Files with Server-Side Includes</a>
</dl>
<hr />
<a name="section1"><h2>What Is Good Site Design?</h2></a>
<a name="section2"><h2>Site Design Begins with Good Content</h2></a>
<a name="section3"><h2>Using Style Sheets to Design Your Site</h2></a>
<h3>Using the &lt;style&gt; Tag</h3>
<h3>Linking to an External Style Sheet</h3>
<h3>Working With Style Classes</h3>
<a name="section4"><h2>Organizing Your Site</h2></a>
<h3>The One-Track Web Page</h3>
<h3>Tie Everything Together with Your Home Page</h3>
<h3>Use a Consistent Layout</h3>
<a name="section5"><h2>Laying Out Your Pages</h2></a>
<h3>What to Include in Each Page</h3>
<h3>Make Your Readers' Lives Easier</h3>
<h3>Anchors Aweigh!: Internal Links</h3>
<a name="section6"><h2>Inserting Files with Server-Side Includes</h2>
</a>
<h3>The Include Tag</h3>
<h3>The Echo Tag</h3>
</body>
</html>
```

Figure 5.8 shows how it looks in Safari.

Although you'll mostly use anchors to link to sections of the same web page, there's no law against using them to link to specific sections of other pages. All you do is add the appropriate anchor to the other page and link to it by adding the anchor's name (preceded, as usual, by #) to the end of the page's file name. For example, suppose you want to put a link in a page and you want that link to whisk the reader immediately to the "Laying Out Your Pages" section of chapter5.htm. I gave that section the anchor name section5, so here's a tag that sets up a link to it:

```
<a href="chapter5.htm#section5">Laying Out Your Pages</a>
```

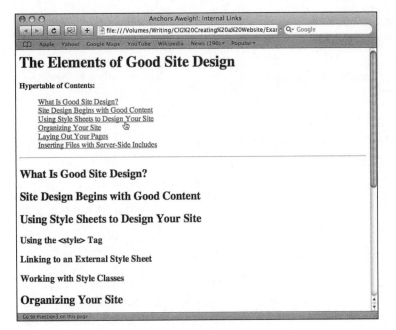

Figure 5.8
The hypertext version of this chapter's headings.

Inserting Files with Server-Side Includes

This section tells you about a clever little technology called server-side includes that enables you to include certain kinds of content automatically in your pages. As you'll see, this can save you *a lot* of time, particularly if you include similar content on all or most of your pages.

The Include Tag

As you've seen, one of the hallmarks of a good site is a consistent layout among your pages, and part of what this means is having certain elements appear on all or most of your pages. Here are some examples:

◆ Links to the major sections of your site

◆ A "header" at the top of each page that includes a logo or some other image, the name of your site, and a motto or slogan

◆ A "footer" at the bottom of each page that includes items such as your name, contact information, and a copyright notice

Adding snippets such as these to each of your pages isn't really a big deal. You just type it out once, copy it, and paste the text into your other HTML files. Ah, but what if you make a change to the text or to a link? In that case, you have to open all your files and edit each one accordingly. That's no big thing if you have only a few pages, but what if you have 20 or 120?

To avoid the mind-numbing drudgery of having to edit a ridiculous number of pages each time you make a small change, consider using something called a *server-side include* (SSI). This involves two things:

◆ A small text file that contains any combination of text and tags.

◆ A special SSI tag you place inside each of your pages. This SSI tag references the text file. Essentially, the tag tells the web server to replace the tag with the entire contents of the text file.

Page Pitfall _____

Remember that SSI requires the services of a server to work properly. If you view your page with the include tag on your own computer, you won't see the inserted file.

What's the advantage here? Simply this: it means you need to edit only that lone text file. Because the server always replaces the SSI tag with the latest version of the text file, all your pages display the edited text automatically.

What's the catch? There are two:

◆ Your web host's server must be set up to handle SSI.

◆ You usually need to use the .shtml extension on any files that have the SSI tag. (SSI also works with ASP or PHP pages, if your web host supports them.)

To use SSI requires two steps:

1. Create a new text file and use it to insert the tags and text you want into your pages. When you're done, be sure to upload this file to your web host directory.

2. In each HTML file you want the text file inserted, add the special SSI tag I've been blathering on about:

```
<!--#include file="TextFileName"-->
```

This is called the *SSI include tag*, and you need to replace *TextFileName* with the name of the text file from step 1. Remember, as well, to position this tag *exactly* where you want the text file's contents to appear.

Let's give an example a whirl. Earlier I showed you the contents of a text file named footer.txt (which you'll find on the CD). Here's the code for a file named include. shtml (also on the CD), which includes an SSI tag that references the footer.txt file:

def•i•ni•tion

An **SSI include tag** is a special HTML tag that points to a text file and tells the browser to include the text from that file in the page.

```
<html>
<head>
<title>Using Server-Side Includes: The Include Tag</title>
</head>

<body>
<p>
The regular page text and graphics go here.
</p>
<!--#include file="footer.txt"-->

</body>
</html>
```

As you can see in Figure 5.9, the server replaces the SSI tag with the contents of footer.txt.

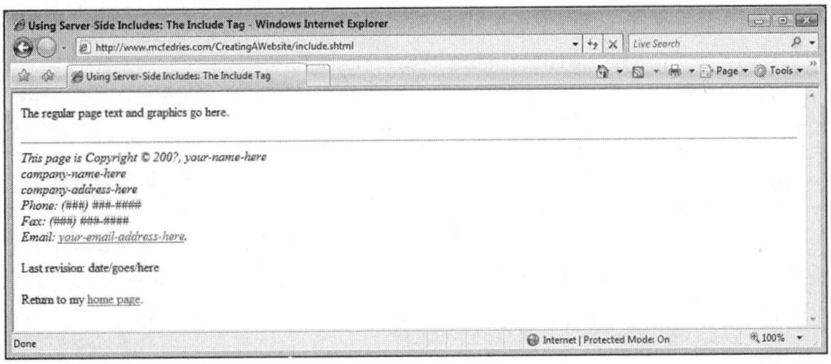

Figure 5.9

When the browser trips over the SSI include tag, it replaces the tag with the entire contents of the file specified by the tag.

The Echo Tag

Most servers that support SSI also support a second SSI tag:

```
<!--#echo var="VariableName"-->
```

This is called the *SSI echo tag*, and you use it to "echo" or write a specific type of data to the page. The data that gets written depends on what you specify for the *VariableName*. For example, you can use the LAST_MODIFIED variable:

```
Last edited on <!--#echo var="LAST_MODIFIED"-->
```

Here, the server replaces the SSI echo tag with the date and time when the file was last modified:

```
Last edited on Friday, August 23 2007 03:02:59
```

Table 5.1 lists some of the more useful echo variable names (as well as a few that are only semi-useful).

Table 5.1   Some SSI Echo Tag Variables

Variable	What It Echoes
DATE_GMT	The current date and time at Greenwich (Greenwich Mean Time)
DATE_LOCAL	The current date and time on the server
DOCUMENT_NAME	The current page's server directory and name
DOCUMENT_URI	The URL of this page (less the host)
LAST_MODIFIED	The date and time this page was last modified
HTTP_REFERER	The address the user came from to get to the current page
REMOTE_ADDR	The IP address of the user

When you're using any of the date and time echo variables, the actual appearance of the output varies depending on the browser and the surfer's computer. Thankfully, you can control the appearance of the date and time by using the SSI config tag:

```
<!--#config timefmt="TimeFormat"-->
```

Place this tag immediately before your SSI echo tag, and replace *TimeFormat* with any of the formats listed in Table 5.2.

Table 5.2   Some SSI Config Tag Formats

Format	What You Get
%a	The abbreviated weekday name
%A	The full weekday name
%b	The abbreviated month name
%B	The full month name
%c	The date and time format that's appropriate for the user's locale
%C	The default date and time format
%d	The day of month (from 01 to 31)
%H	The hour in 24-hour format (00 to 23)
%I	The hour in 12-hour format (01 to 12)
%j	The day of the year (001 to 366)
%m	The month of the year (01 to 12)
%M	The minute (00 to 59)
%p	A.M. or P.M.
%S	The second (00 to 59)
%U	The week of the year, where Sunday is the first day of the week (00 to 51)
%w	The day of the week (Sunday = 0)
%W	The week number of year, where Monday is the first day of the week (00 to 51)
%x	The date format for the user's current locale
%X	The time format for the user's current locale
%y	The year without the century (00 to 99)
%Y	The year with the century (for example, 2007)

Here's the code from a page that puts the SSI echo tag through its paces (see echo.shtml on the CD):

```
<html>
<head>
<title>The SSI Echo Tag</title>
</head>

<body>
```

```
<b>Some useful (and semi-useful) echo variables:</b>
<table border="1">
<tr><th>VARIABLE</th><th>What Gets Echoed</th><th>Description</th></tr>
<tr><td>DATE_GMT</td>
<td><!--#echo var="date_gmt"--></td>
<td>Current date and time at Greenwich (Greenwich Mean Time).</td></tr>
<tr><td>DATE_LOCAL</td>
<td><!--#echo var="date_local"--></td>
<td>Current date and time on the server.</td></tr>
<tr><td>DOCUMENT_NAME</td>
<td><!--#echo var="document_name"--></td>
<td>This page's server directory and name.</td></tr>
<tr><td>DOCUMENT_URI</td>
<td><!--#echo var="document_uri"--></td>
<td>URL of this page (less the host).</td></tr>
<tr><td>LAST_MODIFIED</td>
<td><!--#echo var="last_modified"--></td>
<td>Date and time this page was last modified.</td></tr>
<tr><td>HTTP_REFERER</td>
<td><!--#echo var="http_referer"--></td>
<td>Address the user came from.</td></tr>
<tr><td>REMOTE_ADDR</td>
<td><!--#echo var="remote_addr"--></td>
<td>IP address of the user.</td></tr>
</table>

<b>Formatting the date and time:</b>
<table border="1">
<tr><th>TIMEFMT</th><th>What the Date and Time Look Like</th></tr>
<tr><td>%#c</td>
<td><!--#config timefmt="%#c"--><!--#echo var="last_modified"--></td>
</tr>
<tr><td>%c</td>
<td><!--#config timefmt="%c"--><!--#echo var="last_modified"--></td>
</tr>
<tr><td>%x</td>
<td><!--#config timefmt="%x"--><!--#echo var="last_modified"--></td>
</tr>
<tr><td>%#x</td>
<td><!--#config timefmt="%#x"--><!--#echo var="last_modified"--></td>
</tr>
<tr><td>%X</td>
<td><!--#config timefmt="%x"--><!--#echo var="last_modified"--></td>
</tr>
```

```
<tr><td>%a, %b %d, %Y</td>
<td><!--#config timefmt="%a, %b %d, %y"--><!--#echo var="last_
modified"--></td>
</tr>
</table>
</body>
</html>
```

Figure 5.10 shows how things look in the browser.

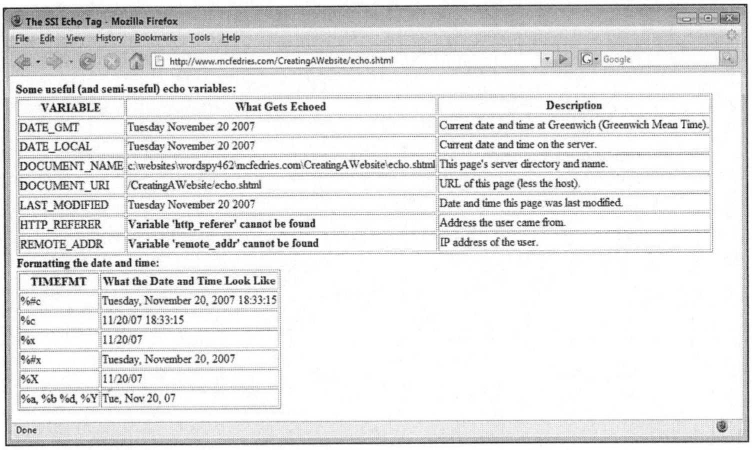

Figure 5.10

Some SSI echo tags.

The Least You Need to Know

♦ Spend most of your site construction time working on the text, and remember to write passionately and in your own voice about topics that interest you.

♦ A style is a collection of formatting instructions for a given tag, and a style sheet is a collection of styles.

♦ An embedded style sheet is a style sheet that resides inside a document and is defined by the `<style>` and `</style>` tags.

♦ An external style sheet is a collection of styles that sits in a separate file. You let the browser know about the existence of this file by using the `<link>` tag.

♦ Keep your pages short and confined to a single topic wherever possible and use a more or less consistent layout on all your pages.

Chapter 6

Getting There from Here: Site Navigation

In This Chapter

- ◆ Understanding directories
- ◆ Cooking up a navigation bar
- ◆ Dropping breadcrumb links
- ◆ Letting surfers search your site
- ◆ Setting up a list of links
- ◆ Drawing up a site map

Having good content wrapped inside good-looking pages is (or should be) the goal of all would-be web authors. Second to that, do your site visitors know where to put their virtual feet when they walk in the front door of your website? Even more important, is it possible for those surfers who enter your site via a side door to find their way to the main entrance? (By a side door I mean they've "deep linked" directly to one of your content pages via, say, a search engine.)

In other words, can people who show up at your website easily navigate it? What do I mean by easy navigation? Really, it's just three things:

◆ Being able to see, at a glance, the main sections of your site.

◆ Being able to easily leap from one site section to another.

◆ Knowing which section of the site you're currently in.

Any website that implements these three navigational goals is going to get a lot of return traffic because web surfers appreciate a site with a simple and easy-to-use navigation system. In this chapter, you learn how to implement these three things on your own site.

Site Organization: Directories

A disorganized site is rarely an easily navigated site, so site navigation always begins with site organization. And site organization always begins with directories. A *directory* is a file storage area that's been carved out of a hard disk. Before getting to the meat of the navigation lesson, let's take a short side trip to understand how directories work in the web world.

> ### Webmaster Wisdom
>
> If you use Windows or a Mac, you may be more familiar with the term *folder* instead of *directory;* it means the same thing. However, *directory* is more often used in web page publishing circles, so that's what I use throughout this book.

When you sign up with a company that will "host" your web pages, that company supplies you with your very own directory on its server. If you're only putting together a few pages, that directory should be more than adequate. If you're constructing a larger site, however, you should give some thought to how you organize your files. Think of your own computer. It's unlikely that you have everything crammed into a single directory. Instead, you probably have separate directories for the different programs you use and other directories for your data files.

There's no reason why you can't cook up a similar scheme in your web home. On my site, to give you an example, I have separate directories for many of my books (such as this book's CreatingAWebSite directory), a directory called Ramblings that stores miscellaneous writings, a Graphics directory to store all my image files, and so on. The basic idea is that you use each directory to store similar pages and files.

However, with this type of multidirectory setup, how you reference files in other directories can be a bit tricky. As an example, consider a website that has three directories:

```
/ (this is the main directory)
things/
stuff/
```

Here, "things" and "stuff" are subdirectories of the main directory. There are three scenarios to watch out for:

Referencing a file in the same directory. This is the easiest because you don't have to include any directory information. Suppose the HTML file you're working on is in the stuff directory and you want to reference a page named tirade.html also in that directory. In this case, you just use the name of the file, like this:

```
<a href="tirade.html">
```

Referencing a file in a subdirectory from the main directory. This is a common scenario because your home page (which is almost certainly in the main directory) is likely to have links to files in subdirectories. For example, suppose you want to link to a page named doggerel.html in the things subdirectory from your home page. Then your `<a href>` tag takes the following form:

```
<a href="things/doggerel.html">
```

Referencing a file in a subdirectory from a different subdirectory. This is the trickiest scenario. For example, suppose you have a page in the things subdirectory and you want to link to a page named duh.html in the stuff subdirectory. Here's the `<a href>` tag:

```
<a href="../stuff/duh.html">
```

The ".." represents what's called the *parent* directory (that is, the one that contains the current directory). It essentially says, "From here, go up to the parent directory, and then go down into the stuff subdirectory."

Setting Up a Navigation Bar

One of the easiest ways to make your website easily navigable is to add a navigation bar on each page. A navigation bar is just a series of links to each of the main sections of your site. By putting these links on every page, your visitors can easily jump from one part of the site and back again. Most web weavers put the navigation part at the top of each page, but there's no reason why you couldn't use a column in a multicolumn site layout (as explained in Chapter 2).

Converting an Image into a Link

There's nothing wrong with using text links for your navigation bar, but many site designers prefer to use images because they often look nicer than plain text. Recall from Chapter 1 that you use the `<a>` tag to build a link into a web page:

```
<a href="url">The link text goes here</a>
```

The *url* part is the Internet address of the web page (or whatever) to which you want to link.

Designating an image as a link isn't very different from using text. You use the same `<a>` tag, but you insert an `<img>` tag between the `<a>` and `</a>` tags, like this:

```
<a href="url"><img src="filename" /></a>
```

Again, *url* is the address of the linked page, but *filename* is the name of the graphics file you want to appear in the page for the surfer to click.

Page Pitfall _____

Always keep the `<img>` tag and the `</a>` end tag on the same line in your HTML file. In other words, don't do this:

```
<a href="url"><img src="filename" />
</a>
```

If you do, you'll see a tiny (yet very annoying) line protruding from the bottom right corner of your image.

For example, it's often a good idea to include a link back to your home page on all your other web pages. This makes it easy for your readers to start over again. Here's a document (backhome.htm on the CD) that sets up an image of a house as the link back to the home page:

```
<html>
<head>
<title>Converting an Image into a Link</title>
</head>
<body>
Click this house <a href="index.htm"><img src="house.gif" /></a>
to return to my home page.
</body>
</html>
```

> ### Webmaster Wisdom
>
> When you use an image as a link, it's a good (possibly even a great) idea to include the `alt` attribute in the `<img>` tag to specify alternate text. This helps the visually impaired use the link and, as an added bonus, it helps search engines index your site.

Figure 6.1 shows what it looks like. Notice how the browser displays a border around the image to identify it as a link.

Figure 6.1

An image masquerading as a link.

The link border that appears around an image link isn't usually very flattering to the image. To keep your images looking good, get rid of the border by adding `border="0"` to your `<img>` tag:

```
<img src="house.gif" border="0" />
```

You can use image links for any number of things on your site, but for our purposes here, we want to use them to add some navigational aids to your site. The next couple of sections provide you with the details.

Setting Up a Web Page Toolbar

Almost all modern programs have toolbars festooned with buttons that give you one-click access to the program's most-used commands and features. You can use image links to provide a similar convenience to the folks who trudge through your site. The basic process for setting this up involves three steps:

1. Use your favorite graphics program to create buttonlike images that represent important sections of your website (your home page, your guest book, your list of links to Ozzy Osbourne sites, and so on).

2. Create `<img>` tags to set up these buttons as image links that point to the appropriate pages.

3. Insert these `<img>` tags consecutively (that is, on a *single* line in the text file) at the top and/or bottom of each page. The consecutive `<img>` tags cause the images to appear side by side. Presto: instant web toolbar!

The design of your buttons is entirely up to you, but most web toolbars use some combination of image and text. I don't have an artistic bone in my body, so I prefer to use "text-only" images, as shown in Figure 6.2. This toolbar is just six linked images displayed on a single line. Here's the HTML code I used to create this toolbar (see toolbar.htm on the CD):

> ### Webmaster Wisdom
>
> Every good graphics program has some kind of "Text" tool that enables you to add text to an image.

```
<html>
<head>
<title>Setting Up a Web Page Toolbar</
title>
</head>
<body>
<a href="/books/index.html">
➥<img src="books.gif" border="0" /></a>
➥<a href="/ramblings/index.html">
➥<img src="ramblings.gif" border="0" /></a>
➥<a href="/toys/index.html">
➥<img src="toys.gif" border="0" /></a>
➥<a href="/guestbook.html">
➥<img src="guestbk.gif" border="0" /></a>
➥<a href="/search.html">
➥<img src="search.gif" border="0" /></a>
➥<a href="/index.html">
➥<img src="homepage.gif" border="0" /></a>
</body>
</html>
```

To be sure the buttons are smushed together, type all the `<a>` tags and `<img>` tags on a single line. (Remember, that's what the ➥ symbol means.)

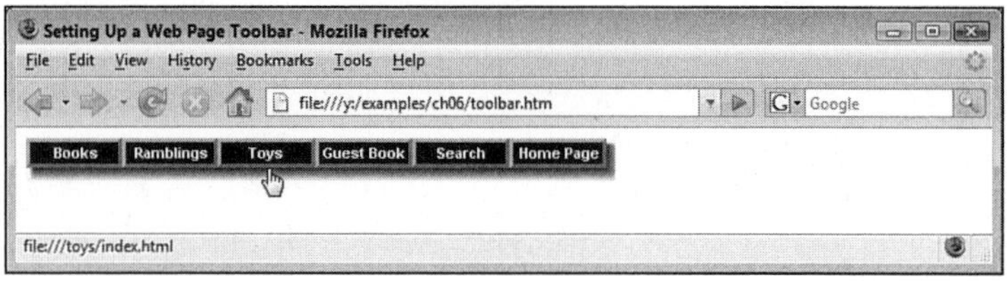

Figure 6.2

Cram consecutive image links together for a handy web page toolbar.

![Screenshot of Mozilla Firefox showing "Setting Up a Web Page Toolbar" with a toolbar containing buttons: Books, Ramblings, Toys, Guest Book, Search, Home Page. Address bar shows file:///y:/examples/ch06/toolbar.htm. Status bar shows file:///toys/index.html]

Creating Navigation Buttons

Some websites contain material that could (or should) be read serially. That is, you read one page and then the next page, and so on. In these situations, it's convenient to give the reader an easy method for navigating back and forth through these pages. The solution many sites use is to set up DVD-style buttons on the page. These are usually arrows that point forward or backward, as well as a "rewind" button that takes the reader to the first page in the series.

For example, Figure 6.3 shows a page from my website. This page is part of a primer on Internet e-mail, and the buttons near the top of each page enable you to navigate to the next installment (the Next button), the previous installment (the Prev button), the first installment (the Top button), or to the home page for this section of my site (the Index button).

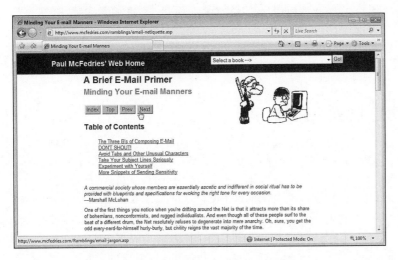

Figure 6.3

This web page uses image links as navigation buttons.

You Are Here: Creating Breadcrumb Links

Breadcrumbing refers to a navigation feature that displays a list of the places a person has visited or the route a person has taken. The term comes from the fairy tale of Hansel and Gretel, who threw down bits of bread to help find their way out of the forest. What does it have to do with your website? If your content is organized as a hierarchy or as a sequence of pages, you can use breadcrumb links to not only show people where they are now, but also to enable them to navigate your site hierarchy or sequence.

The idea is simple: you start with a link to your home page or the opening page of the hierarchy or sequence. Then as the surfer moves down into the hierarchy or through the sequence, you add more links that show the various stops the person has taken along the way. In between each link, add a character that shows that the pages flow from one to the other. Common examples are the greater-than symbol (>; HTML character code >) and the right double-angle quotation mark (»; HTML character code »). Some people also use the vertical bar (|), double colons (::), or the bullet (•; HTML character code •). Figure 6.4 shows an example.

Figure 6.4

This web page uses bread-crumb links.

breadcrumb links ──

Making Your Site Searchable

If your site contains only a single page, or just a few pages, most visitors should be able to find what he or she is looking for. (Assuming, of course, you've set up the necessary links to your pages.) That may not be the case, however, if your site starts getting a bit big for its britches. When you start talking about your total number of pages in the dozens or even the hundreds, finding a specific tidbit may become a real page-needle-in-a-website-haystack exercise.

Adding a Search Feature

To keep your visitors happy, you can add a searching component to your site, just like the big-time websites have. You can find such resources in webland, many of which are free. (However, there are some limitations. For example, maybe a maximum number of pages can be indexed, and you might be required to place an image or ad on your site.)

Before you start checking out specific search services, note that they all return a "results page" after the user runs a search. These results list all the pages on your site that match whatever criteria the user specified for the search. It's important to remember that these results will be useful only if you've done a bit of prep work in advance so your site is search-ready. This means setting up your pages just like you would if you were preparing for the major search engines to come calling: having descriptive titles on every page, using the "Description" and "Keywords" `<meta>` tags, and so on. (See Chapter 11 for details on setting up your site for search engines.)

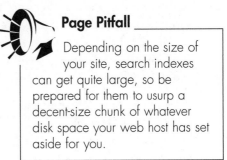

Page Pitfall

Depending on the size of your site, search indexes can get quite large, so be prepared for them to usurp a decent-size chunk of whatever disk space your web host has set aside for you.

Besides the results page, search features also usually include the following three components:

- The search engine
- The search index
- The search form

The search engine is the part that does the actual searching of your site. There are many different types of search engines but two main components are: CGI scripts and search hosting. I discuss these in detail a bit later.

Before the search engine can run searches, it must first "crawl" through your site, reading the text of each page. As it goes along, it compiles a list of the words on each page (usually bypassing common words such as *the* and *and*). The words, along with pointers to the pages in which they appear, are stored in a file called an *index*. When the user searches for a particular word, the search engine looks up the word in the index, grabs a list of the pages in which that word appears, and displays that list to the user.

The search form is the form your visitors use to enter their search criteria. Look for a search service that provides a prebuilt form (ideally, one that can be customized to blend in with your site design).

Searching for a Search Feature

Your search for a good search feature should begin at home. That is, first ask your web hosting provider if it offers a search feature for its customers. If not, it's time to hit the road.

As I mentioned earlier, there are two main search components to consider: a CGI script and a search host. The CGI route involves installing a script on your web host's server, either in your own `cgi-bin` (if you have one) or the host's global `cgi-bin`. Remember that most hosts will want to inspect a CGI script before they'll let you install it. To find a script, see my list of CGI resources in Chapter 4.

A search host is a separate site that hosts not only the search engine, but also the search index. This type of search is marginally slower because the data has to go to and from the other server. However, it's the only way to go if your web host won't allow you to install a CGI program or Java applet, or if your disk space on the server is running low.

Here are some search hosts to check out:

◆ *Atomz* (www.atomz.com) is completely free and indexes up to 10,000 pages! This is probably the most popular of the search servers.

◆ *FreeFind* (www.freefind.com) is free for sites that have up to 32MB data. You're required to place a banner ad (which shows ads for various products) on the search results page.

◆ *FusionBot* (www.fusionbot.com) offers a "Free Package" that lets you index up to 250 pages. The results page has both a banner ad (with ads from FusionBot sponsors) and a FusionBot logo.

◆ *Google* (www.google.com/intl/en_extra/services/free.html) offers a "SiteSearch Companion" for your site. The free version indexes an unlimited number of pages, and the results page (on which Google reserves the right to display an ad) looks just like the regular Google page.

◆ *Master.com* (www.master.com) has a "Search Your Site" feature, the free version of which is happy to index up to 5,000 pages, or 30MB data. You're required to display the Master.com logo on the results page.

◆ *PicoSearch* (www.picosearch.com) offers a free version that indexes up to 250 pages, although you're required to place an ad for PicoSearch on the results page.

Webmaster Wisdom

To help you explore the sites I discussed in this section, I compiled a page with links to the sites. See search.htm on the CD.

Creating Drop-Down Lists of Links

After your site grows to a certain size, you run up against a daunting problem: how do you let surfers navigate to the various nooks and crannies of your site without cluttering each page with tons of links or a massive toolbar? My solution to this problem is the option list you learned about in Chapter 4. Figure 6.5 shows what I mean. As you can see, the list contains all kinds of items that represent pages on my site. The surfer simply picks an item from the list and is immediately whisked to the selected spot. Best of all, it takes up just a small strip of space at the top of each of my pages.

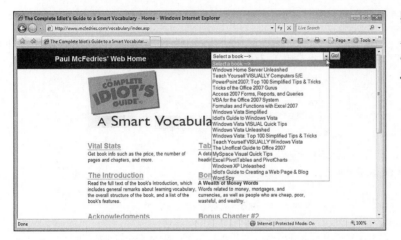

Figure 6.5

Each of my pages uses a drop-down list to help folks navigate my site.

The secret behind this list legerdemain is JavaScript, the programming language that enhances many a website. I give you the full scoop on incorporating JavaScript into your pages in Chapters 12 and 13. For now, let's see how easy it is to set up just such a list on your own site.

Let's begin with the list itself. Start by setting up a more or less standard selection list within a form:

```
<form>
<select width="20" onChange="JumpToIt(this)">
</select>
</form>
```

There are two things you should note about this structure. First, the `<form>` tag is completely naked. That's okay because with this technique you never have to submit any form data to a server. That makes this method as lightning quick as a regular link.

Also, the `<select>` tag houses the JavaScript `onChange` attribute. This tells the browser that whenever the list changes (that is, whenever the user selects a different item), it must run the JavaScript function named `JumpToIt()`. (The `this` part is a reference to the list itself that gets sent to the function.)

Now you need to populate the list with items that represent your pages. You do that with `<option>` tags that take the following form:

```
<option value="url">Item text</option>
```

Here, replace `url` with the address of the page, and replace `Item text` with whatever text you want to appear in the list (such as the page title).

If you want to add nonactive items to the list (such as a "Select an item from this list" message or headings), use `<option>` tags that take the following form:

```
<option value="none">Item text</option>
```

 Again, replace `Item text` with the text you want to appear in the list. Here's the list structure with a few items added (see linklist.htm on the CD):

```
<select width="20" onChange="JumpToIt(this)">
<option value="none">Select a search feature site from this list --->
</option>
<option value="http://www.atomz.com/">Atomz</option>
<option value="http://www.freefind.com/">FreeFind</option>
<option value="http://www.google.com/intl/en_extra/services/free.
html">Google</option>
<option value="http://www.master.com/">Master.com</option>
<option value="http://www.picosearch.com/">PicoSearch</option>
</select>
```

You put all the form code in your page at the place where you want the list to appear.

Here's the JavaScript that's executed when the user selects a list item:

```
<script language="javascript" type="text/javascript">
<!--
function JumpToIt(list)
{
    var selection = list.options[list.selectedIndex].value
    if (selection != "none")
        location.href = selection
}
//-->
</script>
```

The value of the currently selected list item is stored in the selection variable. If the value isn't "none," then the value is a URL, so the `location.href` property is set to that value, and away you go. You put the JavaScript code between the `</head>` and `<body>` tags.

Cyber-Cartography: Adding a Site Map

Site features such as toolbars, breadcrumb links, searching, and link lists make it easy for passersby to find their way around your site. The only problem is that these features tend to show just part of your site, usually just the major sections or, in the case of a search feature, just those parts of the site that match the surfer's search text. This isn't a big whoop on a small site, but if you've built quite a few pages, these visitors may be missing out on some of your good stuff.

To prevent that, you need to give people a true bird's-eye view of your site that shows links to not just a few of your pages, but to *all* of them. You do this by creating what website mavens call a *site map*. Despite the name, a site map isn't an actual map. Instead, it's just a collection of links to every page on your site, organized by category. To give you an idea how this works, Figure 6.6 shows part of the Google site map.

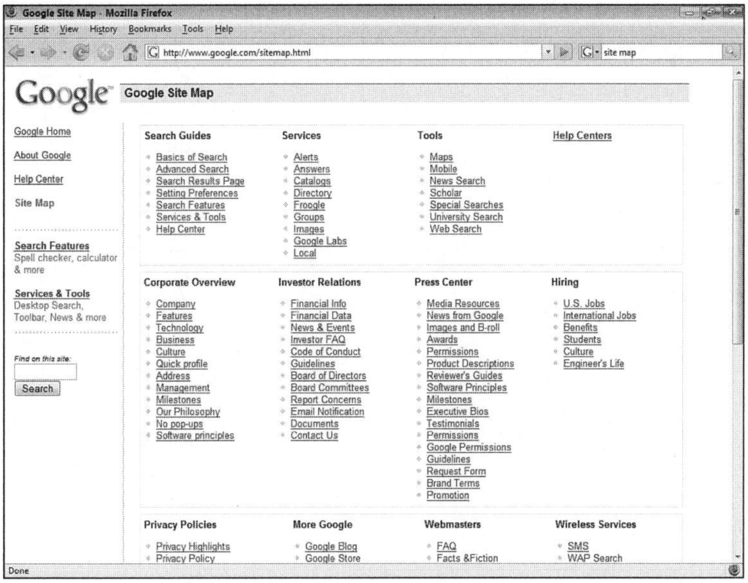

Figure 6.6

The Google site map is a large collection of text links organized into various categories.

Some sites get really ambitious and use images for the site map links. The most common structure is an organization chart (with the site's home page as the "boss"), but there are many other structures, some of them quite interesting and attractive. For example, check out the site map shown in Figure 6.7.

Figure 6.7

An example of an image-based site map.

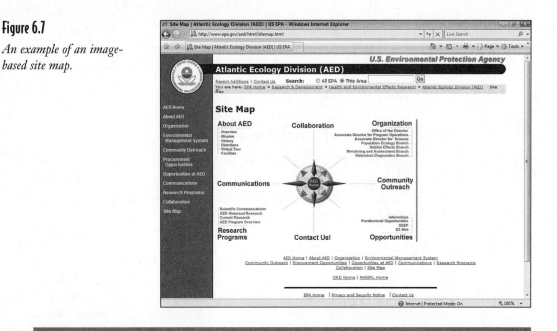

Webmaster Wisdom

Another easy way to create a site map is to use a free program called Xenu's Link Sleuth, available here:

```
http://home.snafu.de/tilman/xenulink.html
```

This program's main purpose in life is to check your site for broken links (that is, links that no longer link to anything), which is very useful. However, the program also comes with a feature that will turn your site's links into a basic text-based site map.

The Least You Need to Know

◆ If the page you're linking to is in the same directory as the current document, you can get away with specifying only the file name in the link's URL.

◆ To set up an image as a link, shoehorn the appropriate `<img>` tag between `<a>` and `</a>`:

```
<a href="url"><img src="filename" /></a>
```

◆ Breadcrumb links are a navigation feature that displays a list of the links to the places a person has visited or the route a person has taken within a site.

◆ There are two main types of search components: a CGI script and a search host.

◆ To set up a site map, use either a categorized list of text links or an image.

Configuring Your Website for Mobile Browsers

In This Chapter

♦ Learning about mobile browsers

♦ Creating a style sheet for a mobile browser

♦ Designing and testing your site for mobile browsing

♦ Hiding images from a mobile browser

Just a few short years ago, web weavers could count on visitors viewing their sites only on computer screens and only using a limited set of screen sizes. So you might design your site to look good at, say, 1024×768, and test it at 800×600 and 1280×1024 just to be sure things didn't go wonky on you at the different resolutions.

Ah, if only life was that simple nowadays! Now folks surf not only using their desktop and notebook machines, but also with devices such as pocket PCs, personal digital assistants (PDAs), and cell phones. This means that a significant portion of your site's visitors will be navigating your pages using a screen that's a *lot* smaller than normal. How in tarnation are you going to cram your whole website into such a tiny space while still allowing folks with big displays to get the full benefit of that extra screen real estate?

The answer to that question is the subject of this chapter. Here you'll learn that it's possible to set up an alternate site configuration that takes mobile devices into account, while still letting other visitors see your site in all its big-screen glory.

A Closer Look at Mobile Browsers

Big-screen visitors surf to your site using a web browser such as Internet Explorer, Firefox, or Safari. However, folks with mobile devices most likely don't use these big-name browsers. Instead, they most often use a browser the device manufacturer has either licensed from a mobile browser vendor or has cobbled together and optimized themselves to work well on the device. Collectively, these are called *mobile browsers* (or sometimes *microbrowsers*).

Popular Mobile Browsers

Here's a list of some of the more popular mobile browsers:

- Opera Mini (www.operamini.com)
- Opera Mobile (www.opera.com/products/mobile)
- Access NetFront Browser (www.access-company.com/products/netfrontmobile)
- Minimo (www.mozilla.org/projects/minimo)
- Openwave Mobile Browser (www.openwave.com)
- Picsel (www.picsel.com/index.php/solutions/view/C11)

In addition to these third-party mobile browsers, there's also Microsoft's Internet Explorer Mobile (see www.microsoft.com/windowsmobile/software/iemobile.mspx), which is the standard mobile browser on Pocket PCs and other Windows Mobile devices, and Apple's Mobile Safari (see www.apple.com/iphone/features/index.html#safari), which is featured on the iPhone and the iPod Touch.

Bad News on the Mobile Browser Front

Although having the web in the palm of you hand is handy, and will bring more traffic to your site, there are a few mobile-browser hiccups to keep in mind.

The implementation of all the mobile browsers is as varied as the companies themselves. Some mobile browsers—such as Opera Mobile, Minimo, Internet Explorer

Mobile, and Mobile Safari—adhere reasonably closely to web standards such as XHTML and CSS, and so render pages consistently. However, standards-compliance for other mobile browsers is all over the map, so you can never be certain how a mobile device will interpret your code.

Also, microbrowser visitors will be viewing your website not on a nice 22-inch desktop monitor, nor on a decent 15-inch notebook display, but with a teensy mobile device display that could be as small as 1.5 inches wide.

Plus, while the majority of desktop and note-book surfers bask in 1024×768 or better screen resolution, mobile device screens can usually muster no better than 240×320, and it's more likely to be 208×208, 176×208, or even a mere 128×128. (Once again, the iPhone is the champ here with its 480×320 resolution.)

> **Webmaster Wisdom**
>
> Some "big" mobile screens are 1.5 inches by 2.5 inches; the largest mobile screen out there right now is the iPhone, which measures a "whopping" 2 inches by 3 inches.

And finally, there's low bandwidth. Although many mobile devices now come with Wi-Fi support baked in (which means they can piggyback on any nearby Internet access by making a wireless connection to that network, if security permits), the reality is that the vast majority of mobile browsing is done via the cellular system, which is usually quite slow. Add to this the fact that almost all mobile devices are hobbled by having a relatively small amount of memory and a slow processor speed, and you have a recipe for a very slow web experience.

So Why Even Bother?

With all these negatives associated with mobile browsers, wouldn't you just be better off ignoring anyone silly enough to try to view your magnificent site on a screen barely bigger than a postage stamp? Isn't modifying your site to handle the mobile mob a lot of work for very little payback? Will these questions just go on and on?

The answer in each case is a resounding "No!" Yes, overall mobile browser use (in terms of page views) is still pretty small, but almost every pundit in the mobile device industry expects mobile browsing to be the Next Big Thing. Even now, almost everyone who has web access via a mobile device browses the web at least occasionally, and a few brave souls use their mobile browsers the majority of the time. In short, mobile browsing is *this close* from jumping into the mainstream.

Happily, as you'll see a bit later, it's not a ton of work to configure your site to make it mobile-friendly. In fact, you just need to set up a style sheet with a few properties and you're more or less good to go. And that work will pay off big time when people who use a mobile browser realize that your site is pro-mobile. Because so few websites are currently optimized for mobile browsing, and because microbrowsing mobile-challenged sites is frustrating and often impossible, folks will come back to your site. They'll appreciate that you took the time to make their browsing lives easier.

Testing ... Testing ...: Mobile Simulators

I mentioned earlier that there's a distressingly wide variety of mobile browsers out there. And while you can easily install, say, Internet Explorer, Firefox, and Safari on your computer to test your site with these major browsers, it's unlikely you've got a bunch of cell phones, PDAs, and pocket PCs lying around for testing purposes. So how will you know whether your mobile modifications are even working? You've got a few choices:

♦ Use whatever cell phones, PDAs, or pocket PCs you have at your disposal to test the site.

♦ Get your friends and family to browse your site using their mobile devices.

♦ Get a few mobile simulators (or emulators).

Mobile simulators are tools that show you what a given site would look like when viewed through the screen of a particular mobile device. Here's a list of mobile simulators you can use:

♦ Opera Mini (www.operamini.com/demo)

♦ NetFront (www.access-company.com/developers/downloads)

♦ BlackBerry (www.blackberry.com/developers/downloads/simulators.jsp)

♦ Openwave (developer.openwave.com/dvl/tools_and_sdk/phone_simulator)

Webmaster Wisdom

If you have the regular Opera browser, you can switch it to small screen view either by selecting **View, Small Screen,** or by pressing **Shift+F11**. This reduces the browser's content area to a display that's about 240 pixels wide.

Setting Up a Mobile Style Sheet

A few years ago, if you were gung-ho enough to want to support mobile browsers on your site, you were forced to learn a variation on the HTML theme called WML—Wireless Markup Language. Unfortunately for those who learned WML, that language is now on the outs. Instead, you just use the standard-issue tags and CSS properties you learned earlier in the book.

Okay, you're probably wondering at this point, if I just use standard HTML and CSS, how the heck do I support mobile browsers? First, you should know that all mobile browsers will do their best to display your pages on their screens. The best microbrowsers—particularly those based on Opera and NetFront—shrink each page so it fits horizontally within the mobile device's screen. This usually involves stripping out columns and shrinking images to fit. Other microbrowsers take a lazier route and just show the page as is, which usually means lots of horizontal scrolling to read the text.

With either method, the resulting page might not have the look you want, and it might not be all that readable. To get more control over how your pages look in a microbrowser, you can specify a separate style sheet file to be used only by mobile devices. Do this by including a `media` attribute either in the `<link>` tag (if you're using an external style sheet) or in the `<style>` tag. Either way, you set that attribute to `handheld`. Here are some examples:

```
<link rel="stylesheet" href="mobile.css" media="handheld" />
<style type="text/css" media="handheld" />
```

For regular users running a browser on a monitor or laptop screen, you should add the `media` attribute to your usual style sheet `<link>` or `<style>` tag, and set the attribute to `screen`, as shown here:

```
<link rel="stylesheet" href="regular.css" media="screen" />
<style type="text/css" media="screen" />
```

In other words, for each page you want to configure for mobile browsing, include two `<link>` or two `<style>` tags. When someone running a microbrowser requests this page, that browser reports to your web server that it's running on a mobile (handheld) device, so the server applies the `handheld` style sheet; other users get the `screen` style sheet.

What do you put in this new `handheld` style sheet? Ah, that's the subject of the next section, so read on.

> **Webmaster Wisdom**
>
> Besides `handheld` and `screen`, other possible values for the `media` attribute include `all`, `print`, `projection`, and `tv`.

Making Mobile Browsers Happy

Before getting to the specific coding choices you might want to use to keep mobile browsers happy, take a step back and think about how browsing on a mobile device is different from browsing on a PC.

Mobiles Versus Full-Sizers

Mobile users don't want "fat" content. The pipe they're using to access your site is a narrow one, and that limited bandwidth means they're not looking for videos, large images, or anything else that would take forever to download.

Mobile users are highly text-focused. Most mobile web services give users only so much total bandwidth that the user can download per month, so mobile users are a frugal bunch. They usually turn off images anyway, but you can't assume that.

Mobile users are almost always in a hurry. One of the things driving the growth of mobile web usage is the handiness of any mobile device. Want to settle an argument at a bar, look up the address of a restaurant, or find out the score of the game? Just whip out your phone or PDA and access the web. However, this only works if information is easily accessible, so don't bury your good stuff many layers deep into your site. All your data should be no more than three or four clicks away.

Mobile users can't click at will. Most mobile browsers require the user to scroll through the links on a page. (This is the same as pressing Tab to navigate page links on your PC's web browser.) Therefore, don't include dozens of links on a page, if you can help it.

Mobile-Friendly Coding

With the preceding differences in mind, how do you code your website to make it mobile-friendly? I'm glad you asked.

Add descriptive alternative text for each image (by including the `alt` attribute in the `<img>` tag). This way, even if a mobile user has turned off images (which is common), he can still tell what each of your images is all about (and might opt to download a specific image, if he thinks it will be useful or interesting).

Keep merely decorative images to a minimum. Just in case a mobile user has images turned on, she's not going to appreciate waiting forever while a 300KB logo loads.

Keep your site design to a single column. Mobile device screens simply aren't wide enough to handle multiple columns. As I said before, many mobile browsers automatically convert a multiple-column page to a single column, but the results aren't always pretty, so you're better off doing this yourself.

Keep navigation as simple as possible. This means having all your content no more than three or four links away, shunning site navigation elements based on technologies such as Flash, not using (or hiding) images or image maps as part of your navigation system, and avoiding (or hiding) JavaScript-based navigation techniques (such as lists of links or dynamic menus).

Hiding Elements from Mobile Browsers

Rather than shunning certain elements altogether to satisfy mobile users, it's better to simply hide some things from mobile browsers and show them to everyone else. You hide an element by setting the `display` property to `none` in a style sheet:

```
.HideImage { display: none }
```

To apply this to an element in a page, specify the `class` attribute:

```
<img src="angst.gif" class="HideImage">
```

But how do you differentiate between a mobile browser and a regular one? That's where the `media` attribute I mentioned earlier comes in. If you only want elements hidden for mobile browsers, include the style class in a style sheet that has the `media` attribute set to `handheld`, like this:

```
<style type="text/css" media="handheld">
.HideImage { display: none }
</style>
```

Here's a complete example (see mobile1.htm on the CD):

```
<html>
<head>
<title>
Hiding an Image from a Mobile Browser
</title>

<style type="text/css" media="handheld">
.HideImage { display: none }
</style>
```

```
</head>

<body>

Do you see it?
</p><p>
<img src="angst.gif" class="HideImage">

</body>
</html>
```

Figure 7.1 shows how the page appears in Internet Explorer running on a regular PC. Figure 7.2 shows the same page running in Internet Explorer Mobile. As you can see, the regular version of Internet Explorer displays the image, but the mobile version doesn't.

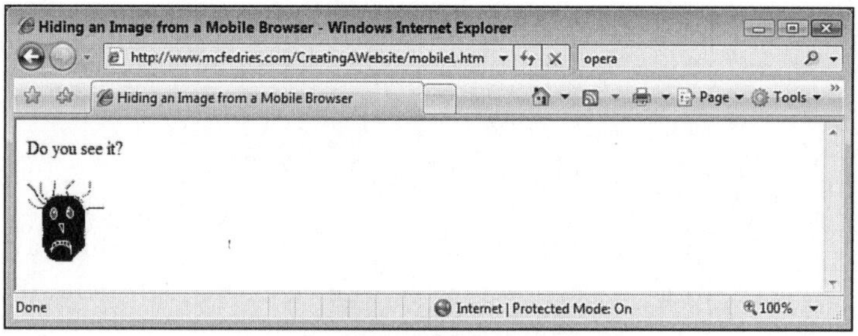

Figure 7.1

When you view this page using regular Internet Explorer, you see the image.

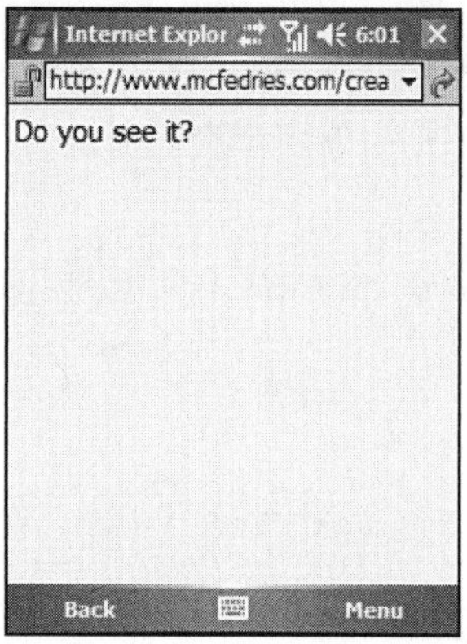

Figure 7.2

When you view the same page using Internet Explorer Mobile, you don't see the image.

Collapsing a Table Structure for a Mobile Browser

In Chapter 2, I showed you how to use tables to define the overall layout of your website. Unfortunately, most mobile browsers don't take kindly to those types of structures. If you don't want to re-jig your entire site to a one-column layout just to keep a few mobile users happy, there's a workaround you can use.

In a `handheld` style sheet, if you apply the `display` property to each table element and set it to `block`, the mobile browser displays the table elements as a series of blocks that run vertically down the page. For example, here's some code from Chapter 2 that creates a three-column table with a header row:

```
<table style="height: 100%;
              width: 100%;
              border-spacing: 0px"
              cellspacing="0">


<tr>
<td style="background-color: LimeGreen;
           height: 100px;
           vertical-align: top"
           colspan="3">
Put your header text, images, and links here.
</td>
</tr>


<tr>
<td style="background-color: PaleGreen;
           width: 200px;
           vertical-align: top">
Put your left column text, links, and images here.
</td>


<td style="vertical-align: top">
Put your main page content (middle column) here.
</td>


<td style="background-color: PaleGreen;
           width: 200px;
           vertical-align: top">
Put your right column text, links, and images here.
</td>
</tr>
</table>
```

To make this work with both a regular browser and a mobile browser, you need to do two things:

◆ Remove the `width` properties from the columns and create a class in a `screen` style sheet.

◆ Create a `handheld` style sheet and apply the `display: block` property to the various table elements. I'll also set the width of those elements to 100 percent so they fill the mobile browser's screen.

Here's the revised code (see mobile2.htm on the CD):

```
<html>
<head>
<title>
Displaying a Table as a Series of Blocks
</title>

<style type="text/css" media="handheld">

table, tr, td, th {
display: block;
width: 100% }

</style>

<style type="text/css" media="screen">

.TDColumn { width: 200px }

</style>

</head>
<body style="margin: 0px; padding: 0px">

<table style="height: 100%;
            width: 100%;
            border-spacing: 0px"
            cellspacing="0">

<tr>
<td style="background-color: LimeGreen;
        height: 100px;
        vertical-align: top"
        colspan="3">
```

```
Put your header text, images, and links here.
</td>
</tr>


<tr>
<td style="background-color: PaleGreen;
          vertical-align: top"
    class="TDColumn">
Put your left column text, links, and images here.
</td>

<td style="vertical-align: top">
Put your main page content (middle column) here.
</td>

<td style="background-color: PaleGreen;
          vertical-align: top"
    class="TDColumn">
Put your right column text, links, and images here.
</td>
</tr>
</table>

</body>
</html>
```

Figure 7.3 shows how the page appears in Opera running with the regular screen mode. Figure 7.4 shows the same page running in Opera's small screen mode. As you can see, the regular screen view displays the table normally, but the small screen view shows the table as a series of blocks.

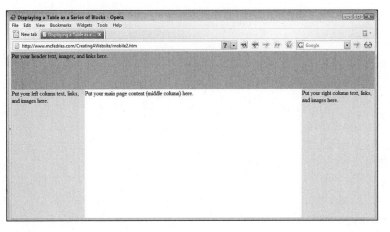

Figure 7.3

When you view this page using Opera's regular screen view, you see the tables as they're defined in the code.

Figure 7.4

When you view the same page using Opera's small screen view, the table elements appears as a series of blocks.

The Least You Need to Know

◆ To accommodate microbrowsers, write detailed alternative text for images; remove or hide decorative or large images; use a single-column site design whenever possible; and avoid navigation elements that require Flash, images, image maps, or JavaScript.

◆ To create a style sheet for a mobile browser, include the `media` attribute in either the `<link>` or `<style>` tag, and set the attribute to `handheld`.

◆ To create a style sheet for a regular browser, include the `media` attribute in either the `<link>` or `<style>` tag, and set the attribute to `screen`.

Publishing Your Website

Well, things are cruising along just swimmingly. You've managed to cobble together a bunch of pages (or perhaps just one page if you're more of a toe-dipper than a deep-end-diver), you've come up with a site design that would make Martha Stewart herself proud, and you've made it this far without a significant onset of insanity. Great! So what's missing? Oh, yeah: you've got to get your website where it belongs—on the web! The chapters in Part 3 help you do that by showing you how to check your site for errors, how to get your site from here to there, and even how to publicize your site.

Chapter 8

Is Your Website Up to Snuff?

In This Chapter

+ Checking your spelling, grammar, and facts
+ Validating your HTML and style sheet code
+ Tips for keeping your links looking good
+ Putting your pages through their paces

Everybody who designs websites—pros, hobbyists, and rookies alike—has had the unpleasant experience of loading a page into a browser and then seeing that something has gone awry. Maybe an image doesn't show up, a table isn't centered, or even a page displays *nothing* despite the fact that you *know* there's lots of text and tags in there somewhere. More often than not, the culprit in these malformed pages is something simple: a missing quotation mark, the lack of an end tag, or a misspelled tag name.

It can be tough to spot these kinds of errors, so if you're having trouble, it's a good idea to submit your page to *page checker*, a service that validates the HTML code on your page. A page checker looks for things like improper or unknown tags, mismatched brackets, and missing quotation marks and lets you know if things are awry. It's the easy way to good HTML mental health! This chapter tells you about a few of these services.

These aren't the only things that can spoil an otherwise-promising web debut. You might misspell a word or two, use outdated or inaccurate information, and send a link to the wrong location. I cover these kinds of gaffes in this chapter, too.

Give Your Site a Once-Over

Before getting to the various web services that can check your code for glitches and goofs, check your site's pages yourself. I'm not talking about going through your site with the digital equivalent of a fine-toothed comb; that would take too long, and the web's validation will do a better job for most stuff, believe me. No, I'm really talking about eyeballing your site to be sure things look right on a broad level, and giving your words a careful proofread.

HTML isn't hard, but it's fussy, persnickety stuff. If you miss even the smallest part of a single tag, your entire page could look bad (or not show up at all). To avoid this, recheck all your tags. In particular, be sure each tag's opening angle bracket (<) has a corresponding closing angle bracket (>). Also, be sure links and `<img>` tags have both opening and closing quotation marks ("") and tags such as `<b>`, `<i>`, `<u>`, `<h1>`, `<ol>`, `<dl>`, and `<a>` have their appropriate closing tags (`</b>`, `</i>`, and so on).

URLs are easy to mistype, so double-check all your links. The best way to do this is to load the page into a browser and try clicking the links.

Different browsers have different ways of interpreting your HTML codes. To be sure your web page looks good to a large percentage of your readers, load the page into as many different browsers as you can. Note that Internet Explorer and Firefox together control well over 90 percent of the browser market, so always run your page through some version of these two programs.

Webmaster Wisdom

The Big Two browsers—Internet Explorer and Firefox—have come out with various versions over the years, and they render HTML in subtly different ways. If possible, check your page with as many different versions as you can. If you have two computers, you should try out Internet Explorer 6 and 7 and Firefox 1.5 and 2.0. If you're launching a big-time site or a site for a company, you might want to invest in a BrowserCam check (www.browsercam.com). BrowserCam shows you how your site looks on all major browsers (and a bunch of minor ones, too) as well as on various versions of the major operating systems. It's expensive (plans start at $39.95 per month, although a free trial is available), but it's a great way to get a broad look at your site.

Pages can also look radically different depending on the screen resolution. If your video card supports them, be sure you view your page using 800×600, 1024×768, and 1280×1024 resolutions. Here's how you change the resolution in various operating systems:

- In *Windows Vista*, right-click the desktop, click **Personalize,** and click **Display Settings.** You can also select **Start, Control Panel** and click the **Adjust screen resolution link** (it's under **Appearance and Personalization**).

- In *Windows XP and earlier*, right-click the desktop, click **Properties,** and select the **Settings** tab.

- In *Mac OS X*, click **System Preferences** in the dock or under the Apple menu, click **Displays,** and click an item in the **Resolutions** list.

One of the advantages of using a word processor to create HTML files is that you usually have access to a spell checker. If so, use it to look for spelling gaffes in your page. Note, too, that some text editors have built-in spell checkers, including the incomparable UltraEdit (www.ultraedit.com).

Besides looking for spelling errors, reread your page text to be sure things make sense and are at least semigrammatical.

It doesn't hurt to check that all your facts are up to date and accurate. And don't just take Wikipedia's word for something; always double- (even triple-) check your facts with other sources.

> **Webmaster Wisdom**
>
> If you've got no spell checker in sight, you can try using a separate spell-check program such as Spell Checker for Edit Boxes (www.quinion.com/mqa/index.htm).

The W3C Validation Service

A good place to start your validation routine is with the W3C itself, which offers validators for both HTML and CSS. The World Wide Web Consortium (W3C) is the home of the folks who create and maintain the HTML standard (among others), so you can be sure they know what they're talking about.

Using the Markup Validation Service

The W3C's Markup Validation Service (validator.w3.org) checks your HTML code to be sure it does what it's supposed to do. Plug in the address of your page and click **Check** to get things moving.

You can test this even if your page isn't on the web yet. Either click **Validate by File Upload** to send your page file directly to the validator, or click **Validate by Direct Input** to plug in the HTML code directly.

To try this out, I'm going to use the following bit of code:

```
<html>
<head>
<title>Using the W3C HTML Validation Service</title>
</head>
<body>
<p>Yo, W3C! Is the page valid, or what?</p>
</body>
</html>
```

This is about as simple a page as you can imagine, so it should pass with flying colors, right? Not so fast! As you can see in Figure 8.1, this page failed miserably.

Figure 8.1

This simple page is a failure in the eyes of the W3C.

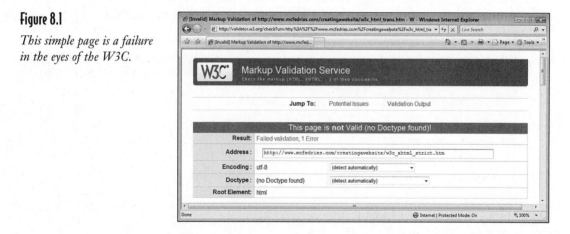

What happened? The validation result offers a cryptic hint: `no Doctype found`. If you scroll down the results page to the Potential Issues section, you see a bit more detail about the reasons behind the failure, as shown in Figure 8.2.

Okay, so the more detailed explanation is just more detailed gobbledygook. In plain English, the W3C's validator is complaining because our page was missing two elements:

- Character encoding
- DOCTYPE declaration

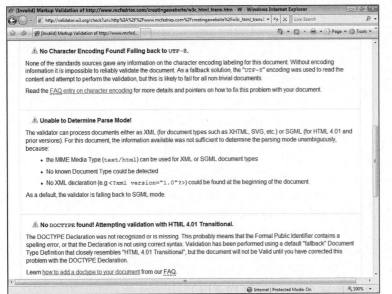

Figure 8.2

Scroll down the results page to get a bit more info about what went wrong.

Character encoding is a `<meta>` tag that tells the browser what type of characters (that is, the character set) you use. Dozens of character sets exist for different languages, different ways of representing characters, and so on. Luckily, you'll be creating your pages using an encoding called the Universal Transfer Format (UTF). So you can satisfy the W3C validator by adding the following tag between the `<head>` and `</head>` tags:

```
<meta http-equiv="content-type" content="text/html;charset=utf-8" />
```

DOCTYPE declaration is a special tag that tells the browser what version of the XHTML (or HTML) standard you used to build your page. The DOCTYPE declaration is out-there stuff, but for our purposes, we can focus on just a few possibilities.

The most straightforward route is via the XHTML 1.0 standards, and there are two ways to go:

- XHTML 1.0 Strict
- XHTML 1.0 Transitional

In XHTML 1.0, you're supposed to use style sheets for the presentation side of a page (as opposed to the structure of the page). For example, instead of using the old `<font>` tag to specify the typeface and size, you use styles such as `font-family` and `font-size`. When you tell the browser you're using XHTML 1.0 Strict, it means you don't have any of the old (*deprecated*, in the vernacular) tags in your document. You tell the browser this by adding the following DOCTYPE declaration to the top of the page (above the `<html>` tag):

```
<!DOCTYPE html PUBLIC "-//W3C//DTD XHTML 1.0 Strict//EN"
    "http://www.w3.org/TR/xhtml1/DTD/xhtml1-strict.dtd">
```

def•i•ni•tion

If a tag or element is no longer part of the HTML standard, it's **deprecated**.

If you're still using a few of the old presentation tags in your pages, you can still get your pages validated by declaring that you're using the XHTML 1.0 Transitional document type. You tell the browser this by throwing the following DOCTYPE declaration on the top of the page:

```
<!DOCTYPE html PUBLIC "-//W3C//DTD XHTML 1.0 Transitional//EN"
    "http://www.w3.org/TR/xhtml1/DTD/xhtml1-transitional.dtd">
```

Note, too, that once you declare your page to be XHTML, you also need to modify your `<html>` tag to the following, which tells the browser the namespace prefix to use (you don't need to worry about what this means):

```
<html xmlns="http://www.w3.org/1999/xhtml">
```

 So now we have everything we need to take another crack at the W3C's validator. Here's the revised code (see W3C_XHTML_Strict.htm on the CD):

```
<!DOCTYPE html PUBLIC "-//W3C//DTD XHTML 1.0 Strict//EN"
    "http://www.w3.org/tr/xhtml1/dtd/xhtml1-strict.dtd">
<html xmlns="http://www.w3.org/1999/xhtml">
<head>
<meta http-equiv="content-type" content="text/html;charset=utf-8" />
<title>Using the W3C HTML Validation Service</title>
</head>
<body>
<p>Yo, W3C! Is the page valid, or what?</p>
</body>
</html>
```

Note that the DOCTYPE declaration must be the very first thing that appears in your page code.

As you can see in Figure 8.3, our page finally satisfies the W3C powers that be.

Figure 8.3

This page is now a fully compliant member of the XHTML community.

Webmaster Wisdom

If your pages pass with flying colors, you might want to brag on your website. At the bottom of the results page, you see some code that you can use to insert the official W3C "Valid" icon for all to see.

There are separate DOCTYPE declarations for pure HTML pages. To get the code for HTML 4.01 Strict and HTML 4.01 Transitional, see the files W3C_HTML_Strict.htm and W3C_HTML_Trans.htm on the CD.

Using the CSS Validation Service

If you've got styles in your pages, it's a good idea to take advantage of another W3C tool called the CSS Validation Service (jigsaw.w3.org/css-validator). It works just like the Markup Validation Service: you type the address of the page and click **Check.** And as with the Markup Validation Service, you can also check your code either by uploading a file or by pasting the code directly.

Fortunately, the style sheet validator isn't anywhere near as picky as the markup validator. You don't need to add any special tags or elements to your pages to get them to validate. As long as you set up your style sheets exactly as I've shown you in this book, your pages will sail through the CSS Validation Service.

Using NetMechanic

The W3C's validation services are free, but they're fairly limited in what they can do. However, some of the more advanced validators on the web really put your site through its paces. One of the better ones is NetMechanic, which offers the following features in its HTML Toolbox product:

- HTML code validation
- Page load time check
- Spell checker
- Browser compatibility check
- Link checker
- Automatic HTML code repair
- Automatic weekly testing of a site

You might think all this would cost big bucks, but the first five features are all part of the free version of the service, which examines up to 5 pages and 125 links. The "Pro" version of the service has two levels: a "small site" level that performs all the above checks on up to 100 pages and up to 5,000 links and costs $60 per year, and a "large site" level that performs all the above checks on up to 400 pages and up to 10,000 links and costs $200 per year.

Here are the steps to follow to give the free version a whirl:

1. Head to www.netmechanic.com/products/HTML_Toolbox_FreeSample.shtml to load the HTML Toolbox Free Sample page.

2. Use the **URL** text box to enter an address. If you want to check a single page, type the address of that page (for example, www.mysite.com/mypage.htm). If you want to check multiple pages, type the address of your site (for example, www.mysite.com).

3. Select either **1 Page** or **5 Pages.**

4. If you selected 5 pages, use the **Email** text box to type the e-mail address where you want the results sent.

5. Click **Test Now** and NetMechanic begins the tests.

If you're checking just a single page, you see the results in the browser window after a minute or two; otherwise, the results are e-mailed to you.

A customized version of the HTML Toolbox enables you to fiddle with things like the specific tests you want to run, whether your site is disabled-friendly, and a custom spell-check dictionary. See the custom version at www. netmechanic.com/toolbox/power_user.htm.

Keeping Your Links in the Pink

Links are a major part of any website, and it's not a stretch to say that the quality of your links goes a long way toward what people think of your site overall. If your site has lots of link errors or your link text isn't straightforward, people will think less of your site. To avoid such a fate, following are a few ideas to keep in mind when using links in your pages.

Make your link text descriptive. Link text really stands out on a page because browsers usually display it underlined and in a different color, which naturally draws the reader's eye. Make the text descriptive so it's easy for readers to know exactly what they're linking to. Always avoid the "here" syndrome, where your link text is just "Here" or "Click here." The following snippet shows you the right and wrong way to set up your link text. Figure 8.4 shows how each one looks in a browser.

```
<h3>Wrong:</h3>
<p>
The Beet Poets page contains various odes celebrating our favorite
edible root, and you can get to it by clicking <a href="beetpoet.
htm">here</a>.
</p>
<h3>Right:</h3>
<p>
The <a href="beetpoet.htm">Beet Poets page</a> contains various odes
celebrating our favorite edible root.
</p>
```

Figure 8.4

Your reader's eye gravitates toward the link text, so be sure your text is descriptive.

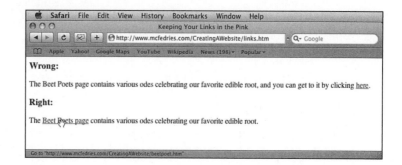

If you're presenting material sequentially in multiple pages, create "navigational links" to help the reader move forward and backward through the pages. For example, each page could have a **Previous** link that takes readers to the previous page, a **Next** link that takes them to the next page, and a **Top** link that returns them to the first page. (See Chapter 6 for a bit more detail on this.)

Webmaster Wisdom

You might be wondering why you'd want to bother with *Previous* and *Next* buttons when most browsers have similar buttons built in (usually called *Back* and *Forward*). Well, they're not really the same things. For example, suppose you surf to a site and end up on a page that's in the middle of a series of pages. If you select the browser's *Back* button, you find yourself tossed back to the site you just bailed out of. If you select the page's *Previous* button, however, you head to the previous page in the series.

For maximum readability, don't include spaces or punctuation marks either immediately after the <a> tag or immediately before the </a> tag.

If you're planning a link to a particular page but you haven't created that page yet, leave the link text as plain text (for example, don't surround it with the <a> and </a> tags). Links that point to a nonexistent page generate an error, which can be frustrating for surfers.

If you move your page to a new site, leave behind a page that includes a link to the new location. Even better, set up the page to automatically redirect people to your new site. I show you how to do this in Chapter 9.

Try to keep all your links, both internal and external, up to date. This means trying out each link periodically to be sure it goes where it's supposed to go and hasn't turned into a *vaporlink*. If you have a lot of links, try Xenu's Link Sleuth (home.snafu. de/tilman/xenulink.html).

Don't link to a page other than the site's home page. Many sites frown upon this because their home pages have banner ads or other material they want all visitors to see. Some sites have been known to sue people who set up *deep links* to their pages. If you want to use a deep link to a site, ask for permission first. If you don't get an answer, just link to the site's home page to be safe.

def•i•ni•tion

A link to a nonexistent page is called a **vaporlink**. A **deep link** is a link that points to a file within a site rather than to the site's home page.

Other Validation Tools

There are lots of validation services and programs around, as a Google search on "html validation" (or "xhtml validation") soon shows. To give you some idea of what's out there, here are a few other validation tools to check out:

- ◆ *HTML Validator* (www.htmlvalidator.com) is a shareware program that enables you to run page checks from your computer. HTML Validator Lite is the free version that checks HTML syntax and looks for spelling errors. It also adds quotation marks around attribute values and converts HTML code to lowercase. The beefier versions—HTML Validator Standard ($69) and HTML Validator Professional ($129)—can also check style sheets, site accessibility, validate links, and much more.

- ◆ *Firefox* offers lots of add-ons (addons.mozilla.org) you can install to validate pages for you right from the friendly confines of the browser. Search for "validator" at addons.mozilla.org.

The Least You Need to Know

- ◆ Give your pages a quick once-over to look for missing closing angle brackets (>) and closing quotation marks (").

- ◆ Check your pages in as many different browsers as you can and using different screen resolutions, particularly 800×600, 1024×768, and 1280×1024.

- ◆ Always check your page spelling and grammar, and double-check your facts and figures.

◆ Use the W3C's Markup Validation Service and CSS Validation Service to check your pages.

◆ To get on the good side of the W3C's Markup Validation Service, you need to add a `<meta>` tag that specifies the character encoding and a DOCTYPE declaration.

◆ Make your link text descriptive, set up navigation links for a series of pages, don't link to nonexistent pages, and keep your external links up to date.

Chapter 9

Ship It! Getting Your Site on the Web

In This Chapter

- Understanding web hosting providers
- A rundown of the various choices for hosting your site
- Choosing the host that's right for you
- A look inside your new web home
- Getting your site to the provider

I've covered a lot of ground in the past few chapters, and no doubt you've worked your fingers to the bone applying the electronic equivalent of spit and polish to buff your website's pages to an impressive sheen. However, you still need to perform a couple related tasks before you can cross "Make website" off your to-do list: you have to find a web home for your site, and you have to move your website files into that new home.

This chapter helps you take care of both tasks. You first learn how to look for and choose a spot on the web where friends, family, and even total strangers from far-flung corners of the world can eyeball your creation.

Then, you learn how to help your web pages emigrate from their native land (your hard disk) to the New World (the web). You learn how to best prepare them for the journey, select a mode of transportation, and settle your pages in when they've arrived.

Intro to Web Hosting Providers

A common question posed by web page publishing neophytes is "Where the heck do I put my website when I'm done?" If you've asked that question, you're doing okay because it means you're clued in to something crucial: just because you've created a website and you have an Internet connection doesn't mean your site is automatically a part of the web.

After all, people on the Net have no way of getting to your computer and, even if they did, your computer isn't set up to hand out documents (such as web pages) to visitors who ask for them. Computers that can do this are called *servers* (because they "serve" stuff out to the Net), and computers that specialize in distributing web pages are called *web servers*. So your web page isn't on the web until you store it on a web server. Because this computer is, in effect, playing "host" to your pages, such machines are also called *web hosts*. Companies that run these web hosts are called *web hosting providers*. (If you're interested in setting yourself up as your own web hosting provider, see Chapter 10.)

def•i•ni•tion

A **web server** is a computer that accepts and responds to remote requests for pages and other web content stored on the server.

Now, just how do you go about finding a web server? Well, the answer to that depends on a bunch of factors, including the type of site you have, how you get connected to the Internet in the first place, and how much money (if any) you're willing to shell out for the privilege. In the end, you have three choices:

- Use your existing Internet provider.
- Try to find a free hosting provider.
- Sign up with a commercial hosting provider.

Use Your Existing Internet Provider

If you access the Internet via a corporate or educational network, your institution might have its own web server you can use. If you get online via an Internet service provider (ISP), phone or e-mail its customer service department to ask whether the company has a web server available. Almost all ISPs provide space so their customers can put up personal pages free of charge.

Try to Find a Free Hosting Provider

If cash is in short supply, a few hosting providers will bring your website in from the cold out of the goodness of their hearts. In some cases, these services are open only to specific groups such as students, artists, nonprofit organizations, and so on. However, plenty of providers put up personal sites free of charge.

What's the catch? Well, there are almost always restrictions both on how much data you can store and on the type of data you can store (no ads, no dirty pictures, and so on). You'll probably also be required to display some kind of "banner" advertisement for the hosting provider on your pages.

Later in this chapter, in the "Free Web Hosts" section, I give you a collection of sites that offer lists of—you guessed it—free web hosts.

Sign Up with a Commercial Hosting Provider

For personal and business-related websites, many web artisans end up renting a chunk of a web server from a commercial hosting provider. You normally fork over a setup fee to get your account going and then you're looking at a monthly fee.

Why shell out all that dough when there are so many free sites lying around? Because, as with most things in life, you get what you pay for. By paying for your host, you generally get more features, better service, and fewer annoyances (such as the ads that most free sites have to display).

I take you through a bunch of sites that provide lists of commercial web hosts later in this chapter. See the "Commercial Web Hosts" section.

A Buyer's Guide to Web Hosting

Unfortunately, choosing a web host isn't as straightforward as you might like it to be. For one thing, hundreds of hosts are out there clamoring for your business; for another, the pitches and come-ons your average web host employs are strewn with jargon and technical terms. I can't help reduce the number of web hosts, but I can help you understand what those hosts are yammering on about. Here's a list of the terms you're most likely to come across when researching web hosts:

Storage space refers to the amount of room allotted to you on the host's web server to store your files. The amount of acreage you get determines the amount of data you can store. For example, if you get a 1MB (1 megabyte) limit, you can't store more than 1MB worth of files on the server. HTML files don't take up much real estate, but large graphics sure do, so you need to watch your limit. For example, you could probably store about 200 pages in 1MB storage (assuming about 5KB per page), but only about 20 images (assuming about 50KB per image). Generally speaking, the more you pay for a host, the more storage space you get.

Bandwidth is a measure of how much of your data the server serves. For example, suppose the HTML file for your page is 1KB (1 kilobyte) and the graphics associated with the page consume 9KB. If someone accesses your page, the server ships out a total of 10KB; if 10 people access the page (either at the same time or over a period of time), the total bandwidth is 100KB. Most hosts give you a bandwidth limit (or "cap"), which is most often a certain number of megabytes or gigabytes per month. (A gigabyte is equal to about 1,000 megabytes.) Again, the more you pay, the greater the bandwidth you get.

Domain name is a general Internet address, such as mcfedries.com or whitehouse.gov. They tend to be easier to remember than the long-winded addresses most web hosts supply you by default, so they're a popular feature. Two types of domain names are available:

♦ A regular domain name (such as yourdomain.com or yourdomain.org)

♦ A subdomain name (yourdomain.webhostdomain.com)

Page Pitfall

If you exceed your bandwidth limit, users will usually still be able to get to your pages (although some hosts shut down access to an offending site). However, almost all web hosts charge you an extra fee for exceeding your bandwidth, so check this out before signing up. The usual penalty is a set fee per every megabyte or gigabyte over your cap.

To get a regular domain, you either need to contact Network Solutions (www.networksolutions.com) directly, or you can use one of the many other registration services such as Register.com. A more convenient route is to choose a web hosting provider that will do this for you. Either way, it will usually cost you $35 per year. (Although some hosts offer cheap domains as a "loss leader" and recoup their costs with hosting fees; also, discount domain registrars such as GoDaddy.com offer domains for as little as $9.99 per year.) If you go the direct route, almost all web hosts will host your domain, which means that people who use your domain name will get directed to your website on the host's web server. For this to work, you must tweak the domain settings on the registrar. This usually involves changing the DNS servers associated with the domain so they point at the web host's domain name servers. Your web host will give you instructions on how to do this.

With a subdomain name, "webhostdomain.com" is the domain name of the web hosting company, and it simply tacks on whatever name you want to the beginning. Many web hosts will provide you with this type of domain, often for free.

Most hosts offer you an *e-mail mailbox* along with your web space. The more you pay, the more mailboxes you get. *E-mail forwarding* enables you to have messages sent to your web host address rerouted to some other e-mail address.

Page Pitfall

If you decide to get your own domain name, be sure *you* own the domain, not the web host. Also, be sure your name is listed as the domain's "administrative" contact.

If the host offers a *shared server* (or *virtual server*), it means that you'll be sharing the server with other websites—dozens or even hundreds of them. The web host takes care of all the highly technical server management chores, so all you have to do is maintain your site. This is by far the best (and cheapest) choice for individuals or small business types.

With a *dedicated server*, you get your very own server computer on the host. That may sound like a good thing, but it's usually up to you to manage the server, which can be a dauntingly technical task. Also, dedicated servers are hideously expensive; they usually start at a few hundred dollars a month.

Operating system refers to the operating system on the web server. You usually have two choices: Unix (or Linux) and Windows (usually Windows Server 2003 or 2008). Unix systems have the reputation of being very reliable and fast, even under heavy traffic loads, so they're usually the best choice for a shared server. Windows systems are a better choice for dedicated servers because they're easier to administer than their Unix brethren. Note, too, that Unix servers are case sensitive in terms of file and directory names, while Windows servers are not.

Almost all free web hosts have *ad requirements*, or require you to display some type of advertising on your pages. This could be a banner ad across the top of the page, a "pop-up" ad that appears each time a person accesses your pages, or a "watermark" ad, usually a semitransparent logo that hovers over your page. Escaping these annoying ads is, by far, the number-one reason webmasters switch to a commercial host.

Webmaster Wisdom

People often ask me if I can supply them with a script or some other means to disable or hide the ads displayed by their free web host. My answer is always an emphatic "No!" because those ads are how the host makes its money. If enough people circumvent the ads, the host eventually loses money and can no longer offer free hosting.

Uptime refers to the percentage of time the host's server is up and serving. There's no such thing as 100 percent uptime because all servers require maintenance and upgrades at some point. However, the best hosts have uptime numbers over 99 percent. (If a host doesn't advertise its uptime, it's probably because it's very low. Be sure to ask before committing yourself.)

If you have problems setting up or accessing your site, you want to know that help—in the form of *tech support*—is just around the corner. The best hosts offer 24/7 tech support, which means you can contact the company—either by phone or e-mail—24 hours a day, 7 days a week.

The *cgi-bin* is a special directory meant to store CGI "scripts" that perform behind-the-scenes tasks. The most common use for these scripts is to process form data, as described in Chapter 4. If you want to use any of the prefab scripts available on the web, or if you want to create your own, you'll need a `cgi-bin` directory in which to store them. You should also check to see if the `cgi-bin` is shared with other sites (this is now rare) or if you have your own. In general, the host places greater restrictions on a shared `cgi-bin` than on a personal one.

Speaking of *scripts*, most good hosts also offer you a selection of ready-to-run scripts for things such as guest books and e-mailing form data.

As you see later in this chapter, you usually use the Internet's *FTP* service to transfer your files from your computer to the web host. If a host offers *FTP access* (some hosts have their own method for transferring files), be sure you can use it any time you like and there are no restrictions on the amount of data you can transfer at one time.

An *anonymous FTP* variation on the FTP theme enables you to set up your own FTP server where other people can log in and download files from or upload files to your site. The more you pay for your site, the more likely you are to get this feature.

FrontPage support means you can use a program called Microsoft FrontPage to manage your website from the comfort of your computer.

Website statistics tell you things such as how many people have visited your site, which pages are the most popular, how much bandwidth you're consuming, which browsers and browser versions surfers are using, and more. Most decent hosts offer a ready-made stats package, but the best ones also give you access to the "raw" log files so you can play with the data yourself.

Some hosts allow for *e-commerce* and offer a service that lets you set up a web "store" so you can sell stuff on your site. That service usually includes a "shopping script," access to credit card authorization and other payment systems, and the ability to set up a secure connection. You usually get this only in the more expensive hosting packages, and you'll most often have to pay a setup fee to get your store built.

Scalability means the host is able to modify your site's features as required. For example, if your site becomes very popular, you might need to increase your bandwidth limit. If the host is scalable, it can easily change your limit (or any other feature of your site).

Finding a Web Host

Now that you understand some of the lingo and concepts that surround this web hosting business, you're ready to start researching the hosts to find one that suits your web style. As I mentioned earlier, there are hundreds of hosts, so how is a body supposed to whittle them down to some kind of short list?

Ask your friends and colleagues. The best way to find a good host is that old standby, word of mouth. If someone you trust says a host is good, chances are you won't be disappointed. (This is assuming you and your pal have similar hosting needs. If you want a full-blown e-commerce site, don't solicit recommendations from someone who has only a humble home page.)

Solicit host reviews from experts. Ask existing webmasters and other people "in the know" about which hosts they recommend or have heard good things about. Sites such as Epinions.com are also good sources of host reviews.

Contact web host customers. Visit sites that use a particular web host, and send an e-mail message to the web author asking what he or she thinks of the host's service.

Peruse the lists of web hosts. A number of sites track and compare web hosts, so they're an easy way to get in a lot of research.

The next couple sections provide you with capsule reviews and addresses of these host lists.

> ### Webmaster Wisdom
>
> For your shopping convenience, I've gathered the links shown here and in the next section and dropped them into a web page. It's called hostlist.htm, and you'll find it on the CD. To check out a list, open the page in your favorite browser, click the link, and you're there!

Free Web Hosts

During the height of the dot-com frenzy, free web hosts seemed to sprout with a weedlike intensity. When the alleged "new economy" became old news and the dot-commers went down in flames, a lot of the free hosts went sneakers up as well. Of the survivors, many converted themselves into commercial hosts to survive. There are still lots of free hosts left, however, and you can find most of them via the following sites that review or compare these hosts (for links to each site mentioned in this chapter, see webhosting.htm on the CD):

◆ *100 Best Free Web Space Providers* (www.100best-free-web-space.com) gives you a summary of the features of each free host, ranks the host on a scale of one to five, and offers a short review of the host.

◆ *FREE Website Providers* (www.freewebsiteproviders.com) lists hundreds of free hosts divided into various categories, including Personal, Business, Nonprofit, and Special Interest. The site provides you with a chart showing the features offered by each host, along with reviews of some hosts.

◆ *Free Web Space 411* (www.freewebspace411.com) includes a large number of capsule reviews for various free web hosts. It does have a ridiculous number of pop-up ads, though. Annoying!

◆ *FreeWebspace.net* (www.freewebspace.net) includes a large number of user reviews for various free web hosts. There are also discussion areas, news stories about hosts, and much more.

◆ *Free Web Site Hosting Providers in the Yahoo! Directory* (dir.yahoo.com/Business_and_Economy/Business_to_Business/Communications_and_Networking/Internet_and_World_Wide_Web/Network_Service_Providers/Hosting/Website_Hosting/Free_Hosting) is one of the best places to go for information. This directory offers an extensive index of free web hosting providers.

Commercial Web Hosts

The world's capitalists—efficient free-market types that they are—smelled plenty of money to be had after the explosive growth of the web became apparent. As a result, there's certainly no shortage of commercial web hosting providers available. Here are some sites that can supply you with lists of such providers:

◆ *C|Net Reviews* (www.cnet.com/internet) divides hosts into various categories and also offers a "Most Popular" list so you can see who's using who.

◆ *Findahost* (www.findahost.com) lets you search for a web host by selecting the features you need.

◆ *HostFinders* (www.hostfinders.com) offers a search feature for finding a web host that has what you want.

◆ *HostIndex* (www.hostindex.com) offers a large index of web hosts. However, its best feature is a monthly ranking of web hosts based on user feedback, features, pricing, and more.

◆ *The List* (www.thelist.com) is *the* site for listings of Internet service providers. For our purposes, it also tells you whether or not the providers host web pages.

◆ *TopHosts* (www.tophosts.com) is impressively comprehensive and lists hosts in various categories, offers a "HostMatch" service to help you find a host that's right for you, has news articles and information related to hosting, and offers much more.

◆ *Web Host Directory* (www.webhostdir.com) not only lists hosts in a wide range of categories, but also offers a quotation service, a search service, news and how-to articles, discussion forums, host awards, and more.

◆ *Web Site Hosting Providers in the Yahoo! Directory* (dir.yahoo.com/Business_ and_Economy/Business_to_Business/Communications_and_Networking/ Internet_and_World_Wide_Web/Network_Service_Providers/Hosting/Website_ Hosting/Directories) offers a list of web hosting directories.

What Does Your Web Home Look Like?

After you sign up with a web hosting provider and your account is established, the web administrator creates two things for you: a directory on the server computer you can use to store your website files, and your very own web address. (This is also true if you're using a web server associated with your corporate or school network.) The directory usually takes one of the following forms:

```
/yourname/
/home/yourname/
/home/yourname/public_html/
```

In each case, `yourname` is the login name (or user name) the provider assigns to you, or it may be your domain name (with or without the .com part). Remember, this is a slice of the host's web server, and this slice is yours to monkey around with as you see fit. This usually means you can do all or most of the following:

- Add files to the directory

- Add subdirectories to the directory

- Move or copy files from one directory to another

- Rename files or directories

- Delete files from the directory

Your web address normally takes one of the following shapes:

> http://*provider/yourname/*
>
> http://*yourname.provider/*
>
> http://www.*yourname/*

Here, *provider* is the host name of your provider (for example, www.hostway.com or just hostway.com), and *yourname* is your login name or domain name. Here are some examples:

> http://www.hostway.com/mywebsite/
>
> http://mywebsite.150m.com/
>
> http://www.mywebsite.com/

Your Directory and Your Web Address

There's a direct and important relationship between your server directory and your address. That is, your address actually "points to" your directory and enables other people to view the files you store in that directory. For example, suppose I decide to store a file named thingamajig.html in my directory and my main address is http://mywebsite.150m.com/. This means someone else can view that file by typing the following URL into his or her browser:

> http://mywebsite.150m.com/thingamajig.html

Similarly, suppose I create a subdirectory named CreatingAWebsite and use it to store a file named index.html. A surfer can view that file by convincing his or her browser to head for the following URL:

> http://mywebsite.150m.com/CreatingAWebsite/index.html

In other words, folks can surf to your files and directories just by strategically tacking on the appropriate file names and directory names after your main web address.

Making Your Hard Disk Mirror Your Web Home

For largish sites, you should divide your stuff into separate subdirectories to keep things organized. (If you have a small site and are planning to keep all your files in a single directory, feel free to leap right over this section without penalty or embarrassment.) If you're going to go this route, you can make your *uploading* duties immeasurably easier if you set up your own computer to have the same directory setup as the one you plan to use at your website. You can go about this in a number of ways, but here's the simplest:

def•i•ni•tion

Moving a file from your computer to a remote location (such as your web host's server) is known in the file transfer trade as **uploading**.

- ◆ Create a folder on your computer that acts as the "home base" for all your HTML files. This is the equivalent of your main directory at your web hosting provider. You can name this folder whatever you like (for example, HTML Stuff or My Web Weavings).

- ◆ Create your subfolders under this home base folder. In this case, the subfolders you create must have the same names and the same capitalization as the ones you want to use on your website. Be sure your folder names don't use any spaces.

Webmaster Wisdom

To help reduce the confusion, in this chapter when I use the word *folder*, I'm referring to a directory on your computer; when I use the term *directory*, I'm referring to a directory on your web host's server.

To see why this is so useful, suppose you set up a subfolder on your computer named graphics that you use to store your image files. To insert into your page a file named mydog.jpg from that folder, you'd use the following tag:

```
<img src="graphics/mydog.jpg" />
```

When you send your HTML file to the server and you then display the file in a browser, it looks for mydog.jpg in the graphics subdirectory. If you don't have such a subdirectory—either you didn't create it or you used a different name, such as images—the browser won't find mydog.jpg and your image won't show. In other words, if you match the subdirectories on your web server with the subfolders on your computer, your page will work properly without modifications both at home and on the web.

Page Pitfall

One common faux pas beginning HTMLers make is to include the drive and all the folder names when referencing a file. Here's an example:

```
<img src="C:\My Documents\HTML Stuff\graphics\mydog.jpg" />
```

This image will show up just fine when it's viewed from your computer, but it will fail miserably when you upload it to the server and view it on the web. That's because the "C:\My Documents\HTML Stuff\" part exists only on your computer.

Uploading Your Site

Now, at long last, you're ready to get your page on the web. If the web server is on your company or school network, you send the files over the network to the directory set up by your system administrator. Otherwise, you send the files to the directory created for you on the hosting provider's web server.

In the latter case, you probably need to use the Internet's FTP (File Transfer Protocol) service. (Note, however, that AOL and some web hosts offer their own file upload services.) For this portion of the show, you have a number of ways to proceed:

◆ Use the demo version of CuteFTP that comes on the CD. This is a Windows FTP program that makes it easy to send files from your computer to the web server. The next couple sections show how to configure and use CuteFTP to get the job done.

◆ If you're an America Online user, you can use AOL's FTP service to ship your files to your "My Place" home directory.

◆ Mac users have a number of FTP programs to try out, including the most popular ones, which are called Fetch and Cyberduck. You can get them via TUCOWS (www.tucows.com). Click the **Mac** link.

Adding Your FTP Address

Before you can send anything to the web server, you have to tell CuteFTP how to find it and how to log on. Thankfully, you only have to do this once and you're set for life (or at least until you move to another web host). Before you begin, you need three pieces of data, which your web host should have given to you when you signed up:

◆ The address of your FTP site on the host. This most often takes the form ftp. myhost.com or ftp.mydomain.com, but in many cases, you use a web address, such as www.myhost.com or www.mydomain.com.

◆ Your FTP user name, which is usually the same as your website user name.

◆ Your FTP password, which, again, is usually the same as your website password.

With that info in hand, here's how it's done:

1. Start CuteFTP. The Site Manager dialog box appears. (If you don't see the Site Manager, select **Tools, Site Manager, Display Site Manager,** or press **F4.**)

2. Click **New, FTP Site** (or press **Ctrl+N**). CuteFTP then prompts you to enter the settings for the new site.

3. Click **Rename,** type a name for the site, and press **Enter.**

4. In the General tab's **Label** text box, enter a name for this site. Something like "My Website" or the name of the web host is fine.

5. In the **Host address** text box, enter the address of your FTP site on the host.

6. Enter your FTP user name in the **Username** text box.

7. Enter your FTP password in the **Password** text box. (Note that, for security reasons, the password appears as dots.) Figure 9.1 shows the General tab with the settings filled in for an example site.

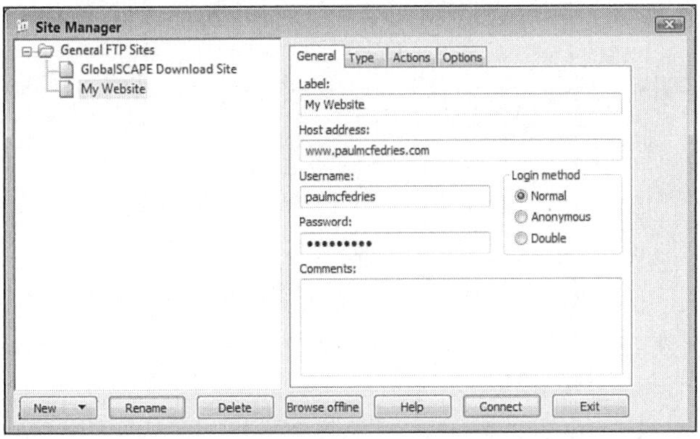

Figure 9.1

An example of a completed General tab for a new FTP site.

8. Click the **Actions** tab.

9. In the **When client connects, switch to this local folder** text box, enter the drive and folder on your computer that contains your website files. (If you're not sure, click the folder icon to the right of this box to pick out the folder using a dialog box.)

10. When you're done with Site Manager, click **Exit** (although you'll need it again in the next section, so you might want to leave it open for now).

Sending the Files via FTP

With CuteFTP ready for action, you can get down to it. Here are the basic steps to follow when sending your files to the web server via FTP:

1. If you haven't done so already, establish an Internet connection with your regular ISP.

2. Select **Tools, Site Manager, Display Site Manager** (or press **F4**) to get reacquainted with the Site Manager.

3. Be sure the site you just added is selected and then click the **Connect** button. After you're logged in to the server, CuteFTP might display a Login Messages dialog box.

4. If so, click **OK.** You're now at the main CuteFTP window. As you can see in Figure 9.2, this window shows your computer's files on the left and your web server files on the right. (The latter will either be empty because you haven't sent anything to the server yet, or it may contain a few default folders created by your web hosting provider.)

Figure 9.2

CuteFTP shows your computer's files on the left and your web server files on the right.

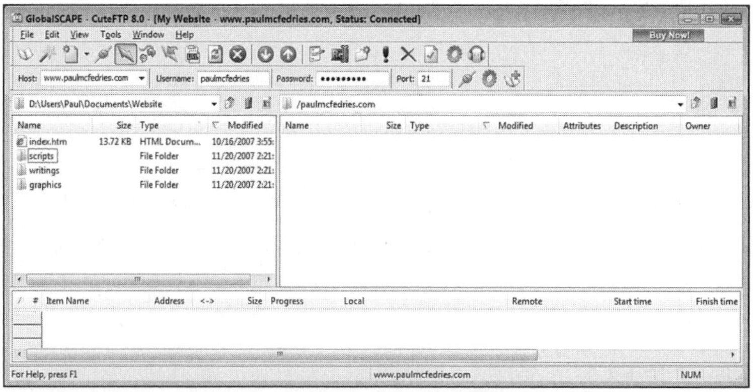

5. Select all the files on your computer you want to send. The easiest way to do this is to hold down the **Ctrl** key, move your mouse into the left box, and click each file you're sending. When you finish select-ing the files, release the **Ctrl** key.

6. Pull down the **File** menu and select **Upload** (or press **Ctrl+Page Up**). CuteFTP sends the files one by one to the web server.

7. After the files have arrived safely, pull down the **File** menu and select **Disconnect** to shut down the connection.

Webmaster Wisdom
A quick way to send files to the server is to use your mouse to drag the highlighted files from the left pane and drop them on the right pane. When CuteFTP asks you to confirm, click **Yes**.

To be sure everything's working okay, plug your web address into your browser and give your page a test surf. If all goes well, then congratulations are in order, because you've officially earned your webmeister stripes!

 Page Pitfall _____

The Unix computers that play host to the vast majority of web servers are down-right finicky when it comes to the uppercase and lowercase letters used in file and directory names. It's crucial that you check your `<a>` tags and `<img>` tags to be sure the file and directory names you use match the combination of uppercase and lowercase letters used on your server. For example, suppose you have a graphics file on your server that's named vacation.gif. If your `<img>` tag points to, say, VACATION.GIF, the image won't appear. To help prevent problems, tell CuteFTP to force all your file names to lowercase letters. In the Site Manager, select your FTP site and click the **Actions** tab. In the **When uploading, apply this rule to files and folder names** list, select **Force lower case**.

Creating a New Directory

If you need to create separate subdirectories for your graphics or HTML files, CuteFTP makes it easy. You have two choices:

♦ If you already have the corresponding subfolder on your computer, upload the entire folder to the server. (That is, select the folder in CuteFTP's left file pane and select **File, Upload.**)

♦ To create a new subdirectory on the server, first open the server directory where you want to work (or just click anywhere inside the right file pane to activate it). Then select the **File, New Folder** command (or press **Ctrl+M**). In the New Folder dialog box that appears, enter the name of the new directory and click **OK.**

Again, remember that your goal is to end up with exactly the same directory structure on both your own computer and on the server. Figure 9.3 shows an example.

Figure 9.3

When you're finished, the list of files and directories on the web server (right) should be identical to the list of files and folders on your computer (left).

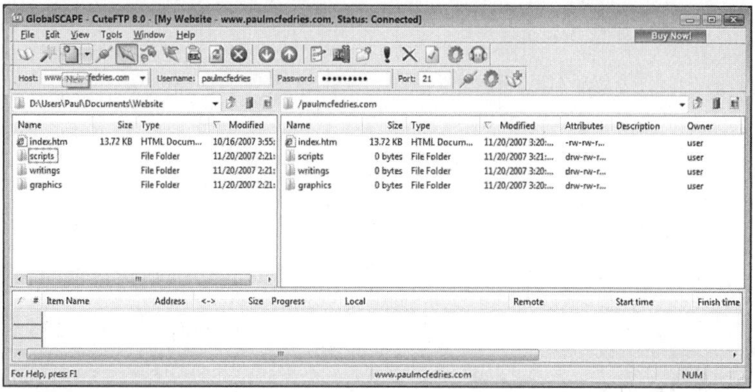

Making Changes to Your Web Files

What happens if you send an HTML file to your web provider and then realize you've made a typing gaffe? Or what if you have more information to add to one of your web pages? How do you make changes to the files you've already sent?

Page Pitfall

Be sure you send the updated file to the correct directory on the server. Otherwise, you may overwrite a file that happens to have the same name in some other directory.

Well, here's the short answer: you don't. That's right, after you've sent your files, you never have to bother with them again. That doesn't mean you can never update your site, however. Instead, you make your changes to the HTML files that reside on your computer and then send these revised files to your web provider. These files replace the old files, and your site is updated with no questions asked.

The Least You Need to Know

- A web hosting provider is a company that runs a web server and supplies you with a chunk of hard disk real estate on that server.

- If you don't want to spend any money to host your site, either ask your ISP if it does web hosting, or try out a free web host.

- The two most important things to bear in mind when shopping for a web host are storage and bandwidth.

- If you want to get your very own domain name, either ask your web host to register one for you or find a host that will create a subdomain.

- Your main web address points to your main directory on the host's web server.

- Be sure the folder structure you use on your computer is identical to the directory structure you set up on the host.

Chapter 10

Hosting Your Own Website

In This Chapter

- ◆ Installing Internet Information Services, the Windows Vista web server
- ◆ Configuring the web server to your liking
- ◆ Setting up directories and other options
- ◆ Setting up security for your website
- ◆ Everything you need to know to serve up piping hot web pages

Web servers are both boon and bane for we webmaestros. Without them, we wouldn't be able to show off our polished pages to the world's web surfers. But they often impose restrictions that hamper our website style. For example, some servers restrict the amount of data we can store in our home directories. That's no big deal for HTML files, which are usually quite small, but it will probably mean you'll have to cut down on graphics files and other fatty web foods. Some servers also enforce bandwidth restrictions that limit the total number of bytes you can ship out to web surfers. Finally, most servers only give you a limited number of configuration options, and if you need anything else changed, you're stuck with a visit to tech support. In most cases, you can solve these problems with money: the more you pay, the less onerous the server's restrictions.

However, you might want to consider an alternative road to server riches: running your own web server. I know this sounds like a for-rich-geeks-only solution and, yes, running a high-end web server is expensive and not for the faint of heart. Fortunately, Microsoft has a web server that won't put a strain on either your heart or your bank account. It's called Internet Information Services (IIS), and it's a big-time server that's also surprisingly easy to use. Best of all, it comes with some versions of Windows Vista (more on that in a sec), which means it costs precisely nothing! This chapter shows you how it works.

Why Host Your Own Site?

Okay, so I'm sure the first question rattling around in your brain right now is, *Why bother?* Do you *really* need to host your own website? No, of course not, but if you think about it, there are some pretty good reasons to give 'er a go:

- You're running a home office or small office and you want to set up an internal website for your employees (that's called an *intranet*).

- You want to set up a simple site with photos and updates for friends and family to access.

- You don't want to fork over your hard-earned money to pay a web hosting company to store your site.

- You want to learn web programming and need a server to practice on.

- You want bragging rights the next time you get together with your friends and another game of "Who's the Geekiest?" breaks out.

def•i•ni•tion

An **intranet** is a website designed to operate and be accessible only over a network.

Yes, for at least some of these scenarios it's easier to use one of the many thousands of web hosting companies to put up your site. However, if you want complete control over the site, you need to roll up your sleeves and get hands-on with IIS. Fortunately, as you see in this chapter, although IIS itself is tremendously complex, the basic features of IIS (which are all you need) aren't hard to grasp.

What Versions of Windows Vista Will Do the Job?

Windows Vista is definitely a client operating system, but it does have its server moments. For example, Vista acts as a kind of server when you set up a folder to be shared with the network. Similarly, Vista also acts as a kind of server when you use it to host an ad hoc wireless network and when you create a meeting using Windows Meeting Space.

However, these are only "serverlike" applications. Surprisingly, there's a way that Vista can act as a full-fledged server: by running the built-in IIS that enables Vista to serve web pages. Note, however, that IIS isn't baked into all versions of Vista. In fact, only three versions can do the IIS thing: Windows Vista Ultimate Edition, Windows Vista Premium Edition, and Windows Vista Business Edition.

Vista Home Premium Edition also comes with a version of IIS, but that version doesn't implement IIS in the same way as the other versions. It doesn't come with some high-end features such as advanced authentication. It also doesn't offer remote administration of IIS, nor does it include the FTP server. Additionally, it's restricted to a maximum of three simultaneous data requests (compared to the limit of 10 simultaneous requests in the Business, Enterprise, and Ultimate versions).

Okay, So Just What *Is* IIS?

As you know from Chapter 9, a web server is a computer that accepts and responds to remote requests for pages and other web content stored on the server. Most of these requests come from remote users running Internet Explorer, Firefox, Safari, or some other web browser. IIS is Microsoft's web server and runs the World Wide Web Publishing Service, which makes a default website available to anyone on your network (or with a bit of tweaking, anyone on the Internet) who uses a web browser. You can add your own pages and folders to the default website, so you can serve almost any type of World Wide Web content from your Vista computer. IIS also comes with the IIS Management Console, which enables you to customize your website to get it set up the way you want.

If you used IIS 5.1 on Windows XP, note that two major restrictions have been lifted from Vista's IIS 7:

♦ *There's no maximum connection limit.* XP IIS 5.1 had a connection limit of 10 users, but there's no such limit in Vista's IIS 7.

♦ *There's no website limit.* XP IIS 5.1 allowed you to create just one website, but Vista's IIS 7 lets you create as many sites as you want.

Webmaster Wisdom

Vista IIS 7's simultaneous data request limit is different from XP IIS 5.1's connection limit. With the connection limit of 10, when an eleventh user tried to access your site, he or she received a `Server Too Busy` error. With the simultaneous data request limit of 10 (3 in Home Premium), if an eleventh (or fourth) request comes in at the same time, that request is simply placed in a queue and is handled when the server is ready for it. How polite!

Installing Internet Information Services

IIS 7 is a feature in the Home Premium, Business, Enterprise, and Ultimate versions of Vista, but it's not installed by default on any of them. To install it, you need to work through the following steps:

1. Select **Start, Control Panel** to open the Control Panel window.

2. Click **Programs** to open the Program window.

3. Under Programs and Features, click the **Turn Windows features on or off** link. The User Account Control dialog box appears.

4. Enter your UAC credentials. Vista displays the Windows Features dialog box, which takes a few moments to populate.

5. Click to activate the check box beside **Internet Information Services.** Vista selects the most commonly used IIS features. If you want to install these default features, skip to step 7.

Figure 10.1

To get IIS on the job, activate the check box beside Internet Information Services.

6. Open the Internet Information Services branch, and activate the check boxes beside each component you want to work with. Here are some suggestions:

   ♦ *Web Management Tools, IIS Management Service.* Install this component to configure your web server from any other computer on your network.

   ♦ *World Wide Web Services, Application Development Features.* The components in this branch represent the IIS programming features. If you're running IIS to build and test web applications, be sure to activate the check box for each development technology you require.

   ♦ *World Wide Web Services, Security, Basic Authentication.* Install this component if you want to restrict website access to users who have a valid Windows user name and password.

7. Click **OK.** Vista gets to work installing IIS 7.

Checking Out Your Newfangled Website

Although there's not much to see, the default website is ready for action as soon as you install IIS. To access the website from the computer running IIS, you can enter any of the following addresses into your web browser:

```
http://127.0.0.1/
http://localhost/
http://IPAddress/
http://ComputerName/
```

Replace *IPAddress* with the IP address of the computer, or replace *ComputerName* with the name of the computer. If you're not sure what the heck I'm talking about with IP addresses and computer name, don't sweat it. I explain it all in the next section.

Figure 10.2 shows the home page of the default IIS website that appears. Note, too, that Internet Explorer displays the Information Bar shown in Figure 10.2. Click the **Information Bar** and then click **Enable Intranet Settings.**

Figure 10.2

It's not much, but it's the default IIS 7 website home page.

IP Addresses and Computer Names

In the previous section, I mumbled something about using the Vista computer's IP address or computer name to access the website. Okay, time to explain myself. An IP (Internet Protocol) address is a unique address your network assigns to every computer. Your Internet ISP also doles out IP addresses to each customer. In both cases, the IP addresses are assigned randomly each time you log on.

On a network, a computer's IP address usually looks like one of the following (where *x* is a number between 2 and 254):

```
192.168.0.x
192.168.1.x
```

To find out your Vista computer's current IP address, select **Start, All Programs, Accessories, Command Prompt**, type `ipconfig` at the command prompt, and press **Enter.** You see results that, in part, look something like this:

```
Ethernet adapter Local Area Connection 2:

    Connection-specific DNS Suffix  . : phub.net.cable.rogers.com
    Link-local IPv6 Address . . . . . : fe80::cdb7:1936:f37d:b501%11
    IPv4 Address. . . . . . . . . . . : 192.168.0.77
    Subnet Mask . . . . . . . . . . . : 255.255.0.0
    Default Gateway . . . . . . . . . : 192.168.0.1
```

The value that comes after `IPv4 Address` is your computer's IP address.

So far so good, now what about the computer name? That's another unique value, but it's one you probably assigned to the Vista machine yourself. If you're not sure of the name, follow these steps to see it:

1. Select **Start, Control Panel.** The Control Panel window shows up for work.

2. Click **System and Maintenance.**

3. Under **System,** click **See the name of this computer.** The System window appears, and the name of the computer appears, not even remotely surprisingly, as the **Computer name** value (see Figure 10.3).

Figure 10.3

The System window tells you the name of the computer.

So you saw earlier that my Vista machine uses the IP address 192.168.0.77, and from Figure 10.3, you can see that I gave the computer the clever name of WebServer. This means I can access my IIS website using the following addresses:

```
http://127.0.0.1/
http://localhost/
http://192.168.0.77/
http://WebServer/
```

Can't Get Here from There: Firewalls

As things stand now, your new website only works properly when you access it using a web browser running on the Windows Vista PC that's running IIS. If you try to access the site on any other computer (or from a location outside your network), you get an error message. Bummer.

Fortunately, we know the identity of the culprit: Windows Firewall. The problem is that the Windows Firewall on the Vista machine hasn't been configured to allow data traffic through the World Wide Web Services used by IIS. For your website to work from any remote location, you need to set up an exception for the World Wide Web Services in Windows Firewall. Here are the steps to follow:

1. Select **Start, Control Panel** to open the Control Panel window.

2. Under Security, click the **Allow a program through Windows Firewall** link. The User Account Control dialog box appears.

3. Enter your UAC credentials. The Windows Firewall Settings dialog box shows up.

4. Select the **Exceptions** tab.

5. Click to activate the check box beside the **World Wide Web Services (*HTTP*)** item, as shown in Figure 10.4.

def•i•ni•tion

HTTP is short for *Hypertext Transport Protocol,* the protocol used to exchange information on the World Wide Web.

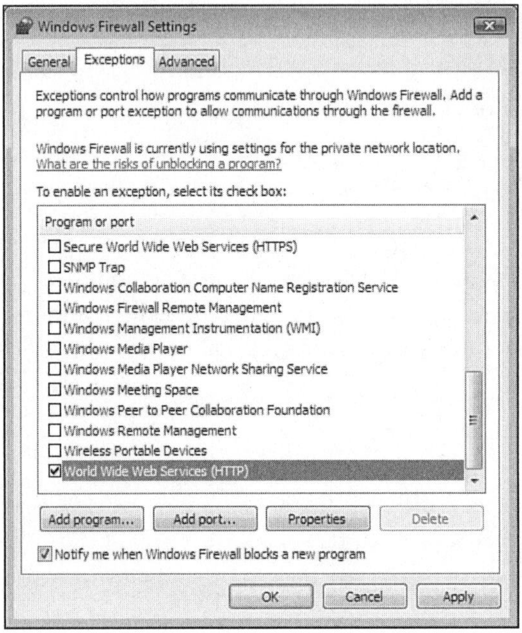

Figure 10.4

You need to configure Windows Firewall on the Vista machine to allow traffic over the World Wide Web Services.

6. Click **OK** to put the exception into effect.

Accessing Your Website over the Network

With the Windows Firewall exception for the World Wide Web Services in place, you can now access the website from any remote computer on your network. Do this by launching your web browser and entering one of the following addresses:

```
http://IPAddress/
http://ComputerName/
```

As before, you need to replace *IPAddress* with the IP address of the computer, or you need to replace *ComputerName* with the name of the computer. Here are some examples:

```
http://192.168.0.77/
http://WebServer/
```

Accessing Your Website over the Internet

People on your network can now access your website, but you may also want to allow website access to people from outside your network (that is, from the Internet). To set this up, you must do three (or possibly four) things:

1. Set up the Vista machine that's hosting the website with a permanent IP address. For the details, see the "Home, Sweet Home: A Permanent IP Address" section, next.

2. Configure your network's router to forward TCP traffic on port 80 to the IP address you specified in step 1. To learn how to do this, see "Configuring Port Forwarding on Your Router," later in this chapter.

3. Get the Internet address of your router. For the particulars, see "Getting Your Router's Public IP Address," later in this chapter.

4. *Optional:* if you want people to access your website using a domain name, you need to sign up for and configure a dynamic DNS (DDNS) service. For the complete lowdown on this, see "Using Your Domain Name with Your Site," later in this chapter.

If you do just the first three steps, an Internet user can access your website by entering the following address into a web browser:

```
http://IPAddress/
```

Here, he or she needs to replace *IPAddress* with your router's public IP address.

If you also do step 4, a surfer can also access your site using your domain name:

```
http://DomainName/
```

Here, the visitor replaces *DomainName* with the domain name you associated with your dynamic DNS account.

Home, Sweet Home: A Permanent IP Address

A bit later you'll be telling your router to send web requests to your Vista computer. However, your router needs to know where to find that computer, and that's tough if its address keeps changing. To fix that, follow these steps to configure the Vista machine with a permanent address:

1. Select **Start, Control Panel.**

2. Click **View network status and tasks.** The Network and Sharing Center shows up.

3. Click **Manage network connections.** The Network Connections window appears.

4. Right-click the connection you want to work with (this is usually **Local Area Connection**), and click **Properties.** The User Account Control dialog box pesters you.

5. Enter your UAC credentials to continue. Vista displays the connection's Properties dialog box.

6. Select **Internet Protocol Version 4 (TCP/IPv4),** and click **Properties.**

7. Click to activate the **Use the following IP address** option.

8. Use the **IP address** box to type the IP address you want to use.

9. Use the Default Gateway box to type the IP address of your network's router. This address is usually 192.168.0.1 or 192.168.1.1, but see your router manual or use the Default Gateway value that appears when you run IPCONFIG at the command prompt.

> **Webmaster Wisdom**
>
> The IP address you use should be the same as the address you saw earlier at the command prompt, but with the last number changed. For example, if the address was 192.168.0.77, change just the 77 to a number between, say, 200 and 225 (for example, 192.168.0.200).

10. Use the Preferred DNS Server box to type the IP addresses of your network's router. Figure 10.5 shows a completed version of the dialog box.

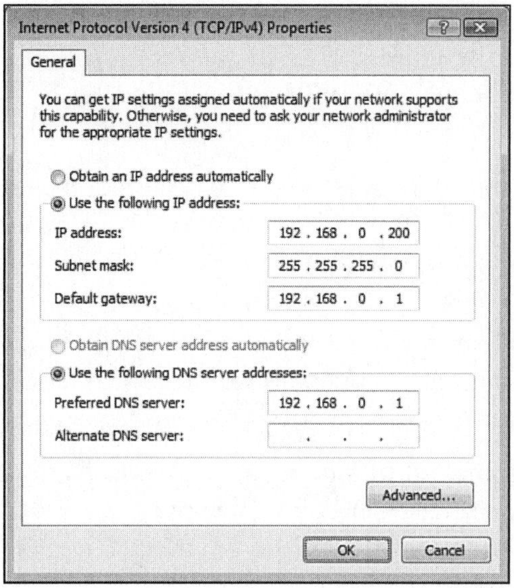

Figure 10.5

You can assign a static IP address to a network connection on a Windows Vista computer.

11. Click **OK** to return to the connection's Properties dialog box.

12. Click **Close.**

Configuring Port Forwarding on Your Router

Now you need to configure your network's router to forward web server data to the Vista computer. This is called *port forwarding*, and the steps you follow depend on the device, so see your manual. Bear in mind that you need to specify three things:

◆ *The port.* This is the connection over which the data is sent. For a web server, the port is 80.

◆ *The protocol.* This is the standard used to make a connection between the surfer and the server. For a web server, the protocol is TCP.

◆ *The web server's IP address.* This is the permanent IP address you assigned to the Vista computer in the previous section.

Getting Your Router's Public IP Address

If your network has a router that serves as your Internet connection point, the router actually has two IP addresses:

- *The private IP address.* This is the address other computers on your network use to communicate with the router. This address is usually 192.168.0.1 or 192.168.1.1.

- *The public IP address.* This is the address assigned to your router from the pool of addresses controlled by your ISP. Internet data sent to any computer on your network is first sent to the router's external IP address.

The big advantage of this setup is that your network is never exposed to the Internet. All communication goes through the router's public IP address; so as far as, say, a web server is concerned, it's communicating with a device at that address.

You've already told your router to forward website requests on port 80 to your Vista machine. But before that can happen, surfers need to know the public IP address of your router. To get that, you need to navigate to any of the free services for determining your current IP. Here are two:

- WhatIsMyIP (www.whatismyip.com)

- DynDNS (checkip.dyndns.org)

Using Your Domain Name with Your Site

In most cases, your ISP assigns your router its public IP address dynamically, which means the address may change over time. If you want other people to access your website over the Internet, then constantly monitoring your dynamic IP address can be a pain. A useful solution is to sign up with a dynamic DNS (DDNS) service, which supplies you with a static domain name. The service also installs a program on your computer that monitors your IP address and updates the service's DDNS servers to point your domain name to your IP address. Here are some DDNS services to check out:

- DynDNS (www.dyndns.org)

- TZO (www.tzo.com)

- No-IP.com (www.no-ip.com)

- D-Link (www.dlinkddns.com)

Getting Comfy with the Default Website

As you saw earlier, the default website set up by IIS isn't much to look at. That's okay because a bit later you'll be adding plenty of your own content to the site. For now, the simplicity of the site is an advantage because it makes it easy for you to look around and see how the default site is constructed. This will help you customize the site and add your own content down the road.

Viewing the Default Website Folder

Let's begin by examining the folder that holds the website content:

1. Select **Start, Computer** to open the computer window.

2. Double-click the hard drive on which Windows Vista is installed.

3. Open the `inetpub` folder.

4. Open the `wwwroot` subfolder.

> ### Webmaster Wisdom
>
> The Vista hard drive is usually the C: drive. If you're not sure, look for the drive icon that has the Windows flag superimposed on it. You may need to pull down the Views menu and select **Large Icons** or **Tiles** to see the flag.

The `wwwroot` folder holds the IIS default website files, as shown in Figure 10.6.

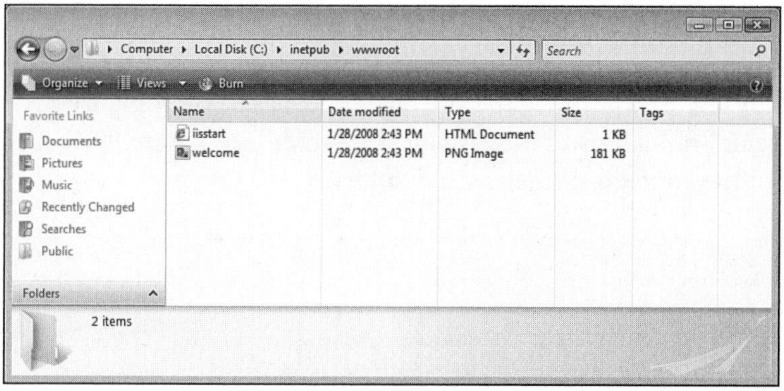

Figure 10.6

The contents of the IIS `wwwroot` *folder.*

The `wwwroot` folder has just two files:

◆ `iisstart.htm` contains the code used to display the home page you saw earlier in Figure 10.2.

◆ `welcome.png` is the image you see in the home page.

Viewing the Default Website with IIS Manager

The wwwroot folder enables you to examine the physical files and subfolders associated with the IIS default website. However, you probably won't often deal with the wwwroot folder (or any folder) directly when creating and configuring your own web pages and websites. Instead, you'll most often use a tool called the IIS Manager.

To display this program and the default IIS website, follow these steps:

1. Select **Start, Control Panel** to open the Control Panel window.

2. Click **System and Maintenance.**

3. Click **Administrative Tools.**

4. Double-click **Internet Information Server (IIS) Manager.** The User Account Control dialog box appears.

> **Webmaster Wisdom**
>
> You can also launch IIS Manager by pressing **Windows Logo+R** (or by selecting **Start, All Programs, Accessories, Run**) to open the Run dialog box, typing inetmgr, and clicking **OK.**

5. Enter your UAC credentials. The Internet Information Services (IIS) Manager window appears.

6. Open the *Computer* branch (where *Computer* is the name of your Windows Vista PC).

7. Open the **Web Sites** branch.

8. Select the **Default Web Site** branch.

IIS Manager gives you two ways to view the website files:

◆ Click the **Content View** button to see the site contents. As shown in Figure 10.7, you see the same subfolder and files as you saw earlier (see Figure 10.6) when you examined the contents of the wwwroot folder.

Figure 10.7

*Click **Content View** to see the site's files and subfolders.*

◆ Click **Features View** to see a collection of icons associated with the site's features, as shown in Figure 10.8. Most of these are advanced features, so you'll be using only a small subset of them.

Figure 10.8

*Click **Features View** to see icons associated with the site's features.*

Much of the rest of this chapter shows you how to use IIS Manager to create and configure Windows Vista website content.

Adding Folders and Files to the Default Website

By far, the easiest way to set up your own web content in Windows Vista is to add that content to the existing default website. This requires no reconfiguration of the server, of IIS, of the Windows Vista firewall, of the client computers, or of the router. You simply add the content, and it's ready for browsing.

Setting Permissions on the Default Website Folder

Somewhat annoyingly, Windows Vista makes it difficult for you to modify the contents of the `wwwroot` folder. For example, if you copy a file to the folder, you need to enter your UAC credentials to allow the copy. Even worse, you get read-only access to the files, so if you edit a file, you can't save your changes.

To avoid these hassles, adjust the Security permissions on the wwwroot folder to give your Vista user account Full Control. Here are the steps to follow:

1. Select **Start, Computer,** and navigate to the inetpub folder on your system drive.

2. Right-click the wwwroot folder, and click **Properties** to open the folder's Properties dialog box.

3. Select the **Security** tab.

4. Click **Edit.** You may see the User Account Control dialog box.

5. Enter your UAC credentials. Vista displays the Permissions for wwwroot dialog box.

6. Click **Add** to display the Select Users or Groups dialog box.

7. In the **Enter the object names to select** text box, type your user name, and click **OK** to return to the Permissions dialog box.

8. Select your user name in the **Group or user names** list.

9. In the **Permissions** list, under the **Allow** column, click to activate the **Full control** check box, as shown in Figure 10.9.

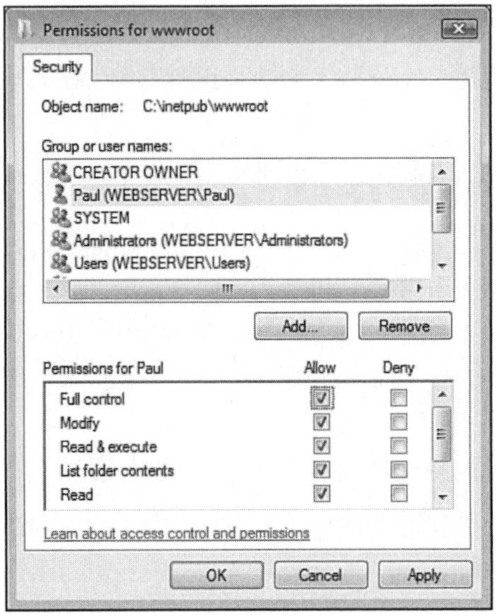

Figure 10.9

For hassle-free editing in the wwwroot *folder, give your user account Full Control permission.*

10. Click **OK** to return to the Security tab.

11. Click **OK** to put the new security settings into effect.

Adding a File to the Default Website

If you have just a few web content files you want to add to the Windows Vista website, you can add them directly to the default website folder. First, create your web content file (HTML, CSS, or whatever). Here's a sample HTML file—which I've named `HelloWorld.htm`—that I'll use as an example:

```
<html>
<head>
<title>Hello World!</title>
</head>
<body>
<p>
<span style="size: 20pt; font-family: Verdana; color: DarkBlue">
Hello Windows Vista World!
</span>
</p>
</body>
</html>
```

Next, save the file to the `wwwroot` folder.

Page Pitfall _____

Don't use spaces in the names of files (or folders) you add to your website. Although Internet Explorer may display such pages successfully, other browsers may not. And if your web content file references other files—for example, an HTML file that uses the `<img>` tag to reference an image file—be sure to copy those files to the `wwwroot` folder. You can either put the files in the root, or you can store them in a subfolder. For example, you might want to create a subfolder named `images` and use it to store your image files. If you store the files in subfolders, be sure you adjust the path in your code, as required. For example, if you place a file named `HelloWorld.jpg` in the `images` subfolder, you need to add the subfolder to the `<img>` tag, like so:

```
<img src="images\HelloWorld.jpg" />
```

Figure 10.10 shows the `HelloWorld.htm` file copied to the `wwwroot` folder, and Figure 10.11 shows the file displayed in Internet Explorer.

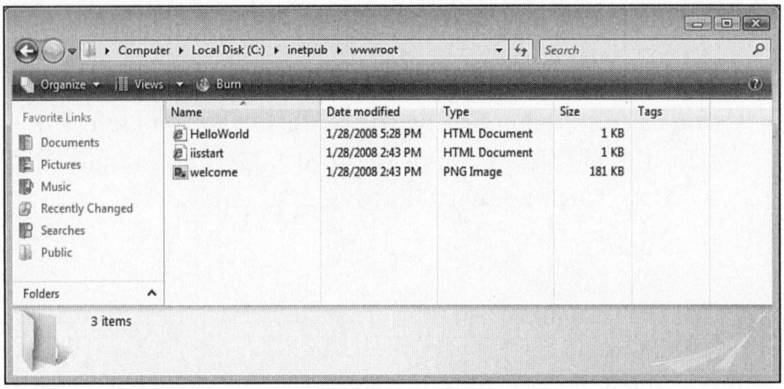

Figure 10.10

You can add individual files directly to the wwwroot *folder.*

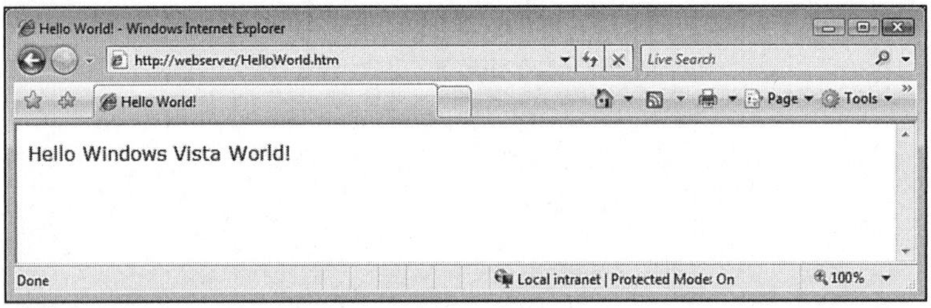

Figure 10.11

Here's the HelloWorld. htm *file displayed in Internet Explorer.*

Changing the Default Website Home Page

One of the first things you'll probably want to do with your new website is change the home page. To do that, you need to create a new HTML file in the wwwroot folder and give the file one of the following names:

```
default.htm
default.asp
index.htm
index.html
```

See "Setting the Website's Default Document," later in this chapter, to learn more about these special file names. For example, here's some bare-bones HTML code I've put in a file named default.htm:

```
<html>
<head>
<title>Home Page</title>
</head>
<body>
<p style="text-align: center">
<span style="size: 24pt; font-family: Verdana; color: Navy">
```

```
Welcome to Our Website!
</span>
</p>
</body>
</html>
```

Figure 10.12 shows `default.htm` added to the `wwwroot` folder, and Figure 10.13 shows the site's new home page in a web browser.

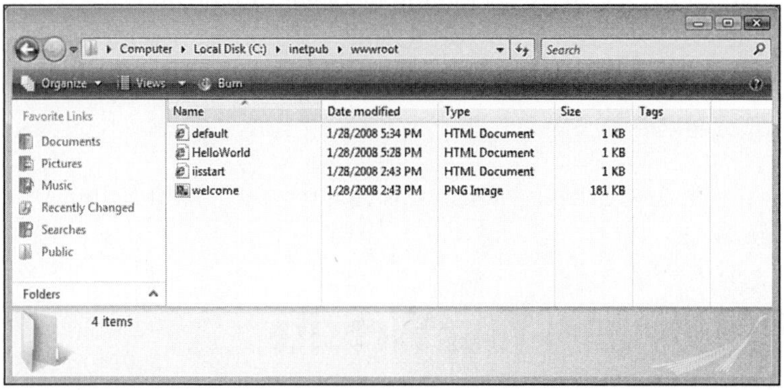

Figure 10.12

The `default.htm` file added to the default website.

Figure 10.13

The `default.htm` file now appears as the website's home page.

Adding a Folder to the Default Website

Adding a folder to the Windows Vista default website is not all that different from adding a file. That is, you can create a new subfolder within the `wwwroot` folder, or copy or move an existing folder and paste it within `wwwroot`.

To access web content within the new folder, tack on the folder name and file name to the default website address. For example, if you create a subfolder named `photos` within the `wwwroot` folder, and the main page is named `photos.htm`, you access the content by entering the following address into the browser:

```
http://localhost/photos/photos.htm
```

Note that you can save some wear and tear on your typing fingers by changing the name of the main content file to one of the following:

```
default.htm
default.asp
index.htm
index.html
default.aspx
```

When you use one of these names, IIS displays the file by default if you don't specify a file name as part of the URL. For example, if you rename the `photos.htm` file to `default.htm`, you can access the file just by specifying the folder path in the URL:

```
http://localhost/photos/
```

I discuss default content files in more detail later in this chapter (see "Setting the Website's Default Document").

Controlling and Customizing Your Website

At this point, you could use your website as is and just continue adding web pages, folders, and other content. However, IIS Manager offers a number of features and settings that enable you to control your website and customize its look and feel. For example, you can stop and start the website and specify the default content page.

The rest of this chapter takes you through the most useful of these IIS Manager features.

Stopping Your Website

By default, when you start Windows Vista, the World Wide Web Publishing Service starts automatically, and that service automatically starts your website. This is reasonable behavior because in most cases you'll want your website available full time (that is, as long as the Vista computer is running).

However, there might be occasions when you don't want your site to be available. If you plan on making major edits to the content, you might prefer to take the site offline while you make the changes. Or you might only want your website available at certain times of the day. If you're developing a web application, certain changes may require that you stop and then restart the website. For these and similar situations, you can stop the website. Here are the steps to follow:

1. Open IIS Manager.

2. Select *Computer,* **Web Sites, Default Web Site** (where *Computer* is the name of the computer running IIS).

3. In the **Actions** pane, click **Stop.** (You can also right-click **Default Web Site** and then click **Stop.**) IIS Manager stops the website.

Webmaster Wisdom
If you'd prefer that your website not start automatically when you log on to Windows Vista, select **Default Web Site,** and click **Advanced Settings** in the **Actions** pane. (You can also right-click **Default Web Site,** and click **Advanced Settings.**) In the **Start Automatically** setting, select **False,** and click **OK.** If you only want your website to not start the next time you launch Windows Vista, stop the site and shut down Vista. When you next log on to Vista, your website won't start. Note, however, that if you then restart the website during the Vista session, the website will start automatically the next time you start Vista.

Restarting Your Website

When you're ready to get your website back online, follow these steps to restart it:

1. Open IIS Manager.

2. Select *Computer,* **Web Sites, Default Web Site** (where *Computer* is the name of the computer running IIS).

3. In the **Actions** pane, click **Start.** (You can also right-click **Default Web Site** and click **Start.**) IIS Manager starts the website.

If your website is stuck or behaving erratically, you can often solve the problem by stopping and restarting the site. However, instead of performing two separate operations—clicking **Stop** and then clicking **Start**—IIS Manager lets you perform both actions in one shot by clicking **Restart.**

Renaming the Default Website

The name Default Web Site is innocuous enough, I suppose, but it's a bit on the bland side. If you prefer to use a more interesting name, follow these steps to change it:

1. Open IIS Manager.

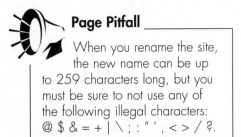

Page Pitfall _____

When you rename the site, the new name can be up to 259 characters long, but you must be sure to not use any of the following illegal characters: @ $ & = + | \ ; : " ' , < > / ?.

2. Open the *Computer,* **Web Sites** branch (where *Computer* is the name of the computer running IIS).

3. Right-click **Default Web Site,** and click **Rename** in the shortcut menu. IIS Manager adds a text box around the name.

4. Type the new name for the website.

5. Press **Enter.**

Setting the Website's Default Document

A normal website URL looks like this:

```
http://name/folder/file
```

Here, `name` is a domain name or hostname, `folder` is a folder path, and `file` is the file name of the web page or other resource. Here's an example:

```
http://localhost/photos/default.htm
```

Intriguingly, you can view the same web page by entering the following address into the browser:

```
http://localhost/photos/
```

This works because IIS defines `default.htm` as one of its default document file names. Here are the others:

```
default.asp
index.htm
index.html
iisstart.htm
default.aspx
```

So as long as a folder contains a file that uses one of these names, you can view the corresponding page without specifying the file name in the URL.

Note, too, that these default documents have an assigned priority, with `default.htm` having the highest priority, followed by `default.asp`, then `index.htm`, then `index.html`, then `iisstart.htm`, and finally `default.aspx`. This priority defines the order in which IIS looks for and displays the default document pages. That is, IIS first looks for `default.htm`; if that file doesn't exist in a folder, IIS next looks for `default.asp`, and so on.

For your own websites, you can add new default documents (for example, `default.html` and `index.asp`), remove existing default documents, and change the priority of the default documents. Here are the steps to follow:

1. Open IIS Manager.

2. Open the *Computer,* **Web Sites** branch (where *Computer* is the name of the computer running IIS).

3. Select **Default Web Site.**

4. Click **Features View.**

5. Double-click the **Default Document** icon. IIS Manager displays the Default Document page, shown in Figure 10.14.

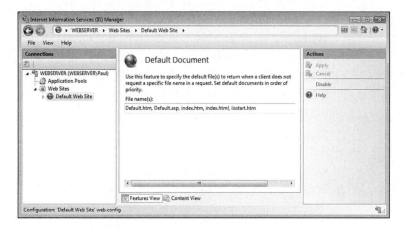

Figure 10.14

Use the Default Document page to add, remove, and reorder a site's default content pages.

6. To specify a new default document, type the file name in the **File name(s)** text box, separating each name with a comma.

7. To delete a default document, select it in the **File name(s)** text box and press **Delete.**

8. To change the default document priority order, cut and paste the items in the **File name(s)** text box.

9. In the **Actions** pane, click **Apply** to put the new settings into effect.

10. Click the **Back** button to return to the website's main page in IIS Manager.

Disabling Anonymous Access

Earlier in the chapter I showed you how to give yourself Full Control permission on the wwwroot folder to make it easier (and in some cases possible) to add and edit content in that folder. When you access your website on the IIS computer using the http://localhost/, http://127.0.0.1/, or http://Computer/ addresses (where Computer is the name of the IIS computer), you access the site using your own user account. Everyone else on your network, and anyone who surfs to your site from the Internet (including you, if you navigate to the site using http://IPAddress/, where IPAddress is your router's external IP address) accesses the site as an anonymous user. This means that IIS gives the person read-only access to the site without requiring a user name and password, a technique called *anonymous authentication*.

> **Webmaster Wisdom**
>
> Remember that you need to install the Basic Authentication component of IIS, as described earlier.

However, you may have content that you want to restrict to people who have user accounts on Windows Vista. In that case, you need to disable anonymous access for the website and switch to basic authentication, which means IIS prompts each user for a user name and password before allowing access to the site.

Follow these steps to disable anonymous access:

1. Open IIS Manager.

2. Open the *Computer,* **Web Sites** branch (where *Computer* is the name of the computer running IIS).

3. If you want to disable anonymous authentication on the entire site, select **Default Web Site;** if you want to disable anonymous authentication only on a specific folder within the site, open the **Default Web Site** branch and select the folder.

4. Click **Features View.**

5. Double-click the **Authentication** icon to display the Authentication page.

6. Select **Anonymous Authentication.**

7. In the **Actions** pane, click the **Disable** link.

8. Select **Basic Authentication.**

9. In the **Actions** pane, click the **Enable** link. The Authentication page should now appear, as shown in Figure 10.15.

Figure 10.15

To secure your website or a folder within the website, disable Anonymous Authentication and enable Basic Authentication.

10. Click the **Back** button to return to the website's main page in IIS Manager.

When an anonymous user attempts to access your website or website folder, he sees a Connect dialog box similar to the one shown in Figure 10.16. The user must enter a user name and password for an account that exists on the Windows Vista machine that's running IIS.

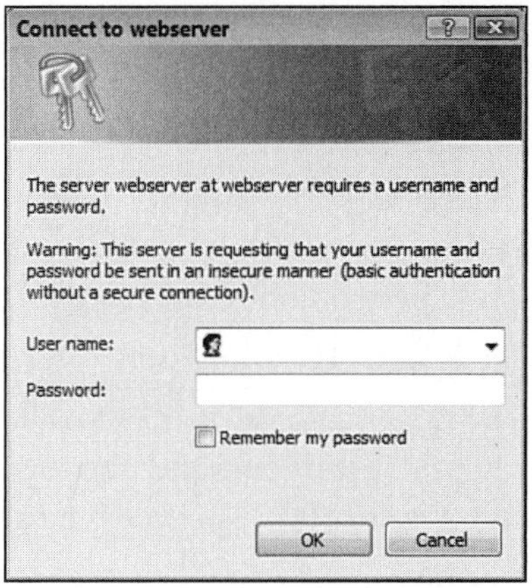

Figure 10.16

With Basic Authentication enabled, users must enter a valid Windows Vista user name and password to access the website or folder.

> **Webmaster Wisdom**
>
> Switching to basic authentication means that any user with a valid account on Windows Vista can access the website. If there are one or more users with Windows Vista accounts that you do *not* want to view the website, you must adjust the security of the website's home folder directly. Use Windows Explorer to display the website's home folder, right-click the folder, and click **Properties.** In the Security tab, click **Edit,** click **Add,** type the name of the user, and click **OK.** Select the user, and activate the **Full Control** check box in the Deny column. This tells Windows Vista not to allow that user to view the folder.

Viewing the Server Logs

After your web server is chugging along and serving up pages, you might start to wonder which pages are popular with surfers and which ones are languishing. You might also want to know whether users are getting errors when they try to access your site.

You can tell all this and more by working with the IIS logs. A log is a text file that records all the activity on your website, including the IP address and computer name (if applicable) of the surfer, the file that was served, the date and time the file was shipped to the browser, and the server return code (see the next sidebar). For each server request, the log file writes a sequence of space-separated values, which makes it easy to import the file into a database or spreadsheet program for analysis.

The log files are stored in the `\inetpub\logs\LogFiles\W3SVC1` folder of your Windows Vista system drive. (As you navigate to this folder, you may see one or two dialog boxes telling you that you don't have permission to open a particular folder. In each case, click **Continue** and enter your UAC credentials.)

Each file name takes the form `u_ex`*`yymmdd`*`.log`, where *yy* is the two-digit year, *mm* is the two-digit month, and *dd* is the two-digit day. For example, the log for August 23, 2008, would be stored in `u_ex080823.log`. Figure 10.17 shows a typical log file.

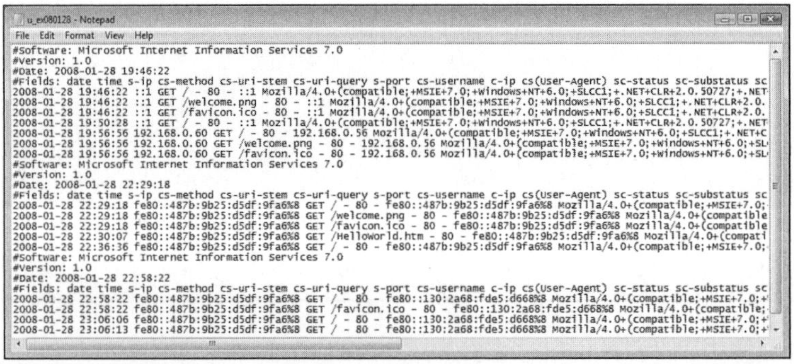

```
#Software: Microsoft Internet Information Services 7.0
#Version: 1.0
#Date: 2008-01-28 19:46:22
#Fields: date time s-ip cs-method cs-uri-stem cs-uri-query s-port cs-username c-ip cs(User-Agent) sc-status sc-substatus sc
2008-01-28 19:46:22 ::1 GET / - 80 - ::1 Mozilla/4.0+(compatible;+MSIE+7.0;+Windows+NT+6.0;+SLCC1;+.NET+CLR+2.0.50727;+.NET
2008-01-28 19:46:22 ::1 GET /welcome.png - 80 - ::1 Mozilla/4.0+(compatible;+MSIE+7.0;+Windows+NT+6.0;+SLCC1;+.NET+CLR+2.0.
2008-01-28 19:46:22 ::1 GET /favicon.ico - 80 - ::1 Mozilla/4.0+(compatible;+MSIE+7.0;+Windows+NT+6.0;+SLCC1;+.NET+CLR+2.0.
2008-01-28 19:50:28 ::1 GET / - 80 - ::1 Mozilla/4.0+(compatible;+MSIE+7.0;+Windows+NT+6.0;+SLCC1;+.NET+CLR+2.0.50727;+.NET
2008-01-28 19:56:56 192.168.0.60 GET / - 80 - 192.168.0.56 Mozilla/4.0+(compatible;+MSIE+7.0;+Windows+NT+6.0;+SLCC1;+.NET+C
2008-01-28 19:56:56 192.168.0.60 GET /welcome.png - 80 - 192.168.0.56 Mozilla/4.0+(compatible;+MSIE+7.0;+Windows+NT+6.0;+SL
2008-01-28 19:56:56 192.168.0.60 GET /favicon.ico - 80 - 192.168.0.56 Mozilla/4.0+(compatible;+MSIE+7.0;+Windows+NT+6.0;+SL
#Software: Microsoft Internet Information Services 7.0
#Version: 1.0
#Date: 2008-01-28 22:29:18
#Fields: date time s-ip cs-method cs-uri-stem cs-uri-query s-port cs-username c-ip cs(User-Agent) sc-status sc-substatus sc
2008-01-28 22:29:18 fe80::487b:9b25:d5df:9fa6%8 GET / - 80 - fe80::487b:9b25:d5df:9fa6%8 Mozilla/4.0+(compatible;+MSIE+7.0;
2008-01-28 22:29:18 fe80::487b:9b25:d5df:9fa6%8 GET /welcome.png - 80 - fe80::487b:9b25:d5df:9fa6%8 Mozilla/4.0+(compatible
2008-01-28 22:29:18 fe80::487b:9b25:d5df:9fa6%8 GET /favicon.ico - 80 - fe80::487b:9b25:d5df:9fa6%8 Mozilla/4.0+(compatible
2008-01-28 22:30:07 fe80::487b:9b25:d5df:9fa6%8 GET /HelloWorld.htm - 80 - fe80::487b:9b25:d5df:9fa6%8 Mozilla/4.0+(compati
2008-01-28 22:36:36 fe80::487b:9b25:d5df:9fa6%8 GET / - 80 - fe80::487b:9b25:d5df:9fa6%8 Mozilla/4.0+(compatible;+MSIE+7.0;
#Software: Microsoft Internet Information Services 7.0
#Version: 1.0
#Date: 2008-01-28 22:58:22
#Fields: date time s-ip cs-method cs-uri-stem cs-uri-query s-port cs-username c-ip cs(User-Agent) sc-status sc-substatus sc
2008-01-28 22:58:22 fe80::487b:9b25:d5df:9fa6%8 GET / - 80 - fe80::130:2a68:fde5:d668%8 Mozilla/4.0+(compatible;+MSIE+7.0;+
2008-01-28 22:58:22 fe80::487b:9b25:d5df:9fa6%8 GET /favicon.ico - 80 - fe80::130:2a68:fde5:d668%8 Mozilla/4.0+(compatible;
2008-01-28 23:06:06 fe80::487b:9b25:d5df:9fa6%8 GET / - 80 - fe80::130:2a68:fde5:d668%8 Mozilla/4.0+(compatible;+MSIE+7.0;+
2008-01-28 23:06:13 fe80::487b:9b25:d5df:9fa6%8 GET / - 80 - fe80::130:2a68:fde5:d668%8 Mozilla/4.0+(compatible;+MSIE+7.0;+
```

Figure 10.17

A typical IIS log file.

At first glance, an IIS log file appears to be nothing but a jumble of letters, numbers, and symbols. However, there's a bit of method in the apparent madness. First, know that each line (that is, each line that doesn't begin with #) represents an object that IIS served. This could be a file, an image, or some other content on the website. Second, remember that each field is separated by a space. Third, notice the #Fields line, which appears from time to time in the log:

```
#Fields: date time s-ip cs-method cs-uri-stem cs-uri-query s-port cs-
username
➡c-ip cs(User-Agent) sc-status sc-substatus sc-win32-status
```

This line tells you the name of each log field. To help you make sense of what you're looking at, Table 10.1 gives you a summary of what you see in each field.

IIS Log File Fields

Field	Description
date	The date on which the item (file or folder) was served.
time	The time at which the item was served.
s-ip	The IP address of the computer that's running the web server.
cs-method	The method used to request the item. (This is almost always GET.)
cs-uri-stem	The name of the requested item.
cs-uri-query	The query used to generate the item request. (This will usually be blank, represented by a dash.)
s-port	The port used to exchange the data. (This will always be 80.)
cs-username	The name—and sometimes the computer name—of the authenticated user. You only see values in this field if you turn on basic authentication for the website or a folder.
c-ip	The IP address of the user who requested the item.
cs(User-Agent)	A string that identifies the user's web browser.
sc-status	A code that specifies whether the request was handled successfully and, if not, what the error was.
sc-substatus	A secondary error code if the request failed.
sc-win32-status	The Windows status during the request.

A sc-status code of 200 means the document was sent successfully to the browser. For unsuccessful operations, the following table offers a summary of some of the return codes you'll find in the log.

Return Code	What It Means
204	File contains no content.
301	File moved permanently.
302	File moved temporarily.
304	File not modified.
400	Bad request.
401	Unauthorized access.
402	Payment required.
403	Access forbidden.
404	File not found.
500	Internal server error.
501	Service not implemented.
502	Bad gateway.
503	Service unavailable.

The Least You Need to Know

- A full version of the Internet Information Services web server is part of Windows Vista Ultimate, Enterprise, and Business, while a slightly scaled-down version is part of Vista Home Premium.

- To install IIS, select **Start, Control Panel, Programs, Turn windows features on and off,** and activate the check box beside **Internet Information Services.**

- You can view the IIS website locally using any of the following addresses:

    ```
    http://127.0.0.1/
    http://localhost/
    http://IPAddress/
    http://ComputerName/
    ```

- You can view the IIS website over the network using any of the following addresses:

    ```
    http://IPAddress/
    http://ComputerName/
    ```

- Add content to your website by adding files and folders to the wwwroot folder.

Chapter 11

Publicizing Your Site

In This Chapter

- ◆ Measuring your readership
- ◆ Getting your site noticed
- ◆ Marketing your website
- ◆ Syndicating your site content

Unlike certain baseball diamonds in Iowa cornfields, in the website field, if you build it, they won't necessarily come. That may not matter much to you if you built your website only for a select group of family, friends, or colleagues. But if you're like most website proprietors, you want (okay, you *crave*) an audience. What's the point of slaving over your pages if no one else reads them? You may as well be scribbling away in a *paper* diary, for gosh sakes.

So how does a budding website maven convince a bunch of perfect strangers to stop by for a visit? It's a tough chore in this busy website world, but it *can* be done, and that's the topic of this chapter. In the following pages, you learn all kinds of tips and techniques that will have them packing the aisles—and have you putting out the "Standing Room Only" sign.

Measuring the Size of Your Audience

Before implementing any of the nifty techniques in this chapter, you must have some way of knowing whether they're working for you. That is, you need to know if your website is attracting hordes or merely collecting dust. You need to know if you've hit the big time, or just hit the skids. In other words, you need to know the number of people who've accessed your website. There are two ways to go:

♦ *Ask your hosting provider.* Many companies can supply you with statistics that tell you the number of "hits" your site has taken.

♦ *Include a counter in your website pages.* A counter is a little program that increments each time a surfer requests the page.

 Page Pitfall _____

Counters are fun, and they're certainly a handy way to keep track of the amount of activity your website is generating. There are, however, two counter-related caveats you should know about. The counter program sits on another computer, so it takes time for the program to receive and send its information. This means your page loads a little more slowly than usual. And if the computer that stores the counter program goes "down for the count" (pun intended), the count won't appear on your page.

Creating a counter program is well beyond the scope of this humble book (insert sigh of relief here). However, a few community-minded programmers have made counter programs available on the web. Happily, you don't even have to copy or install these programs. All you have to do is insert a link to the program in your page, and the counter updates automatically whenever someone checks out the page. Here are some counter programs to try:

♦ *Site Meter* (www.sitemeter.com) is a free, website-friendly counter that gives a lot of juicy site stats, including the number of unique visitors and the total page views they generate. You also get a list of "referring URLs," which are addresses of pages that are linking to your website.

♦ *eXTReMe Tracker* (extremetracking.com) offers a wide range of tracking options, including referrer tracking.

♦ *Motigo Webstats* (webstats.motigo.com) is free for noncommercial sites and gives you all the basic stat stuff in a nice, neat package.

◆ *WebCounter* (www.digits.com) is a nicely implemented, no-frills counter. Note that busy sites (those getting more than 1,000 hits a day) should use the commercial version.

◆ *Yahoo!'s Access Counter Index* (dir.yahoo.com/Computers_and_Internet/Internet/ World_Wide_Web/Programming/Access_Counters), as usual, offers a long list of sites that supply counters.

Webmaster Wisdom

This chapter contains tons of web addresses. To save you from having to type them in by hand, I have links to each site on sites.htm on the book's CD.

Getting Your Site on the Search Engines

The web is a massive place that boasts billions (yes, I said *billions*) of pages. So even though your magnificent and hard-won work is on the web, all you've really done at this point is add your own needle to the web's digital haystack.

How are people supposed to know your new cyberhome is up and running and ready for visitors? Well, people won't beat a path to your door unless you tell them how to get there. For starters, you can spread the news via word of mouth, e-mail notes to friends and colleagues, and by handing out your shiny, new business cards that have your home page address plastered all over them. Also, it's worth checking to see if your hosting provider has a section devoted to announcing new customer pages.

However, if you want to count your visitors in the hundreds or even the thousands, you need to cast a wider net. That is, you need to get your site listed in the web's major search engines so other people can find you when they search for sites that have content similar to yours. This section takes you through the fine art of getting on the search engines and getting good rankings once you're there.

Submitting Your Site

The most straightforward way to get your site listed on a search engine is to stick the search engine's nose in it, so to speak. Most search engines have a page you can use to submit the particulars of your site. Here are the addresses of the submission pages for some of the top search engines:

◆ *AllTheWeb* (www.alltheweb.com/help/webmaster/submit_site)

◆ *AltaVista* (www.altavista.com/addurl/default)

◆ *Ask.com* (submissions.ask.com/ping?sitemap=*URL*; replace *URL* with the address of your page)

◆ *Google* (www.google.com/intl/en_extra/addurl.html)

◆ *MSN Live Search* (search.msn.com/docs/submit.aspx)

◆ *Yahoo!* (search.yahoo.com/info/submit.html)

Two notes to bear in mind with these search engines: the Ask.com address is the ping address that alerts the Ask.com search crawler to the existence of a sitemap file (see "Creating a Sitemap File for Search Engines," later in this chapter). In the ping address, you need to replace *URL* with the address of your sitemap file. Also, you might want to try and get your site listed in the famous Yahoo! Directory. Yahoo! doesn't have a single submit page for the Directory. Instead, find the category that best suits your site and click **Suggest a Site.** See help.yahoo.com/help/us/dir/suggest/index.html for more info.

Your page won't necessarily show up on a search engine immediately after you make your submission. Some search engines are remarkably fast at updating their databases, but others can take weeks or even *months*, so patience is the key.

Also, don't submit *all* your pages to the search engine; your main page is enough. The search engine's crawler will visit your main page and then follow your links to get to your other pages.

> **Webmaster Wisdom**
>
> Rather than submitting your site to the search engines by hand, services can perform this drudgery for you. Although some charge you a fee, many free services are available, although most of the freebies submit your site to only a limited number of search engines. Add Me! (www.addme.com) and Submit Express (www.submitexpress.com) are two popular ones. See also the Yahoo! Promotion index (yahoo.com/Business_and_Economy/Business_to_Business/Marketing_and_Advertising/Internet/Promotion).

Getting Noticed Using the `<meta>` Tag

The big search engines such as Google and Yahoo! scour the web for new and updated sites. If you haven't submitted your site by hand, chances are they'll stumble upon your humble home one of these days and add your pages to their massive databases. Either way, is it possible to ensure that your pages will come out near the top if someone runs a search for topics related to your site? Well, no, there isn't any way to guarantee a good placement. However, you can help things along tremendously by adding a couple special `<meta>` tags you insert between the `<head>` and `</head>` tags.

The first of these tags defines a description of your site:

```
<meta name="description" content="your description goes here" />
```

Some search engines use this description when they display your page in the results of a web search.

The second `<meta>` tag defines one or more keywords that correspond to the key topics in the page. The search engines use these keywords to match your page with keywords entered by users when they perform a web search. Here's the syntax:

```
<meta name="keywords" content="keyword1, keyword2, etc." />
```

Here's an example:

```
<html>
<head>
<title>Wii-Robics</title>
<meta name="description"
content="This page examines the use of the Wii gaming console as a
training aid for Olympic sports such as tennis and the modern
pentathlon." />
<meta name="keywords" content="wii, gaming, olympics, pentathlon" />
</head>
<body>
etc.
```

Composing Search Engine-Friendly `<meta>` Tags

The mere fact that you're conscientious enough to add `<meta>` tags to your pages is no guarantee that you'll get excellent positions within search results. Instead, you need to take a bit of extra time to craft your `<meta>` tags for maximum effect. Here are some pointers:

Watch the length of your `<meta>` content. Most search engines have a limit on the length of the `<meta>` tag `content` values. For the `description` tag, don't go longer than about 200 characters; for the `keywords` tag, a maximum of 1,000 characters will keep you in good stead.

Use lowercase keywords. To ensure compatibility with most search engines, you should put all of your keywords in lowercase.

Spread your keywords around. Search engines rank sites based not only on the words in the keywords `<meta>` tag, but also on those found in the `<title>` and in the page text, especially the first few lines.

Don't go keyword crazy. You might think you could conjure yourself up a better search result placement by repeating some of your keywords a large number of times. Don't do it! Search engines *hate* this (they call it *spamdexing*), and they'll usually disqualify your site if they think you're trying to pull the web wool over their eyes. Use a word no more than six or seven times max.

def•i•ni•tion

Including a keyword an excessive number of times is called **spamdexing.**

You can't fool them. Over the years, webmasters have tried all kinds of tricks to fool search engine rankings. For example, they've included important keywords numerous times in the body of the page, but changed the text color to match the background so the user doesn't see the repeated words. Search engines are hip to this and other tricks.

Include keyword variations. Include different parts of speech for important keywords (for example, play, plays, and playing). Also, you might want to allow for the different spelling used by American and Canadian or British users (for example, *color* and *colour*).

Place crucial keywords first. Search engines tend to prioritize keywords in the order they appear. Therefore, if you have one or more important keywords, put them at the beginning of the `<meta>` tag.

Use your keywords in your text. If you use a keyword, you can make the search engine happy by also using that keyword somewhere in the page text. Ideally, surround the word with the `<strong>` and `</strong>` tags and, if possible, include the word in the page's main `<h1>` tag.

Perhaps the best advice I can give you is to try and get your head inside the searcher. If it was *you* who was searching for data similar to what's on your page, what keywords and phrases would you use?

Creating a Sitemap File for Search Engines

Okay, so a search engine spider crawls to your site. Great! But how can you guarantee that the bot will index all your pages? Well, in short, you can't. However, you can give your site a better shot at getting fully indexed by creating a listing of all its pages. Such a list is called a *sitemap*, but don't confuse this with the site maps I yammered on about back in Chapter 6. The kind of sitemap I'm talking about here is a special XML file that follows the Sitemaps XML Protocol. (See "What Is Syndication?" later in this chapter, for a bit of background on this XML business.)

To create this file, begin with the following code:

```
<?xml version="1.0" encoding="UTF-8"?>
<urlset xmlns="http://www.sitemaps.org/schemas/sitemap/0.9">
</urlset>
```

Now, between the `<urlset>` and `</urlset>` tags, create a URL entry for each page you want the search engine to index. At its simplest, a URL entry looks like this:

```
<url>
    <loc>http://www.yourdomain.com/
yourpage.html</loc>
</url>
```

That is, between the `<url>` and `</url>` tags, include `<loc>` and `</loc>` tags and place the address of the page between them.

> **Webmaster Wisdom**
>
> The Sitemaps XML protocol also includes tags that let you specify when the page was last modified, how often it changes, and the relative priority of the page on your site. For the details, see the Sitemaps XML site at www.sitemaps.org/protocol.php.

Here's an example (see sitemap.xml on the CD for a sitemap template):

```
<?xml version="1.0" encoding="UTF-8"?>
<urlset xmlns="http://www.sitemaps.org/schemas/sitemap/0.9">
    <url>
        <loc>http://www.yourdomain.com/</loc>
    </url>
    <url>
        <loc>http://www.yourdomain.com/page1.html</loc>
    </url>
    <url>
        <loc>http://www.yourdomain.com/speeches/speech1.html</loc>
    </url>
</urlset>
```

After you've done that, you need to let a passing spider know you've got a sitemap file for it to digest. Create a text file named robots.txt, and add the following line:

```
SITEMAP: http://www.yourdomain.com/sitemap.xml
```

Replace *yourdomain* and *sitemap* with the correct values for your site.

Announcing Your Site

To help your website stand out, you need to blow your own horn by doing a little advertising and promotion. This doesn't mean paying for a 30-second ad during next year's Super Bowl (although feel free if you got a few million lying around you don't know what to do with).

By far the best marketing tool in existence is a little thing called word of mouth, so you can get things off to a good start by spreading the word about your website to friends, family, co-workers, and cocktail party conversationalists. Tell them not only to visit your site, but also to tell their friends about it.

There are many other things you can do to spread the gospel of you even further. You could include a brief "ad" about your website at the bottom of all your e-mail messages. Even just the URL of the website page would suffice. (Remember, too, that most e-mail programs can be set up to automatically tack on a "signature" to the bottom of each outgoing message.)

Page Pitfall

Please resist the temptation to broadcast an e-mail about your new website at work. Sending out an announcement to your department or even the entire company is in poor taste, and is probably not a good career move.

Join mailing lists and participate in newsgroups and discussion lists related to your website topic. Also, look out for online communities that discuss themes related to your website. Establishing a track record of thoughtful, helpful, and on-topic commentary (*not* useless and annoying "Check out my website!" posts) will do wonders to encourage other participants to visit your site. Note, too, that many community sites have a "member profiles" section you can use to talk up your website.

Volunteer to help out at any site that has content related to your website or participants whom you think might be interested in your website. Write articles, create programs, suggest new features, design a logo, or do anything that helps the site with its day-to-day chores. People who work at larger online community sites tend to be well connected; impressing these people might lead them to share your website information with their long list of friends.

Get all your friends and relatives to link to your site. The more links that point to you, the greater your ranking will be in some search engines—particularly Google.

Syndicating Your Site

You can steer perfect strangers to your website by allowing other sites to publish bits of your content along with a link back to your page. If people like what they read, they'll probably click the link so they can see what else you have up your online sleeve.

Sharing content seems easy as pie at first glance. The other site just views your page source code, copies the material they want, and pastes it somewhere on their site along with a link back to you. (I'm assuming you've given this person permission to do this.) That *is* relatively easy for a static page, but it can become mind-numbingly tedious for a frequently updated page such as a blog or journal. For example, if someone wants to display the most recent headlines from your blog and you post daily, that person has to visit your site every day to get your headlines. That's bad enough, but they might be a *news aggregator* that lists headlines from a number of different blogs. Imagine the hassle it would be to grab headlines from 10 or 20 different blogs.

The solution to this is something called *syndication*, which automates the process of grabbing headlines (or whatever) from a site. This section shows you how to set this up on your website.

def•i•ni•tion

A **news aggregator** is a service that collects and displays headlines from many different blogs. **Syndication** is the distribution of website content in a format that enables others to gather and read that content.

What Is Syndication?

You're probably familiar with the term *syndication* from the world of television. When a show is starting out, it appears at a scheduled time each week. When the show has been around for a while, the producers can make big bucks by selling to television stations the right to broadcast the older shows. Those stations can then broadcast the shows whenever they want. Web page syndication is similar, although unfortunately big bucks are never involved.

By syndicating your site, you're giving implicit permission for other people to "rebroadcast" portions of your content on their sites. This sounds the same as giving people permission to copy bits of your site source code, but there's a big difference. With syndication, the gathering and broadcasting of your content is done automatically—there's no cutting and pasting involved.

The secret to this is something called *Rich Site Summary* (or possibly *Real Simple Syndication* or *RDF Site Syntax*—nobody really knows). RSS is based on the eXtensible

Markup Language, or XML. XML uses tags, like HTML, but they serve a different purpose. HTML tags tell a web browser *how* text is supposed to appear to the user (bold, as a link, and so on); XML tags tell the browser *what* the text represents. For example, in HTML you might surround headline text with a `<span>` tag that contains several style properties to distinguish the headline from the other elements of the page. In an XML document, you might surround the headline text with a `<headline>` tag.

What XML means and how it's implemented are beyond the scope of this book. However, figuring out RSS is well within our purview.

The important point to keep in mind is that RSS automates the syndication of website content. It does that by enabling you to specify exactly which elements of the website are to be syndicated—usually, one or more headlines and all or part of their corresponding entries. It also provides for links back to your website, so people who like your syndicated material will drop by your site for more. To perform this magic, you need to create an RSS file.

Building an RSS File

RSS is actually very simple to learn and is, in fact, no more difficult than any of the HTML tags you've mastered elsewhere in this book. Like an HTML file, an RSS file is a simple text document. So go ahead and launch your favorite text editor, create a new file, and save it. Give the file a name that ends with the .xml or .rss extension.

Always begin this text file with the following tag:

```
<?xml version="1.0" encoding="UTF-8" ?>
```

This isn't necessary, but it's good to include because it declares to the world that this file conforms to the XML standard.

You're building an RSS document, so the next thing you do is declare the RSS version. We'll use version 2.0:

```
<rss version="2.0">
```

You also need the closing `</rss>` tag, so now your file looks like this:

```
<?xml version="1.0" encoding="utf-8" ?>
<rss version="2.0">
</rss>
```

In RSS, a *channel* is just the data feed provided by a site. You declare the beginning and end of your channel by using, appropriately enough, the `<channel>` tag and its `</channel>` end tag. Here's where we stand:

```
<?xml version="1.0" encoding="utf-8" ?>
<rss version="0.92">
    <channel>
    </channel>
</rss>
```

Notice that I've indented the `<channel>` and `</channel>` tags a few spaces. This is purely to make the file easier to read and has absolutely no effect on how it's interpreted.

Your next task is to describe the channel, which you do with five tags:

- ◆ `<title>` provides a name for the channel.

- ◆ `<link>` provides the address of your website.

- ◆ `<description>` provides a short summary of your website.

- ◆ `<language>` declares the language of your website. Use **en-us** for U.S. English.

- ◆ `<copyright>` specifies a copyright message for the feed.

Here's the channel information I use on my Word Spy site's Recent Words RSS feed:

```
<title>Word Spy</title>
<link>http://www.wordspy.com/</link>
<description>Recent Words</description>
<language>en-us</language>
<copyright>Copyright 2008 Logophilia Limited and Paul McFedries
</copyright>
```

Here's how the skeleton RSS file looks now:

```
<?xml version="1.0" encoding="utf-8" ?>
<rss version="2.0">
    <channel>
        <title>Your Website Title</title>
        <link>Your Website Address</link>
        <description>Your Website Description</description>
        <language>en-us</language>
        <copyright>Your Copyright Message</copyright>
    </channel>
</rss>
```

Finally, you need to add some tags that represent each of the website entries you want to include in the RSS feed. These are called *items*, and you begin and end them with the `<item>` and `</item>` tags. In between, you define the item using the `<title>`, `<link>`, `<pubDate>`, `<description>`, and `<guid>` tags:

- `<title>` is the headline of the website entry.

- `<link>` is the permanent address of the website page or the blog entry in your archives.

- `<pubDate>` is the date you published or posted the item. Use the following date format:

    Sat, 23 Aug Jan 2008 06:12:35 EST

- `<description>` is the website entry, or perhaps just a sentence or two if the entry is a long one.

- `<guid>` is the globally unique identifier, an overly fancy way of saying that it's a value that's unique to the item. Most people use the permanent address of the website page or blog entry.

Here's a simplified example of an item from Word Spy:

```
<item>
    <title>defictionalization</title>
    <link>http://www.wordspy.com/words/defictionalization.asp</link>
    <pubDate>Thu, 24 Jan 2008 05:31:58 EST</pubDate>
    <description>When a product or object from a movie, book, or other
    fictional source is made in the real world.</description>
    <guid>http://www.wordspy.com/words/defictionalization.asp</guid>
</item>
```

 I've put together a skeleton RSS file you can use as a starting point. See rss.xml on the CD. Figure 11.1 shows how Internet Explorer 7 renders an RSS file.

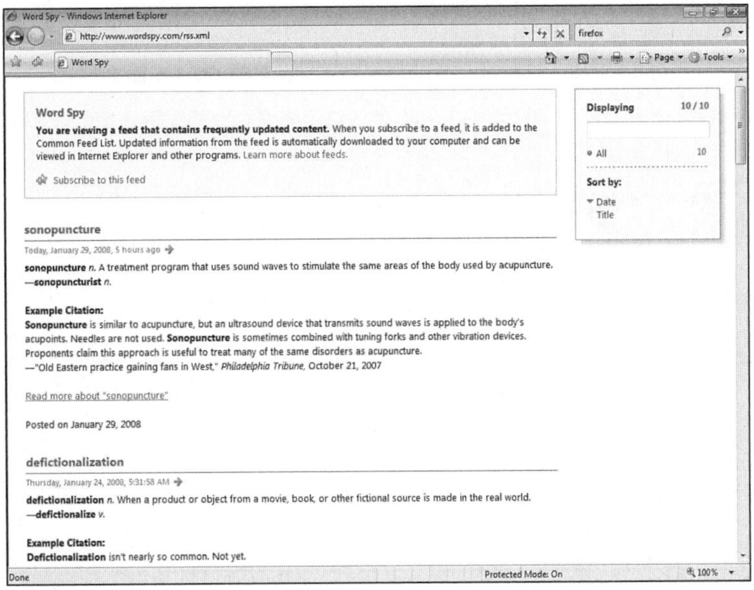

Figure 11.1
How Internet Explorer 7 displays an RSS file.

Putting Your Feed Online

After you've completed your RSS file, you have to give other people access to the feed. The first thing to do is upload the RSS file to your website. When that's finished, check to be sure your RSS code is valid. Numerous RSS code validators are available on the web, and you can find one by entering "RSS validator" into any search engine. Here are a couple validators to get you started:

◆ *Feed Validator* (feedvalidator.org)

◆ *RSS Validator* (rss.scripting.com)

Next, load your RSS file into an RSS reader to be sure the feed text and links look and behave the way you want. Search for "RSS reader" in any search engine, or use the following page as a starting point:

```
blogspace.com/rss/readers
```

When your RSS files are checked out and ready for public consumption, you need to let people know you have an RSS feed by setting up a link to the RSS file. For example, if your RSS file is named rss.xml and you stored it in your site's main directory, you'd set up a link like this one:

```
<a href="rss.xml">RSS Feed</a>
```

Note, too, that many web designers flag their RSS feed link by placing a standard "XML" image beside the link. Figure 11.2 shows an example.

Figure 11.2

Create a link to enable visitors to find your RSS feed.

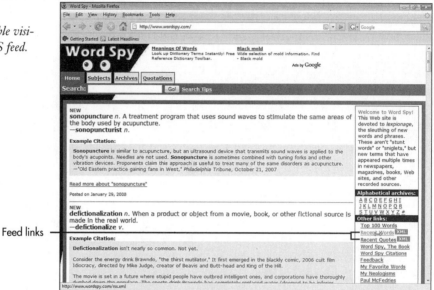

Feed links

 Finally, you also want to make it easy for news aggregators that crawl sites automatically to find your feed. Do that by adding a special `<link>` tag inside your page header (that is, between the `<head>` and `</head>` tags):

```
<link rel="alternate" type="application/rss+xml" title="rss"
href="RSS File" />
```

> **Webmaster Wisdom**
>
> The CD contains a sample "XML" image. Look for the xml.jpg file.

Here, replace *RSS File* with the full URL of your RSS file.

Setting up an RSS feed is not difficult, but if you post frequently, you'll begin to wonder if there's an easier way to generate the RSS file. Yup, there is. Many blogging sites and tools come with automatic RSS generators built right in. You can also use the RSS Channel Editor, which is available from www.webreference.com/cgi-bin/perl/rssedit.pl.

More Strategies for Drawing a Crowd

You've seen quite a few strategies for tooting your own website horn, but we're not done yet. The rest of this chapter takes you through a few more techniques you can use to get yourself heard above the din.

Get in the Blog-Specific Indexes

If your website is a blog, submitting your site to general search engines (particularly Google) is a must, but there are also several blog-specific indexes and searching tools you should know about—and that need to know about you. Blog fans use these resources all the time to find specific blog content or blogs that cover a particular subject area. Here are the ones to check out:

◆ *BlogHop* (bloghop.com/account/join.htm) is a directory of blogs that also enables visitors to rate each blog.

◆ *Eatonweb Portal* (portal.eatonweb.com/add.php) was one of the first blog directories to attempt to impose some order on the early blog chaos. It organizes blogs by category, language, country, and alphabetically, and it also includes visitor ratings for each blog.

◆ *Globe of Blogs* (www.globeofblogs.com/register.php) lists thousands of blogs by title, topic, location, and even date of birth!

◆ *Technorati* (www.technorati.com/signup) is the main blog index site, so if you only register with one index, make it this one.

> ### Webmaster Wisdom
> Find a large list of blog indexes and search engines at www.aripaparo.com/archive/000632.html.

Join a Webring or Blogring

A *webring* is a collection of related websites that use special links to create a kind of chain that connects one site to another. For example, Site A would have a link to Site B; Site B would have links to Site A (usually labeled "Previous") and Site C (usually labeled "Next"); Site C would have links to Site B and Site D, and so on. Site Z would have links to Site Y and Site A, thus completing the ring.

The advantage to this kind of setup is that it enables users to easily surf through a group of sites that are all focused on a particular topic.

Although webrings exist for all kinds of sites, they're popular in the blogosphere and a lot of readers use them to access many blogs that relate to a favorite theme. So you can drive a nice chunk of traffic to your site by joining an appropriate blog webring, or *blogring*.

> ### Webmaster Wisdom
> A site that lets you keep up to date on your favorite weblogs is blo.gs. It not only displays a constantly updated list of recently changed blogs, but can also send you an e-mail notifying you that your favorite blog has new content. The address is its name: blo.gs.

def•i•ni•tion

A webring that consists of a collection of related blogs is often called a **blogring**.

To find a webring or blogring, use your favorite search engine to search for "*topic* blogring" or "*topic* webring," where *topic* is a word or phrase that describes the topic of your blog. You can also try RingSurf (www.ringsurf.com), a directory of webrings. When you find one you want to join, the main site will give you instructions (note that you may need to be approved) and the code for the "Previous" and "Next" links.

Join a Geographic Index

Vacationers on cruise ships and in resorts often exhibit a strange behavior: if they meet people who hail from the same town, region, or country, they'll strike up a friendship and hang out with those people for the rest of their stay. It seems weird to travel thousands of miles only to end up vacationing with your own kind, but that's human nature for you.

This bonding instinct also shows up among webmasters in the form of the *geographic index*, a collection of websites and blogs from people who live in a particular city, state, region, or country. Sometimes these indexes consist of sites that discuss the common geographical area, so they're a great resource for people interested in learning more about that area. But these indexes increasingly serve a larger social function, with the webmasters exchanging e-mails and sometimes even getting together offline.

Whether your site deals with a geographic area or you just want to strike up a friendship with neighboring webmesiters, joining a geographic index can be a great way to drum up a bunch of new visitors. To find one, visit a search engine and look for "*area* blog," where *area* is the geographic location you're interested in.

Send a Note to an A-List Blogger

If you've been hanging around blogdom for a while, you probably have a few A-list bloggers (A-LBs) you like and admire. You probably also know that the mention of a site by a big-time blogger can generate a *ton* of traffic to that site. Your goal is obvious: get one of your favorite A-LBs to talk up your site. Of course, getting the blogger to do this isn't easy. A slightly easier goal is to get the A-LB to visit your site; occasionally you can make that happen just by dropping a line to the blogger via e-mail.

Tell the A-LB not only that you like and admire his or her blog, but *why* you like it. Don't flatter just for the sake of it; instead, be sincere and focus on those things you truly do enjoy about the site. Writing with humor or wit certainly helps get you noticed, too. Finally, be sure to include the address of your own blog and cross your fingers that the A-LB deigns to take a look.

You could, of course, come right out and *ask* the A-LB to visit your site, but the subtlety and mystery of an otherwise unmentioned address would very likely be too much for the A-LB to resist. (Remember that most bloggers *love* links and find it hard to resist clicking a new address.)

Link to Other Sites

Referrer URLs are the addresses of pages that link to your page. For example, if Site X has a link to your blog and a user clicks that link, Site X becomes a *referrer* and its address is recorded in the "Referrer" field of your website statistics.

Of course, it works the other way, too. That is, if you link to another site and someone clicks that link, your site address shows up as a referrer URL for the other site. Many site operators keep track of their referrers so they know who's linking to them. If they're curious about your referrer address, they may check out your page to see what you're all about. If the person likes what he or she sees, you might get a reciprocal link on his or her site, or even a mention in a blog entry. And if that other site happens to be a well-read blog, that could send a lot of new readers your way.

Page Pitfall

It goes without saying that you should only link to sites you're comfortable recommending to other people. Never link to a big-time site you dislike, because that level of naked ambition and dishonesty will certainly come back to haunt you in this life or the next one.

So when you're constructing your own list of favorite sites, be sure to include a few links to some high-traffic sites.

The Least You Need to Know

◆ Before trying to attract new visitors, use a site statistics tool or service to measure how many people are visiting your site.

◆ Use the pages provided by most search engines to tell them about your new site.

◆ For search engines to properly index your site, and for surfers to find it, include both a description and a keywords `<meta>` tag on all of your pages.

- Give the gift of you by creating an RSS feed that enables other sites to post summaries of your recent entries.

- Encourage friends, relatives, and willing co-workers to tell two friends about your website.

- Get your website in every website and blog index; join an appropriate webring or geographical index; drop a line to one of the blogerati you admire; and link to major websites you enjoy reading.

Part 4

Automating Your Website with JavaScripts

At this point on your website learning curve, you know pretty much everything there is to know about making your pages look their best. From fonts to images to tables to style sheets, you've got the know-how to turn out well-buffed websites. The problem, though, is that your pages just kind of sit there. Outside of adding a few animated GIFs, how can you make your pages seem more dynamic? You find at least part of the answer in Part 4. These two chapters show you how to add a bit of "software" to your pages in the form of scripts written in the JavaScript programming language. Without doing any actual programming yourself (insert sigh of relief here), you'll see just how easy it is to display messages to the user, validate form content, store data about the user, and much more.

Adding JavaScripts to Your Pages

In This Chapter

- ◆ Inserting scripts into a page
- ◆ Using scripts to display messages to the surfer
- ◆ Writing text to the page on the fly
- ◆ Detecting the user's browser

You now know that HTML stands for Hypertext Markup Language, a phrase that surely could only warm the cockles of a geek's heart, particularly the word *Language*. Many people interpret this to mean that HTML is a programming language, and they wash their hands of the whole thing right off the bat. "You mean I gotta learn *programming* to get my two cents worth on the web?"

Fortunately, as you've seen, HTML has nothing whatsoever to do with computer programming. Rather, HTML is a "language" in the sense that it has a small collection of two- and three-letter combinations and words you use to specify styles such as bold and italic.

Now, however, it's time to get ever so slightly acquainted with a *real* programming language. It's called *JavaScript*, and you use it to add tiny little programs called *scripts* to your pages. You can use these scripts to pop up a welcome message whenever someone visits your site, display the current time, find out which browser a visitor is using, and tons more.

Does this mean you have to learn how to program in JavaScript? Well, no, not if you don't want to. You can always go the "black box" route where you simply add a script to your page without understanding exactly how the script does its thing. That's the approach I take in this chapter. You won't learn any programming here. Instead, I show you how to add a script to your page, and I run through a few examples of some useful scripts. (You'll see even more examples in the next chapter.)

Using the `<script>` Tag

JavaScript code goes right inside the web page, just like HTML tags. When a browser accesses the page, the JavaScript code is executed and the program does its thing. For example, the program might check the time of day and display an appropriate welcome message, or you could embed a calculator right on the page.

JavaScripts reside between the `<script>` and `</script>` tags and always take the following form:

```
<script language="javascript" type="text/javascript">
<!--
The script commands go here.
//-->
</script>
```

Note the use of HTML comment tags: `<!--` and `-->`. These ensure that JavaScript-feeble browsers don't try to read the JavaScript commands.

Webmaster Wisdom

In the same way that HTML has comment tags that tell the browser to ignore the text and tags between them, programmers can also add comments to scripts. To do so, they insert two slashes (`//`) at the beginning of each line they want ignored. A common example is the line just above the `</script>` end tag:

```
//-->
```

You have to put the comment slashes at the beginning to prevent JavaScript from trying to "execute" the end tag of the HTML comment (`-->`).

Inserting the Script

Where you store the script in your page depends on what it does. If the script writes text to the page, position the script where you want the text to appear. Otherwise, position the script inside the page header (that is, between the `<head>` and `</head>` tags).

Using an External JavaScript File

Besides having your scripts snuggle up to your regular page tags, in some cases, it's also possible to plop the scripts into a separate file. Although this is really only for advanced users who know what they're doing, it's worthwhile because it has three benefits:

♦ It makes it easier to reuse a script because you need to tell the browser only the name and location of the separate file. You don't have to insert the script itself into all your pages.

♦ If you need to adjust the script, you have to adjust it only in the separate file. Every page that accesses the script automatically uses the edited version.

> **Webmaster Wisdom**
>
> This section on using an external JavaScript file is advanced stuff, so don't worry if it makes no sense to you now. Just skip over it and come back to it later, after you've had some experience working with JavaScripts.

♦ It makes your page's source code look less cluttered, so it's easier to read.

The key thing about all this is that you can put only what are known as *functions* in the external file. A JavaScript function looks like this:

```
function Name() {
A bunch of programming statements go here.
}
```

Here, `Name` is the name of the function.

To tell the browser about the external file, add the `src` attribute to the `<script>` tag. For example, if your functions are all in a file named scripts.js (it's traditional to use the .js extension for these files; they're just text files, however), you'd put the following into your page between the `<head>` and `</head>` tags:

```
<script language="javascript" type="text/javascript" src="scripts.js">
</script>
```

Some JavaScript Examples

The real purpose of this chapter isn't so much to show you how to insert scripts (although that's clearly important). No, what I really want to do is give you a good supply of scripts to use, at no extra charge, in your own pages. To that end, the next few sections take you through quite a few JavaScripts that perform all manner of interesting and useful functions. (Remember, too, that you get even more script examples in the next chapter. See also my JavaScript code for a drop-down list of links in Chapter 6.)

Webmaster Wisdom

If you would like to learn a bit of JavaScript, good for you! It's actually not as hard as you might think, especially if you learn it using a book written by your favorite computer book author (that's me). My book *Special Edition Using JavaScript* (Que, 2001) can teach you JavaScript even if you've never programmed before. To find out more about the book, please see www.mcfedries.com/UsingJavaScript.

Displaying a Message to the User

Let's begin with the simplest of all JavaScript functions: displaying a message to the user in a simple dialog box (also called a *pop-up box* or an *alert box*). Here's the JavaScript code that does the job:

```
alert("Insert your message here")
```

In other words, between the quotation marks you enter whatever message you want to display. For example, suppose you want to have a message pop up each time a user visits your home page. You can do that by inserting the following script between the </head> and <body> tags (see jsalert1.htm on the CD):

```
<script language="javascript" type="text/javascript">
<!--
alert("Welcome to my website!")
//-->
</script>
```

Figure 12.1 shows what happens when the user loads your page.

Figure 12.1

The JavaScript alert() *statement displays a little dialog box like this one.*

Windows Internet Explorer

⚠ Welcome to my website!

OK

Writing Data to the Page

After displaying a dialog box message to the user, the second most common JavaScript chore is to write some data to the page. This is really powerful because it means you can display *dynamic* text on your page. For example, you could write the current date and time (see the next section to learn how to do this).

The JavaScript statement that performs this magic is document.write(), which looks like this:

```
document.write("The stuff you want to write goes here.")
```

The idea is that you place this statement at the spot within your page where you want the text to appear.

For example, many web spinners like to include in their page the date and time the page was last modified. This helps the surfer know whether he's dealing with recent data. JavaScript has a special statement called document.lastModified that returns the date and time the file was last edited. Here's a script (see jswrite1.htm on the CD) that shows you one way to use it with document.write():

```
<script language="javascript"
type="text/javascript">
<!--
document.write("This page was last
monkeyed with on " + document.
lastModified)
//-->
</script>
```

In JavaScript you use the plus sign (+) as the *concatenation operator*, which is geekspeak that just means it combines two bits of text. Figure 12.2 shows how things shake out in Firefox.

Page Pitfall

JavaScript is *really* finicky about uppercase versus lowercase letters. So when entering JavaScript statements, always use precisely the same combination of uppercase and lowercase letters I show you. For example, you must use document.lastModified, not Document.LastModified or document.lastmodified.

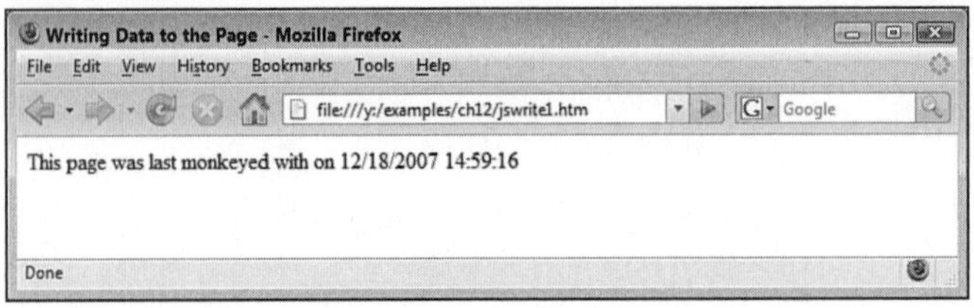

Figure 12.2

Use document.write() *to add text to your page on the fly.*

![Firefox browser window titled "Writing Data to the Page - Mozilla Firefox" showing URL file:///y:/examples/ch12/jswrite1.htm and text: This page was last monkeyed with on 12/18/2007 14:59:16]

What's that? The text in the previous example is a bit plain? No problem. We can put some fancy pants on it. You can easily add HTML tags within the document.write() statement. Here's a revised script (see jswrite2.htm on the CD) that does just that:

```
<script language="javascript" type="text/javascript">
<!--
document.write("<span style='font-family: arial; font-size: 14pt'>
➥<b>This page was last monkeyed with on <tt>" +
➥document.lastModified) + "</tt></b></font>"
//-->
</script>
```

Webmaster Wisdom

This seems like a good time to remind you about the ➥ character you see in the jswrite2.htm code. Publishing types call this a *code continuation character*. All it means is that the current line and the line above it are to be considered a *single* statement. So if you're typing in the statement by hand, be sure you keep everything on one line.

I added the <span>, <b>, and <tt> tags to produce the effect shown in Figure 12.3.

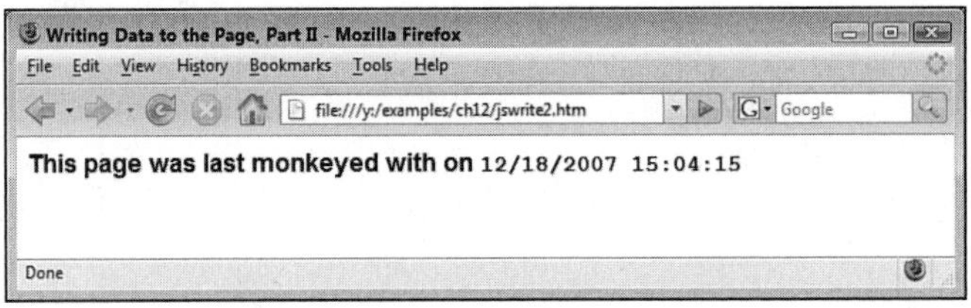

Figure 12.3

There's no problem adding tags within your document. write() *statements.*

![Firefox browser window titled "Writing Data to the Page, Part II - Mozilla Firefox" showing URL file:///y:/examples/ch12/jswrite2.htm and text: This page was last monkeyed with on 12/18/2007 15:04:15]

Page Pitfall

One thing you have to watch out for in `document.write()` (and indeed, in most JavaScript statements) is when you use quotation marks within quotation marks. In the previous example, I had to use `<font face='arial'>` instead of `<font face="arial">` because `document.write()` already has its own double quotation marks ("), and it would seriously confuse things to use `<font face="arial">`. Always use single quotation marks (') within JavaScript statements such as `document.write()`.

Hiding Your E-Mail Address from Spam Crawlers

As you might know, *spam* is the whimsical name given to a nonwhimsical thing: unsolicited commercial e-mail messages. If you put up a website and include your e-mail address on it somewhere, I'll bet you dollars to doughnuts you'll start receiving more spam in your inbox. Why? Because programs called *spam crawlers* troll the web looking for pages containing e-mail addresses they can harvest for their evil intentions. They look for @ signs and mailto links.

You can foil spam crawlers by using a simple bit of JavaScript code to write your e-mail address to the page. Here's the code (see jsnospam.htm on the CD):

```
<script language="javascript" type="text/javascript">
<!--
var addr = "mai"
addr = addr + "lto:"
addr = addr + "YourUserName"
addr = addr + "@"
addr = addr + "YourDomainName.com"
document.write('<a href=' + addr + '>')
document.write('E-mail Me!</a>')
//-->
</script>
```

Place this script at the spot in the page where you want your mailto link to appear. Of course, you need to edit things for your own e-mail address. (That is, you replace `YourUserName` and `YourDomainName` with the appropriate values from the e-mail address you want to use.) As you can see in Figure 12.4, what you end up with is a mailto link that works normally, as far as the surfer is concerned.

Figure 12.4

The JavaScript code creates a standard mailto link.

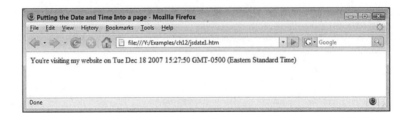

Putting the Date and Time into a Page

 A similar example involves putting the current date and time into the page. The current date and time is produced by JavaScript's `Date()` statement. Here's a simple example that uses `Date()` (see jsdate1.htm on the CD). Figure 12.5 shows the Firefox interpretation.

```
<script language="javascript" type="text/javascript">
<!--
document.write("You're visiting my website on " + Date())
//-->
</script>
```

Figure 12.5

A simple script inserts the current date and time.

That's not bad, but the date and time display is a bit ugly. To get more control, you need to break out the various components of the date and time: the day of the week, the month, the hours and minutes, and so on. Here's a quick summary of the JavaScript statements that do this:

- `getDay()` returns a number between 0 and 6, where 0 is Sunday, 1 is Monday, and so on.

- `getMonth()` returns the month number, where 0 is January, 1 is February, and so on.

- `getYear()` returns the year component of a date. If the year is before 2000, it returns a two-digit year (such as 99); if it's in 2000 or later, Internet Explorer returns the four-digit year, but Netscape 4 and later subtract 1900 from the year (for example, 2001 returns 101).

- `getSeconds()` returns the seconds component of a time.

◆ `getMinutes()` returns the minutes component of a time.

◆ `getHours()` returns the hours component of a time. Note that this is military time, so if it's 5:00 in the afternoon, it returns 17.

To use these statements, you must first store the current date in what programmers call a *variable*, like so:

```
d = new Date()
```

You can then apply one of the statements to this variable. Here's how you'd get the current day:

```
d.getDay()
```

Note, too, that after you go to all this trouble, it becomes relatively easy to display a custom message to the user based on the current time. For example, you might want to add "Good morning!" if the current date and time is before noon.

Here's a long script that takes advantage of all this (see jsdate2.htm on the CD):

```
<script language="javascript" type="text/javascript">
<!--
// Store the date in a variable
d = new Date()
dateText = ""

// Get the current day and convert it to the name of the day
dayValue = d.getDay()
if (dayValue == 0)
    dateText += "Sunday"
else if (dayValue == 1)
    dateText += "Monday"
else if (dayValue == 2)
    dateText += "Tuesday"
else if (dayValue == 3)
    dateText += "Wednesday"
else if (dayValue == 4)
    dateText += "Thursday"
else if (dayValue == 5)
    dateText += "Friday"
else if (dayValue == 6)
    dateText += "Saturday"

// Get the current month and convert it to the name of the month
monthValue = d.getMonth()
```

```
dateText += " "
if (monthValue == 0)
    dateText += "January"
if (monthValue == 1)
    dateText += "February"
if (monthValue == 2)
    dateText += "March"
if (monthValue == 3)
    dateText += "April"
if (monthValue == 4)
    dateText += "May"
if (monthValue == 5)
    dateText += "June"
if (monthValue == 6)
    dateText += "July"
if (monthValue == 7)
    dateText += "August"
if (monthValue == 8)
    dateText += "September"
if (monthValue == 9)
    dateText += "October"
if (monthValue == 10)
    dateText += "November"
if (monthValue == 11)
    dateText += "December"

// Get the current year; if it's before 2000, add 1900
if (d.getYear() < 2000)
    dateText += " " + d.getDate() + ", " + (1900 + d.getYear())
else
    dateText += " " + d.getDate() + ", " + (d.getYear())

// Get the current minutes
minuteValue = d.getMinutes()
if (minuteValue < 10)
    minuteValue = "0" + minuteValue

// Get the current hours
hourValue = d.getHours()

// Customize the greeting based on the current hours
if (hourValue < 12)
    {
    greeting = "Good morning!"
    timeText = " at " + hourValue + ":" + minuteValue + " AM"
```

```
        }
    else if (hourValue == 12)
        {
        greeting = "Good afternoon!"
        timeText = " at " + hourValue + ":" + minuteValue + " PM"
        }
    else if (hourValue < 17)
        {
        greeting = "Good afternoon!"
        timeText = " at " + (hourValue-12) + ":" + minuteValue + " PM"
        }
    else
        {
        greeting = "Good evening!"
        timeText = " at " + (hourValue-12) + ":" + minuteValue + " PM"
        }
    // Write the greeting, the date, and the time to the page
    document.write(greeting + " It's " + dateText + timeText)
    //-->
    </script>
```

Whew! That's some script! It works quite nicely, though, as you can see in Figure 12.6.

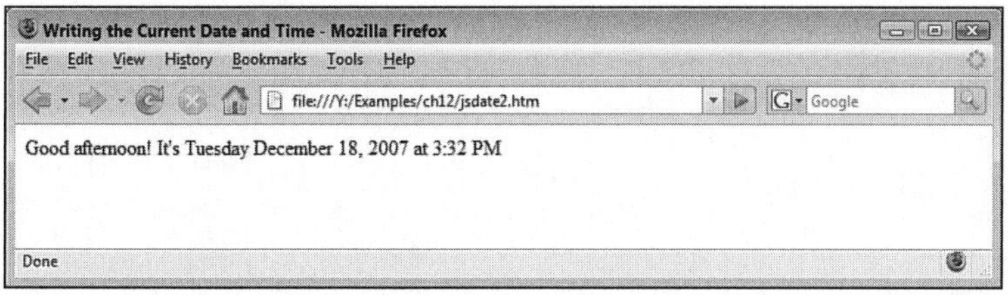

Figure 12.6

This page uses JavaScript to display the date and time and an appropriate message based on the time of day.

Understanding JavaScript Functions

In the examples you've seen so far, how did the browser know it was supposed to run the JavaScript statements? Because the browser routinely scours the page for a `<script>` and `</script>` combo. If it sees one, it goes right ahead and runs whatever JavaScript statements are stuffed in there.

The exception to this is when the statements reside inside a JavaScript function. In that case, the browser ignores the function's statements. So how do they get executed? You have to put in a statement that says to the browser, "Hey, you! Run this function for me, will ya!" In geek-speak, this is known as *calling* the function.

Let's check out a simple example. Instead of displaying a dialog box when the user loads your page, what if you want to display a message when the user *leaves* your page? The browser has already processed your page, so it doesn't do anything to it when the user leaves. Therefore, to execute some JavaScript code at that point, you have to create a function and then call it. Here's an example function called SayGoodbye():

```
function SayGoodbye() {
    alert("Thanks for visiting my website!")
}
```

Here's how it looks within the page (see jsalert2.htm on the CD):

```
<html>
<head>
<title>Displaying a Message to the User, Part 2</title>
</head>

<script language="javascript" type="text/javascript">
<!--
function SayGoodbye() {
    alert("Thanks for visiting my website!")
}
//-->
</script>

<body onUnload="SayGoodbye()">
<a href="/">Click here to reload this page and see the alert</a>
</body>
</html>
```

The thing to notice here is the special onUnload statement in the <body> tag. This tells the browser to execute the SayGoodbye() function when the user leaves ("unloads") the page.

So to summarize, here's how the browser executes JavaScript statements:

♦ If the statements aren't within a function, the browser executes them as soon as the page loads.

♦ If the statements are within a function, the browser doesn't execute them until the function is called.

Detecting the User's Browser

For the final example in this chapter, I'll show you how to determine which browser the user is surfing with. Why would you care? Well, you might want to send the surfer to a page that's been customized for his or her browser.

JavaScript offers three statements that return browser info:

◆ *navigator.userAgent* returns the complete information about the browser, including its name, version number, and operating system.

◆ *navigator.appName* returns the name of the browser. This isn't all that useful nowadays because many browsers return "Netscape" for this value.

◆ *navigator.appVersion* returns the version number of the browser.

Here's a script (see jsbrowser.htm on the CD) that determines the browser name and version and then displays a custom message (shown in Figures 12.7, 12.8, and 12.9).

```
<script language="javascript" type="text/javascript">
<!--
    // Get the browser infor
    var browserInfo = navigator.userAgent
    //
    // Is it Internet Explorer?
    //
    if (browserInfo.indexOf("MSIE") != -1) {
        var start = browserInfo.indexOf("MSIE") + 5
        var end = browserInfo.indexOf(";",start)
        browserVer = browserInfo.substring(start,end)
        alert("Welcome Internet Explorer user!" + "\n\n" + "You are
➥ using version " + browserVer)
        }
    //
    // Is it Firefox?
    //
    else if (browserInfo.indexOf("Firefox") != -1) {
        var start = browserInfo.indexOf("Firefox") + 8
        browserVer = browserInfo.substring(start)
        alert("Welcome Firefox user!" + "\n\n" + "You are using version
➥ " + browserVer)
        }
```

```
        //
        // Is it Safari?
        //
        else if (browserInfo.indexOf("Safari") != -1) {
            var start = browserInfo.indexOf("Safari") + 7
            browserVer = browserInfo.substring(start)
            alert("Welcome Safari user!" + "\n\n" + "You are using version
➥ " + browserVer)
            }
        //
        // Hmmm, it must be some other browser
        //
        else
            {
            var browserName = navigator.appName
            var browserVer = navigator.appVersion
            alert("Welcome " + browserName + " user!" + "\n\n" + "You are
➥ using version " + browserVer)
            }
        //-->
        </script>
```

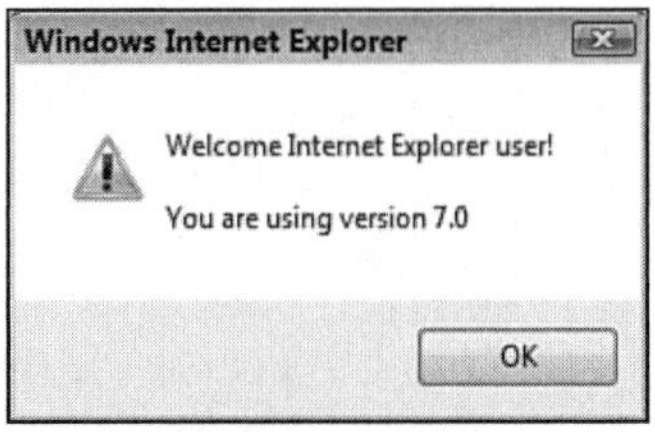

Figure 12.7

The alert message for the
Internet Explorer browser.

Windows Internet Explorer

⚠ Welcome Internet Explorer user!

You are using version 7.0

OK

Figure 12.8

The alert message for the
Firefox browser.

[JavaScript Application]

⚠ Welcome Firefox user!

You are using version 2.0.0.11

OK

Figure 12.9

The alert message for the
Safari browser.

JavaScript

Welcome Safari user!

You are using version 523.10

OK

> **Webmaster Wisdom**
>
> If you want to modify this script to send the user to another page based on his or her browser, use the `location.href` statement:
>
> ```
> location.href = "url"
> ```
>
> Here, `url` is the name or full URL of the page to which you want to send the surfer.

The Least You Need to Know

- You insert scripts by using, not surprisingly, the `<script>` and `</script>` tags:

  ```
  <script language="javascript" type="text/javascript">
  <!--
  The script commands go here.
  //-->
  </script>
  ```

- If your script writes text or tags to the page, insert the script at the exact spot where you want the text or tags to appear; otherwise, place the script inside the page header (that is, between the `<head>` and `</head>` tags).

- When you're using the `document.write()` method for inserting text on the fly, feel free to toss in a tag or two if you want to format the text.

More JavaScript Fun

In This Chapter

◆ Changing images on the fly with mouseovers

◆ Password protecting your pages

◆ Using JavaScript to work with forms

◆ Calculating mortgage payments

The previous chapter showed you that although programming JavaScript is tough, just inserting a script or two into a page isn't a big deal. If you liked the examples I took you through in that chapter, wait until you see what I have in store for you here. By necessity, these are much more complex scripts, but you'll see that they do much more interesting things. Don't worry if some of the scripts look intimidating. Remember: you don't have to understand their inner workings to get them to work. Just follow my instructions, and you'll have your JavaScript-enhanced pages up and at 'em in no time.

A Script for Mouseovers

Have you ever visited a site, sat your mouse over an image, and noticed that image magically transform into a different graphic? This neat effect is called a "mouseover," and it's all done with JavaScript.

There are several ways to go about this, but one method is relatively simple and straightforward. You begin by entering a normal `<img>` tag, except you name it by inserting the `name` attribute:

```
<img src="whatever.gif" name="somename" />
```

For the example I'm using, I have two images:

◆ *mouseout.gif* is the regular image that appears without the mouse pointer over it.

◆ *mouseover.gif* is the image that appears when the user puts the mouse pointer over mouseout.gif.

Here's the `<img>` tag (each attribute is on a separate line for easier reading):

```
<img src="mouseout.gif"
    width="157"
    height="39"
    border="0"
    name="mypicture" />
```

As you can see, I've used mouseout.gif to start, and I've given the name "mypicture" to the `<img>` tag. Now you construct an `<a>` tag (mouseovers work only with images that are set up as links):

```
<a href="jsmouse.htm"
    onmouseover="mypicture.src='mouseover.gif'"
    onmouseout="mypicture.src='mouseout.gif'">
```

There are two extra JavaScript attributes here: `onMouseover` and `onMouseout`. The `onMouseover` attribute says, essentially, "When the user moves the mouse pointer over the image named mypicture, change its `src` attribute to mouseover.gif." Similarly, the `onMouseout` attribute basically says, "When the user moves the mouse pointer off (out of) the image named mypicture, change its `src` attribute to mouseout.gif."

Here's how the whole thing looks (see jsmouse.htm on the CD):

```
<a href="jsmouse.htm"
    onmouseover="mypicture.src='mouseover.gif'"
    onmouseout="mypicture.src='mouseout.gif'">
<img src="mouseout.gif"
    width="157"
    height="39"
    border="0"
    name="mypicture" />
</a>
```

Figure 13.1 offers two Internet Explorer windows showing the same page (jsmouse. htm). In the top window, I don't have the mouse over the image, so Internet Explorer shows mouseout.gif. In the bottom window, I've put my mouse over the image, so Internet Explorer displays mouseover.gif.

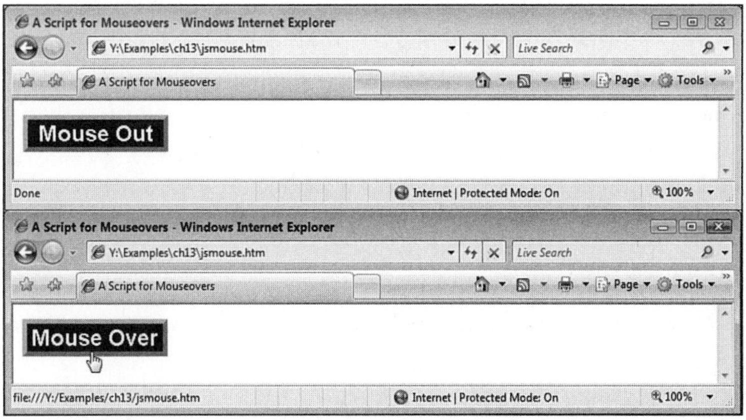

Figure 13.1

Internet Explorer showing the <img> tag without the mouse over it (top window) and with the mouse over it (bottom window).

Webmaster Wisdom

You might be wondering where the heck is the `<script>` tag I told you in the previous chapter you had to use for JavaScript. It's nowhere in sight because sometimes you can just enter a JavaScript statement directly, without needing a `<script>` tag. For example, consider the following chunk from the `<a>` tag in this example:

```
onMouseover="mypicture.src='mouseover.gif'"
```

The `onMouseover` part is called an *event*, and the rest of the line is an honest-to-goodness JavaScript statement. In other words, when the `onMouseover` event occurs (that is, when the user places the mouse over the image), the JavaScript statement is executed automatically.

When working with mouseovers, don't use large images for your mouseover effects. When the user puts the mouse over the image for the first time, the browser delays while it downloads the mouseover image. If you use a large image, that delay can be several seconds or longer, which spoils the effect. Mouseovers are best used with images that weigh only a few kilobytes or so.

Also, if you must use a larger image, or if you have a lot of mouseover images on your page, it's possible to "preload" images (that is, have the browser load the images and keep them waiting in memory when it first opens the page). I show you how this works at www.mcfedries.com/JavaScript/mouseover3.html.

Creating a Password-Protected Page

Many readers have written to me over the years and asked how they can set up a page that can be accessed only if the user enters the appropriate password. "That depends," I always respond, "on how bulletproof you need your password to be."

If you have sensitive information that must be protected at all costs, ask your web hosting provider if it can establish a password-protected portion of your site. If that's not possible, you might need to hire a CGI programmer to create a password-protection script. There are also some password scripts available on the web. (See Chapter 4's "Getting the Data Delivered to Your Door" section for some resources.)

If your needs aren't so grandiose, you can set up a reasonably strong password system using just a few dollops of JavaScript.

Hold on just a sec, mister! JavaScript stuff sits right inside the page. Won't someone be able to see the password if he looks at the page source code?

That's very perceptive of you. However, in the system I show you, the password never appears in the JavaScript code! Why? Because the password is just the name of the protected page (minus the .htm or .html extension). Because it's just as hard to guess the name of a web page as it is to guess a password, you get basically the same level of protection.

Page Pitfall

For this password scheme to work, it's absolutely crucial to have a default page in the same directory as the password-protected page. Why? Well, recall that a default page is the one the server sends out if the user doesn't specify a page. For example, suppose the user enters the following address:

    http://www.yourserver.com/finances

Most servers use index.html as the default page, so the above is equivalent to the following address:

    http://www.yourserver.com/finances/index.html

If you don't include the default page in the directory, most web servers simply return a list of all the files in the directory! This would obviously defeat our password protection scheme.

The system I'm going to show you requires three parts:

- ◆ A page that has a link to the password-protected part of your site. I use a page titled TestPassword.htm (it's on the CD) for this example.

- ◆ A page that asks the user for the proper password (GetPassword.htm on the CD).

- ◆ The password-protected page (idiot.htm on the CD). When you name this file, you must use lowercase letters only.

The next sections show you how to set everything up.

Linking to Password-Protected Parts of Your Site

You can send people to the password-protected page by including a link in one or more pages on your site. Other than the password-protected page itself, this is the only thing you need to create yourself. Here's the `<a>` tag to use:

```
<a href="javascript:GetPassword()">
```

As you can see, this link calls a JavaScript function named `GetPassword()`. Here's the code for that function (place this in the header section of the page that includes the link):

```
<script language="javascript" type="text/javascript">
<!--
function GetPassword()
{
    window.open("GetPassword.htm", "", "width=225,height=70")
}
//-->
</script>
```

All the `GetPassword()` function does is open a new window that contains the GetPassword.htm page. Figure 13.2 shows a page that uses this link and function (see PasswordTest.htm on the CD) and shows the window that appears when you click the link.

Figure 13.2

When you click this link, the
GetPassword() function
displays a window.

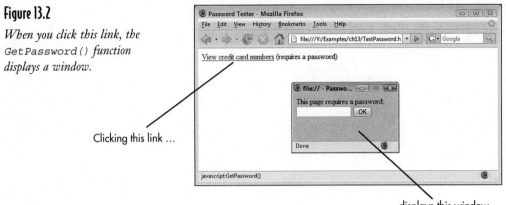

Clicking this link ...

... displays this window.

The Password-Processing Script

The little window that shows up contains a simple form that asks the user to enter the password:

```
<form>
This page requires a password:<br>
<input type="text" name="pw" size="15">
<input type="button" value="OK"
onClick="submitpassword(this.form)">
</form>
```

There are two things to note here for future use:

◆ The text box is named pw.

◆ The button uses the JavaScript onClick event to run a function. That is, when the user clicks the button, the JavaScript function named SubmitPassword() is called.

Here's the code for the SubmitPassword() function:

```
<script language="javascript" type="text/javascript">
<!--

function SubmitPassword(frm) {
    //
    // Get the value entered into the text box
    //
    var password = frm.pw.value
```

```
//
// Convert it to lowercase
//
password = password.toLowerCase()
//
// Add the .htm extension
//
var loc = password + ".htm"
//
// Make sure the user entered something
//
if (password != "")
{
    //
    // If so, send the browser there
    //
    opener.location.href = loc
}
//
// Close this window
//
window.close()
}

//-->
</script>
```

Here's what happens:

1. The value in the pw text box is stored in the `password` variable.

2. The `password` value is changed to all lowercase letters (just in case the user entered any uppercase letters).

3. The .htm extension is tacked on to `password`. (You might need to change this to ".html" if your pages use that extension.)

4. If `password` isn't blank, the main browser window is sent to the password-protected page.

5. The little window is closed.

> **Webmaster Wisdom**
>
> I give the details of a sturdier version of this password-protection scheme in my book *Special Edition Using JavaScript* (www.mcfedries.com/UsingJavaScript).

If you try out the example page that's on the CD, enter **idiot** as the password.

JavaScript and Forms

In the previous example, you saw how I used a small form to get the password and then I used JavaScript to process that value. As you'll see over the next few sections, JavaScript is quite happy to work with forms for all kinds of things.

Making Form Fields Mandatory

One of the problems we webmasters face when constructing forms is getting our users to fill in all the required fields. We can augment the form with all kinds of notes that warn the user of the dire consequences that can result from leaving a field blank, but users have a way of ignoring these things.

A better approach is to use a little JavaScript know-how to make one or more form fields mandatory. That is, make it so the browser won't submit the form unless the user puts something in those fields.

For example, suppose you have a contact form where users can enter an e-mail address so you can send them a reply. Whatever script you're using to process the form may not have any way to detect whether the user's e-mail address is present, which means you have to rely on your readers to enter their e-mail address so you can contact them. One thing you can do is use JavaScript to make your form's e-mail field mandatory.

To set this up, you first need to make two adjustments to your `<form>` tag:

- Add the `name` attribute, and set it to whatever you want to name your form.

- Add the JavaScript `onSubmit` attribute, like so (here, *FormName* is the name you gave your form):

```
onSubmit="return Validate(FormName)"
```

Here's an example:

```
<form
    action="http://www.mcfedries.com/scripts/formtest.asp"
    method="post"
    name="MyForm"
    onSubmit="return validate(MyForm)">
```

The `onSubmit` event means that when the user clicks the form's Submit button, the function specified by `onSubmit` is executed before the form data is shipped out to the server. This enables you to check that a particular field has been filled in (or whatever). If it hasn't, the JavaScript can tell the browser not to submit the form.

Set up the rest of your form in the usual manner. You just need to pay attention to the names you supply each field because you use those names in the JavaScript procedure. Here's the example field I'll use:

```
<b>Please enter your email address:</b><br />
<input type="text" size="35" name="Email" />
```

Here, at long last, is the script (see jsform.htm on the CD):

```
<script language="javascript" type="text/javascript">
<!--
function validate(frm)
{
    //
    // Check the Email field to see if any characters were entered
    //
    if (frm.Email.value == "")
    {
        alert("Tsk tsk. Please enter an email address.")
        frm.Email.focus()
        return false
    }
}
//-->
</script>
```

The `Validate()` function checks the value the user entered into the specified field (Email, in this case). If the value is empty (""), it means the user didn't enter a value. So the script displays an alert (see Figure 13.3), puts the cursor back in the Email field (this is called setting the "focus" in programming parlance), and returns false, which tells the browser not to submit the form.

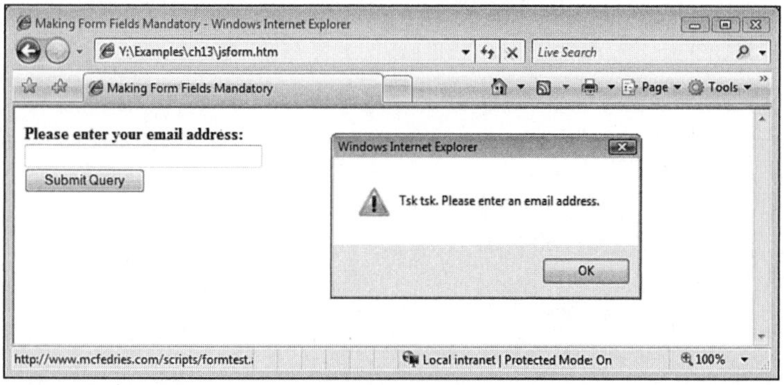

Figure 13.3

If the user doesn't enter anything in the text box, he or she sees this message.

To use this script on your own form, you need to adjust two things:

◆ The `if` statement checks the value of the form field named Email. When setting this up for your own use, change `Email` to the name of your field.

◆ The same goes for the `frm.Email.focus()` statement. Change `Email` to the name of your field.

Webmaster Wisdom

The user can easily thwart this script by entering a trivial value (such as a single letter) in the text box. My site offers a more sophisticated version of the script that checks to see if the user entered the @ sign (which is part of every e-mail address). See www.mcfedries.com/JavaScript/mandatory.html.

Confirming Form Data with the User

It's important that the data submitted in a form be as accurate as possible. However, lots of web surfers have short attention spans (present company excepted, of course), so they tend to fill in form data haphazardly. To help boost the accuracy of submissions, it's a good idea to display the entered data to the user before submitting it. If everything looks good, the user can submit the data; otherwise, he or she can cancel and make changes.

 Before getting to the JavaScript, let's set up a sample form that includes the four main form controls: a text box, an option list, radio buttons, and a check box (see Chapter 4). Here it is (see jscheck.htm on the CD):

```
<form
    action="http://www.mcfedries.com/scripts/formtest.asp"
    method="post"
    name="MyForm"
    onSubmit="return checkdata(MyForm)">

Please enter your name:<br />
<input type="text" name="UserName" />
<p>
Who is your favorite Beatle?<br />
<select name="Beatle">
<option value="George" selected>George</option>
<option value="John">John</option>
<option value="Paul">Paul</option>
<option value="Ringo">Ringo</option>
```

```
<option value="Pete Best">Pete Best</option>
<option value="Hunh?">Who the heck are the Beatles?</option>
</select>
<p>
Have you ever gotten jiggy with it?<br />
<input type="radio" name="Jiggy" value="yes" checked/>Yes
<input type="radio" name="Jiggy" value="no"/>No
<input type="radio" name="Jiggy" value="shhh"/>Not Telling
<p>
<input type="checkbox" name="Spam"/>Send tons of spam?
<p>
<input type="submit" value="Fire!"/>
</form>
```

Note, in particular, that I added the JavaScript `onSubmit` attribute to the `<form>` tag:

```
onSubmit="return CheckData(MyForm)"
```

This tells the browser that when the user submits the form, it must run the `CheckData()` JavaScript function. The `return` part means the browser should examine the value returned by `CheckData()` to see whether the form submission should proceed or be cancelled. Here's the JavaScript:

```
<script language="javascript" type="text/javascript">
<!--
function CheckData(frm)
{
    //
    // Get the text box value
    //
    var tb = frm.UserName.value
    //
    // Get the selected option
    //
    var opt = frm.Beatle.options[frm.Beatle.selectedIndex].value
    //
    // Get the selected radio button
    //
    for (var i = 0; i < frm.Jiggy.length; i++)
    {
        if (frm.Jiggy[i].checked)
            var rb = frm.Jiggy[i].value
    }
```

```
//
// Get the check box value
//
if (frm.Spam.checked)
    var cb = "On"
else
    var cb = "Off"
//
// Construct the message to display
//
var msg = "Your name: " + tb + "\n"
    + "Favorite Beatle: " + opt + "\n"
    + "Jiggy with it? " + rb + "\n"
    + "Send spam: " + cb + "\n"
//
// Show the data to the user
//
return confirm("Here is the form data you entered:" + "\n\n"
    + msg + "\n"
    + "Do you want to submit this data?")
}
//-->
</script>
```

Webmaster Wisdom

In case you're wondering, all those \ns in the script are just the JavaScript code for starting a new line. This makes the displayed message easier to read.

Most of the function is spent getting the various form values. After that's done, a message containing all the values is constructed and shown to the user via the `confirm()` statement. Figure 13.4 shows the dialog box that pops up. If the user clicks **OK**, the `confirm()` statement returns `true`, and the form gets submitted; if the user clicks **Cancel**, `confirm()` returns `false` and the form doesn't do anything.

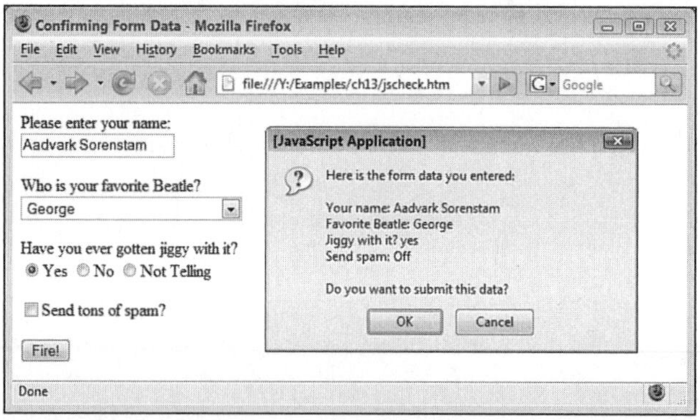

Figure 13.4

When the user submits the form, he or she sees this confirmation message.

A Mortgage Calculator

For the final example, I'll show you a particularly powerful script that sets up a mortgage calculator. Figure 13.5 shows the calculator, which I created using form and table tags.

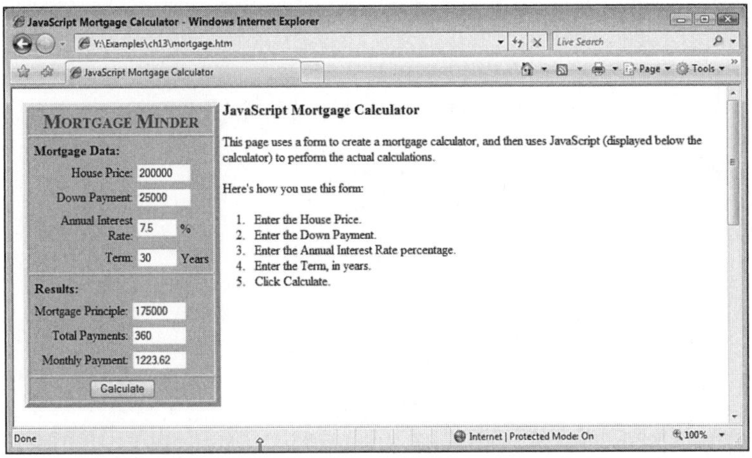

Figure 13.5

I created this mortgage calculator using standard form and table tags. JavaScript makes the calculator calculate.

The calculator looks pretty enough, but can it calculate anything? Sure! Using the following JavaScript, you can actually compute the monthly mortgage payment based on the values you input:

```
<script language="javascript" type="text/javascript">
<!--
function checkForZero(field)
{
    if (field.value == 0 || field.value.length == 0) {
        alert ("This field can't be 0!");
        field.focus(); }
    else
        calculatePayment(field.form);
}

function cmdCalc_Click(form)
{
    if (form.price.value == 0 || form.price.value.length == 0) {
        alert ("The Price field can't be 0!");
        form.price.focus(); }
    else if (form.ir.value == 0 || form.ir.value.length == 0) {
        alert ("The Interest Rate field can't be 0!");
        form.ir.focus(); }
```

```
        else if (form.term.value == 0 || form.term.value.length == 0) {
            alert ("The Term field can't be 0!");
            form.term.focus(); }
        else
            calculatePayment(form);
    }

    function calculatePayment(form)
    {
        princ = form.price.value - form.dp.value;
        intRate = (form.ir.value/100) / 12;
        months = form.term.value * 12;
        form.pmt.value = Math.floor((princ*intRate)/
➡ (1-Math.pow(1+intRate,(-1*months)))*100)/100;
        form.principle.value = princ;
        form.payments.value = months;
    }//-->
    </script>
```

That's a complex chunk of code, to be sure, but luckily, you don't have to understand how it works. The only thing you need to be sure of when using this script in another page, is that you use the same names for the form controls that I use in the example mortgage.htm file (which is, of course, on the CD).

The Least You Need to Know

◆ When using mouseovers, keep your images small so the browser can quickly download the second image.

◆ If you have strict password needs, ask your web host or a CGI programmer to rustle you up some heavy-duty protection.

◆ If you have a field the user *must* fill in, make that field mandatory by intercepting the submission using the onSubmit attribute.

◆ If you want users to enter the correct data into your form, show them the contents of each field before submitting the form.

Part 5

Turning Your Website Skills into Cash

This final part of the book shows you how to convert your newfangled website creation prowess into cold, hard cash. You'll learn four different "get-rich-click" schemes. The first (Chapter 14) tells you how to lose your amateur status and become a professional website designer. The second (Chapter 15) gives you the scoop on making money by taking advantage of your site's popularity and putting up banner ads. The third scheme (Chapter 16) goes the joint venture route by showing you how to make a few bucks through affiliate marketing programs. The fourth scheme (Chapter 17) gives you a step-by-step tutorial on setting up your site for e-commerce—selling actual goods and services from your humble website home.

14

Becoming a Paid Website Designer

In This Chapter

◆ Getting a web design business off the ground

◆ How to set rates

◆ Learning about contracts, advertising, and certification

> Dear Paul,
>
> Just want to let you know that I am actually getting paid to design and produce websites, and it's all your fault for writing your HTML book.
>
> —Patsy West (www.websitewiz.com)

That's a real note sent to me from a real reader of my book *The Complete Idiot's Guide to Creating a Web Page and Blog*. And it's no fluke, either, because I've received dozens of similar messages from readers over the years. I'm not at all surprised, because website designing is one of *the* hottest fields right now. Lots of tech jobs burst right along with the high-tech bubble a few years ago, but that meltdown hasn't changed one thing: small businesses and individuals still want either to get on the web or to have a better website than the one their cousin's kid pasted up a few years ago.

Because of this undiminished demand, people who know how to cobble together websites have remained popular. If you've read the whole book and if you have at least a bit of design skills, you, too, can get work as a website producer.

This chapter gives you some tips and pointers on becoming a paid site spinner. My focus here is on setting up a freelance website design business. You will learn how to set up your business, how to find contracts, what to charge, and more.

Getting Started: Your Business Plan

If you want to do this freelance website design business thing right, there's one step you shouldn't skip: creating a business plan. This doesn't mean you have to forge a 50-page tome with all kinds of charts and economic analyses. No, all you really want is to get a handle on the type of business you're creating and running. To that end, ask and answer these 10 basic questions:

> **Webmaster Wisdom**
>
> If your interest lies more in "going captive"—getting a full-time job as a crafter of a corporate website—read this chapter anyway. For one thing, it helps immensely if you have a page portfolio you can show to prospective employers. For another, many full-time site designers got their start by doing a great job on a freelance project for a company.

What's my goal? It's tough to get anywhere if you don't have a final destination in mind. You need a concrete, realistic goal: to be able to quit the corporate rat race, to save up enough for the family vacation, to pay your way through school, to have a steady supply of Doritos and Jolt cola, etc.

What's my target market? Although general website design is still a reasonable area to shoot for, your chances of success improve immensely if you can target one or more smaller markets. Do you have a particular field of expertise? Do you design particular kinds of websites better than others?

What's my name/domain? Think long and hard about the name you want to use. Lots of rookie website weavers seem to change their business name every 6 months or so, which is no way to build your "brand." As soon as you've thought of a great name, *immediately* go to a registration service such as Register.com or GoDaddy.com and register the corresponding domain name. Having a "dot com" domain instantly makes your business look more solid and respectable. You think anyone's going to give money to someone with a 100-character-long URL from GeoCities? I don't think so.

What are my expenses? This is crucial, particularly because your income might take a while to build. Do you need to upgrade your computer or your Internet connection?

Do you need other equipment, such as a scanner or a digital camera? What about software such as HTML editors or graphics programs? If you don't know JavaScript or Flash, will you have to hire someone to program for you? Or will you buy a bunch of books and figure things out yourself? Break everything down into two categories: start-up costs and ongoing expenses.

What will I charge? This is one of the most important questions, and it's also one of the toughest to answer. See "Getting Paid: Website Design Rates" later in this chapter.

> **Webmaster Wisdom**
>
> You could set up shop with a web host that specializes in business sites because those hosts usually offer domain registration as well. Check out Yahoo! Small Business (smallbusiness.yahoo.com), Verio (www.verio.com), or Microsoft Office Live (www.microsoft.com/smallbusiness/products/office/microsoft-office-live).

How will I allocate my time? Come up with realistic estimates for how long it takes you to forge various kinds of pages: simple text-only pages, heavily designed graphics pages, forms, and so on. You also need to budget time for client discussions, accounts receivable, and other business-related tasks. And of course, please remember that you have a life ....

What will my income be? After you've settled on your rates and allocated your time, you can then come up with a realistic projection of your income.

Do I need professional help? No, not a psychiatrist! I'm talking about an accountant and a lawyer. An accountant can help you set up books and can tell you whether some expenses are deductible (particularly if you work out of your home). You need a contract for each job, and a lawyer can help you create one that suits you and your business. (See "Legalese: Notes About Contracts" later in this chapter.)

How will I promote my business? This isn't a better mousetrap you're building, so people won't automatically beat a path to your web door. You need to advertise not only online, but also in the real world, too. (See "Getting the Word Out: Advertising and Promotion" later in this chapter.)

What about customer service? No matter how you look at it, website design is a service business. Therefore, you need to be prepared to offer a high level of customer service. Think about your policies regarding project updates, postproject follow-up, complaints, and so on.

Getting Paid: Website Design Rates

What you charge for your services is obviously a critical part of your business success (or lack thereof). If you charge too much, people won't hire you; if you charge too little, you'll leave money on the table (at best) or fail due to lack of profits (at worst). Unfortunately, the web design business is still relatively wet behind its electronic ears, so there are no set rates. In any case, what you charge depends on a number of factors:

◆ *Your level of experience.* The more, the monetarily merrier.

◆ *What skills you have.* Someone with good writing, graphics, or programming skills can charge more than someone who just knows HTML inside and out.

> **Webmaster Wisdom**
>
> It's a rare web designer who has the Big Four skills: HTML and CSS, writing, graphics, and programming. If you lack one or more of these assets, you can always hire someone to work with you on a project-by-project basis.

◆ *The type of client.* You can get away with charging more to a corporation than you could to a Mom-and-Pop shop or a nonprofit organization.

◆ *What type of site you're creating.* You should charge one (lower) price for simple text pages or for converting existing documents to HTML; you should charge another (higher) price for pages that require creative writing, custom graphics, or programming.

◆ *How much consulting is involved.* You can boost your rate if a job requires long consultations with the client.

With all that in mind, the next question to think about is how you want to charge the client: by the hour or by the project?

Per-hour pricing is the most common, particularly for new web designers. Before delving into this, you should be familiar with one crucial concept: *billable hours.* These are hours you actually work on a project. They don't include activities such as selling the client in the first place, eating lunch, or blowing away nasty aliens in a rousing game of Crysis. With that in mind, coming up with that all-important hourly rate is tough.

def•i•ni•tion _____

> **Billable hours** are hours you actually work on a project.

You could see what other designers are charging. Visit the sites of other page designers and check out their rates. See what kinds of sites they've produced. If you think you can do as good a job, you might be able to charge the same amount.

Page Pitfall

Be diligent about tracking even small blocks of time where you do real work. Most time-billers work to the nearest tenth of an hour—that is, in 6-minute blocks of time—because it's just easier to keep track of such chunks. (So if a client call lasts just 2 minutes, you still bill 6 minutes.) You'd be surprised to see how 6 minutes here and there really add up. (That said, don't get all lawyerly and start billing to the nearest 15 minutes; nobody will appreciate that.)

Or you could use the expenses-and-profits method. With this method, you calculate your average weekly expenses, add the amount of profit you'd like, and divide by the weekly billable hours. For example, suppose your weekly expenses work out to $600. If you want to make a minimum 25 percent profit (a not-unreasonable figure), you need to add another $150, for a total weekly net of $750. If you figure your week has 30 billable hours, you'd set your rate at $25 per hour.

After you've gained enough experience, you might consider moving to a per-project fee. This means you charge a single fee for all the work you do in a particular project. Most web designers I've talked to say they usually make much more profit this way than they do using an hourly rate. However, going this route isn't for rookies in the field:

♦ You need to have top-notch skills. Per-project contracts are usually for a large number of pages, and you won't get those kinds of contracts unless your portfolio is of the highest quality.

♦ You need to be very experienced so you can estimate with some exactitude just how long the project will take. You won't help your cause if you charge $1,000 for a project you thought would take you 20 hours, and it ends up taking 100 hours.

♦ These kinds of projects are really sellable only to large businesses.

Webmaster Wisdom

To see what other website designers charge, check out Yahoo!'s huge list of website designers at dir.yahoo.com/Business_and_Economy/Business_to_Business/ Communications_and_Networking/Internet_and_World_Wide_Web/Website_ Designers. You can also get a bit of pricing data from Real Rate Survey (www.realrates. com/survey.htm) or About.com Salaries and Pricing for Web Designers (webdesign. about.com/cs/salaries/a). You could also run a Google search on "(web OR website) design (pricing OR rates)." All the links in this chapter can be found in the file pro.htm on the CD.

Legalese: Notes About Contracts

Having a contract for each project is something new website designers rarely think about. However, it's absolutely crucial because it helps ensure that you get paid, it prevents your client from suing your pants off because of a misunderstanding, it specifies copyright issues, and it outlines everyone's rights and responsibilities.

By far the best advice I can give you in this area is this: *see a lawyer!* Although I give you a few good resources to check out in a sec, don't fool yourself into thinking you can do this on your own. By all means put together a contract that makes sense for your business, but be sure you run it by a lawyer versed in this type of thing. I guarantee you'll be glad you did.

With that out of the way, here are some resources devoted to web design contracts and legal issues:

◆ *Ivan Hoffman's Articles for Web Site Designers and Site Owners* (www.ivanhoffman. com/web.html)—designed by Mr. Hoffman, *the* expert on legal issues involving creative adventures, including website design—is loaded with truly useful data on web design contracts, copyrights, and much more.

◆ *HTML Writers Guild Contract FAQ* (www.hwg.org/resources/faqs/contractFAQ. html) answers a few standard contract questions and provides a link to an FTP site that shows a very basic contract that offers a good place to start.

◆ *Web Developer's Contract Swap File* (provider.com/contracts.htm) is a great resource with tons of links to contract info.

◆ *Website Design Contract* (www.wilsonweb.com/worksheet/pkg-con.htm) has an elaborate design contract by Ralph Wilson.

◆ *Bulletproof Web Design Contracts* (www.sitepoint.com/article/bulletproof-web-design-contract) is an outstanding article by John Tabita, chock-full of smart and useful advice about creating contracts for site design jobs.

◆ *Zenful Creations Web Site Design Contract* (www.zenfulcreations.com/resources/worksheets/design_contract.htm) is Lori Leach's standard web design contract for all to peek at.

◆ *Create a Watertight Web Site Design Contract* (www.ecommerceattorney.com/web-contract.html) is lawyer David M. Adler's collection of best practices for putting together a solid website design contract.

Be sure your clients understand that any design or content changes that aren't in the contract result in extra charges. Put it in writing, too.

Getting the Word Out: Advertising and Promotion

With site design being such a growing concern, you better believe thousands of like-minded souls are out there competing for those client bucks. To help your business stand out from the herd, you need to blow your own horn by doing a little advertising and promotion.

By far the best marketing tool in existence is a little thing called word of mouth. Impressed clients naturally sing your praises to other people, and that recommendation might be all some soul needs to come knocking on your virtual door. In other words, the most effective advertising is to do the highest-quality work, meet your deadlines, operate responsibly and ethically, and offer great customer service.

Online Promotion

There are also plenty of other things you can do to spread the gospel of you even further afield. Here are some ideas for online promotion:

- Include at the bottom of all your e-mail messages a brief ad about your business—nothing too elaborate. Even just the URL of your business home page is good.

- Join mailing lists and participate in newsgroups and discussion lists related to your area of expertise.

- Be sure to use `<meta>` tags on your pages so search engines index your site (see Chapter 11). When constructing your keywords, use words and phrases related to the market or markets in which you specialize. This helps differentiate your site.

> **Webmaster Wisdom**
>
> Most e-mail programs can be set up to automatically tack on a signature to the bottom of each outgoing message.

- Even with `<meta>` tags, don't assume all search engines will find you. Register your site with the major search engines directly.

- Be sure your contact information is present and easy to find on your own website.

- Write articles for other sites or online magazines. Along similar lines, you could create your own e-newsletter that offers site tips, business ideas, and whatever else you think might interest prospective customers.

- Look for sites that list local businesses in your area and register your business with them.

- Get all your friends and relatives to link to your site.

- Be sure your own site is always up to date and well designed. Nothing turns off a prospective client more than an ill-maintained business home page.

- At the bottom of every client page, put a small, tasteful logo that links back to your site. (Be sure your client is okay with this.)

- Show samples of your work on your site.

Real-World Promotion

You don't have to restrict all your promotion efforts to cyberspace. Here are some ideas for advertising your business in the real world:

- Get business cards or flyers made up and plaster them around town in grocery stores, community centers, and other appropriate public spaces.

- Check to see if local businesses have a web presence. If not, send them a proposal.

- Create free pages for churches, charitable organizations, community groups, and schools.

- Chat up the nerds at the local computer or electronics store. Be sure to leave them a stack of business cards so they can refer people your way.

- Advertise in community newspapers.

- Give talks or presentations to local computer user groups, community groups, clubs, or even the chamber of commerce.

> **Webmaster Wisdom**
>
> If you decide to start your own web design shop, or even if you're seriously thinking about it, you'd do well to check out a mailing list called hwg-business. It's run by the HTML Writers Guild and it covers most aspects of running a web design business. Find out more about it here: www.hwg.org/lists/hwg-business/index.html.

Street Cred: Web Design Certification

As I said in the previous section, getting your new business noticed is vital if you want a steady stream of contracts. One good way to do that and to assure prospective clients that you really know what the heck you're doing is to get some kind of web design certification. Tons of certification programs are available, but the following are among the most respected:

- *International Webmasters Association* (www.iwanet.org) offers Certified Web Professional (CWP) certification for many different "tracks," including Site Designer and Web Developer.

- *Society of Internet Professionals* (www. sipgroup.org) offers Accredited Internet Professional (AIP) certification "streams" for Web Technology, Web Design, Web Management, and Web Development (among others).

Page Pitfall

When you examine web certification programs, beware of hidden costs and fees. If a program seems reluctant to tell you how much it will cost, the chances are that it's very expensive and you should consider looking elsewhere if you don't have the funds.

- *Certified Internet Web Professional Program* (www.ciwcertified.com) offers a Certified Internet Web (CIW) program for Site Designer.

- *World Organization of Webmasters* (www.joinwow.org) offers Certified Professional Webmaster and Certified Professional Web Designer programs.

The Least You Need to Know

- Putting together a solid business plan will get your new venture off to the proper start.

- When deciding what to charge, take into account your level of experience, your skills, the client, and the types of pages you'll be cranking out.

- Put together a web design contract you're comfortable with and then wave it in a lawyer's face to be sure it passes legal muster.

- Advertise the heck out of your new business. When jobs do come your way, do high-quality, professional work to get the old word-of-mouth advertising working for you.

- Consider getting some kind of certification or accreditation so people know that *you* know what the heck you're doing.

Chapter 15

Putting Ads on Your Site

In This Chapter

- ◆ Why web ads work
- ◆ Understanding ad jargon
- ◆ Pointers for selecting a banner exchange or ad network
- ◆ Getting Google AdSense ads on your site

The previous chapter showed you how to get started as a professional website cobbler. But what if you like your day job, or are a student and don't have time to go into full-time webmastering? An alternative is to turn your home page into an electronic money machine. One way you can do that is by selling ad space on your site. It's unlikely to make you rich, but it's a great way to earn some extra income, and doesn't require a ton of work. This chapter explains how web ads work and shows you how to get Google's AdSense ads working for you.

Are Website Ads a Good Thing?

Web page advertising has gotten a bad rap or two over the past couple years.

Bad rap #1: You shouldn't put ads on your site because they'll just annoy your visitors. I think most web surfers have learned to live with ads (even if they don't exactly *like* them), so nobody's going to shun your site just because of a few page promos. (Although there *are* ways to truly annoy your readers; I talk about some of them a bit later.)

Bad rap #2: Okay, if people ignore ads, doesn't that prove that web advertising is dead? Nope. For one thing, we all still see *tons* of ads on sites, right? If they weren't working, we wouldn't see them. This whole notion of the death of web ads is a myth. What *is* dead is the idea of basing a company's income entirely on web advertising. That's why you see fewer freebies on the web these days. Companies are generating revenue not only from advertising, but also from fees, subscriptions, content licensing, and other e-commerce economics. In other words, businesses are still making money from web advertising; they're just not making *all* their money that way.

As an individual, you don't have to worry about diversifying your web-based income. (I'm assuming here that you have a day job.) All that matters is that, yes, it's still possible to make a bit of extra cash doing the web advertising thing.

Some Ad Lingo You Should Know

The waters of the web advertising business are infested with brain-bending buzzwords and sanity-sapping jargon. To survive, you first need to learn the lingo so you know what the devil these people are jabbering on about. Here's a short lexicon of the most important terms you need to know:

action Occurs when the user clicks an ad to visit the advertiser's site and then performs some action such as purchasing a product, filling in a form, registering, subscribing, or whatever.

ad format The dimensions of the ad. There are 18 standard ad formats divided into three categories—rectangles and pop-ups, banners and buttons, and skyscrapers—as defined by the Interactive Advertising Bureau (IAB; www.iab.net).

Here are the seven ad formats in the rectangles and pop-ups category (see Figure 15.1):

Format Name	Dimensions (Height×Width)
Large rectangle	336×280 pixels
Medium rectangle	300×250 pixels
Rectangle	180×150 pixels
3:1 rectangle	300×100 pixels
Vertical rectangle	240×400 pixels

Square pop-up   250×250 pixels

Pop-under   720×300 pixels

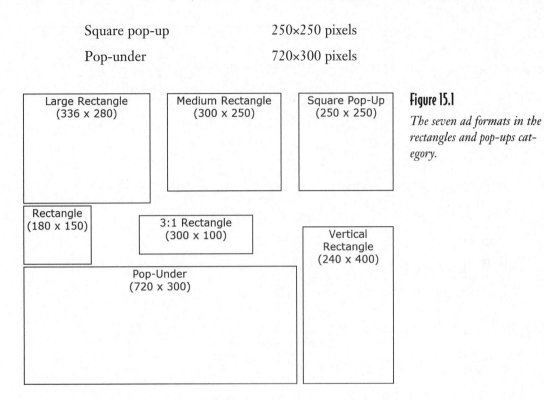

Figure 15.1

The seven ad formats in the rectangles and pop-ups category.

Here are the eight ad formats in the banners and buttons category (see Figure 15.2):

Format Name	Dimensions (Height×Width)
Leaderboard	728×90 pixels
Full banner	468×60 pixels
Half banner	234×60 pixels
Vertical banner	120×240 pixels
Square button	125×125 pixels
Button 1	120×90 pixels
Button 2	120×60 pixels
Micro bar	88×31 pixels

Figure 15.2

The eight ad formats in the banners and buttons category.

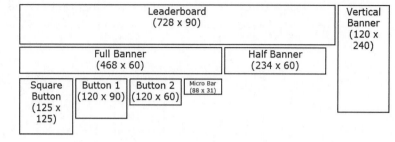

Here are the three ad formats in the skyscrapers category (see Figure 15.3):

Format Name	Dimensions (Height×Width)
Skyscraper	120×600 pixels
Wide skyscraper	160×600 pixels
Half-page ad	300×600 pixels

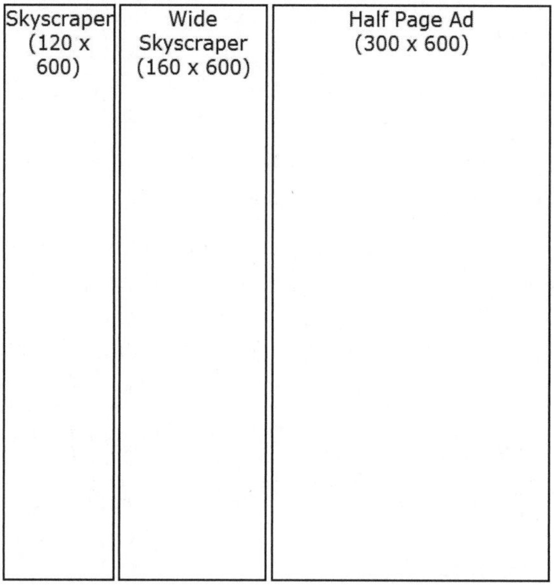

Figure 15.3

The three ad formats in the skyscrapers category.

Skyscraper (120 x 600)	Wide Skyscraper (160 x 600)	Half Page Ad (300 x 600)

banner ad An ad that appears in a web page as a rectangular, clickable image.

click-through When the user clicks an ad.

click-through ratio (CTR)   The rate at which users click an ad. It's calculated by dividing the number of click-throughs by the number of impressions.

cost-per-action (CPA)   How much an ad costs you per action if you're an advertiser (a company that creates ads for marketing its products or services), or how much an ad pays you per action if you're a publisher (a person or company that creates a website on which an advertiser or ad network can display ads).

cost-per-click (CPC)   How much an ad costs you per click-through if you're an advertiser, or how much an ad pays you per click-through if you're a publisher. This is calculated using the CTR (click-through ratio) and the CPM (cost-per-thousand): CPC = CPM ÷ CTR × 1,000. For example, if your CPM is $20 and your CTR is 1 percent, the CPC is $2.

cost-per-thousand (CPM)   How much an ad costs you per thousand impressions if you're an advertiser, or how much an ad pays you per thousand impressions if you're a publisher. For example, if you charge $100 for an ad and that ad gets 20,000 monthly impressions, the CPM is $5.

effective cost-per-thousand (eCPM)   This is a measure of how much revenue an ad generates per 1,000 impressions. You calculate it using the ad's revenue (R) and its impressions (I): eCPM = R ÷ I × 1,000. For example, if an ad generates $2.83 on 432 impressions, the eCPM is $0.83 ÷ 432 × 1,000, which gives $6.55. In other words, the ad generates $1.92 for every 1,000 impressions it gets. You use eCPM to compare the performance of the ads on your site.

impression   An instance of an ad being displayed to a user. For example, if a person views one of your pages that has an ad and then a second person views the same page, you chalk up two impressions. Similarly, if one person views that page and then refreshes the page, that would also count as two impressions because the ad was displayed to the user twice. This is also called an *ad view*.

interstitial   An ad that appears in a separate browser window, especially one that appears while the regular page is loading.

run-of-site   This means that an ad can appear on any page of your site and not just a specific page such as your home page.

unique users   The number of separate individuals who have viewed a page or ad.

Now let's see how all these terms add up to revenue from ad space.

Selling Your Ad Space

When you've decided to give up a chunk of your page real estate for an ad or two, you need to make a decision about how you go about attracting advertisers. That means deciding which of the following approaches best suits both you and your site:

Banner exchange network is a free network in which sites submit their banner ads and agree to display the banner ads from the other sites in the network. This benefits you not with a direct monetary gain, but by sending more traffic to your site, which means you can make more money in other ways (such as selling stuff or selling ads). The network also sends out ads from paying customers, which is how the network makes its money.

Ad network is a company that contracts with a number of advertisers and so generates a pool of ads. It then uses an "ad server" to distribute those ads to sites that have signed up with the ad network. Your site typically gets a percentage of whatever revenue the ad network generates, typically 40 to 60 percent.

Direct selling is where you contact advertisers directly and ask them if they want to advertise on your site.

Choosing a Banner Exchange or Ad Network

Thousands of banner exchange and ad networks are on the loose. How do you choose one that's right for you? Here are some things to look for:

Credit ratio   On a banner exchange network, this is the number of ad impressions your site has to generate to have one of your ads displayed by someone else. The usual ratio is 1:2, which means your ad gets displayed once for every two impressions you generate.

Payment   Does the ad network use CPM or CPC to determine how much you get paid? Are there different rates for different ad formats? How do they pay you (check, PayPal, direct deposit, and so on)? Is there a minimum payment? For example, most networks won't send payment unless your account is at or above some minimum amount (such as $100).

Minimums   Does the network require a minimum number of monthly impressions, a minimum number of unique daily or monthly visitors, or a minimum click-through ratio?

Image specifications   Does the banner exchange network have any specific requirements for the image files you use as an ad? For example, it may want only GIFs or JPEGs, it may require file sizes to be a certain number of kilobytes or less, or it may not allow animated GIFs.

Ad formats   What types of ad formats does the network serve, and can you choose the formats served to your site? For example, if you think your site visitors will hate pop-unders (most people do), avoid a network that serves them or doesn't allow you to choose a different format.

Ad position   Does the network require that ads be positioned *above the fold?* Are *below the fold* ads used?

Multiple ads   Does the network restrict the number of ads that can appear on the page?

Site type   Does the network restrict the type of sites it deals with? For example, many networks won't serve ads to sites on free servers; sites where the proprietors don't own their domain names; or sites that are composed only (or mostly) of chat rooms, bulletin boards, or links to other sites. Also, many banner exchange networks are geared to sites with specific types of content, such as business or sports.

def•i•ni•tion

Above the fold describes an ad the user sees without having to scroll down. (This is based on the newspaper term *above the fold,* where it refers to stories that appear in the top half of the front page.) Ads that don't appear until the user scrolls down are **below the fold.** Similar terms are *above the scroll* and *below the scroll.*

Some Ad Networks to Check Into

There are probably hundreds of ad networks scattered around the web, so how do you know where to start? My advice is to stick with the best-known companies, because there are some pretty shady operators out there. To help you get started, here's a quick look at a half dozen of the best ad networks:

BurstMedia (www.burstmedia.com) is one of the oldest ad networks around (it started up in 1995), so the fact that it's still around tells you something about the quality of the company and its network. It offers both CPM and CPC campaigns. BurstMedia requires a minimum of 5,000 page views per month, and pays out 50 percent of ad revenue. (If you sign up to use BurstMedia as your exclusive ad network for 1 year, you get 55 percent; a 3-year commitment will get you 60 percent.) The minimum check size is $50.

Casale Media (www.casalemedia.com) is a relatively new ad network that's already generating a lot of positive buzz among publishers. That's partly because Casale offers high-quality ads and unique features such as setting the maximum number of times ads from a particular advertiser appears (so your visitors don't see the same ad over and over) and complete control over your ad inventory. However, it also has to do with Casale being a CPM-only network (great if your site gets lots of page views), and it pays a whopping 70 percent of ad revenue. Unfortunately, Casale Media requires a minimum of 10,000 unique visitors per month.

def•i•ni•tion

A **contextual** ad is one that offers a product or service that's related to the content of the page on which the ad appears.

Google AdSense (www.google.com/adsense) is by far the most popular because it offers ads that are *contextual*: that is, they're targeted at the specific content of the page on which the ad appears. There are no page view or visitor minimums, you get 50 percent of the ad revenue, and the threshold for the first payment is $100. See more about AdSense in the "Making Sense (and Cents) Out of Google AdSense" section, later in this chapter.

Tribal Fusion (www.tribalfusion.com) is a CPC network that delivers top-notch ads to selected sites. The network requires a minimum of 2,000 unique visitors per day, so it's aimed at relatively popular sites. However, its CPM rates are considered among the highest in the industry, and you get 55 percent of the revenue. The first payment threshold is $50.

ValueClick (www.valueclickmedia.com) is a CPC network that has an excellent reputation for delivering high-quality ads and decent eCPM rates. In fact, you get to choose from various ad campaigns, each of which has its own CPM. ValueClick requires at least 3,000 impressions per month, and there are various restrictions about where the ads can be placed on your site. You get 50 percent of the ad revenue and the threshold for the first payment is $50.

Yahoo! Publisher Network (publisher.yahoo.com; see Figure 15.4) offers text ads targeted to your site content. It's a CPC network, and its CPC rate is usually a bit higher than Google's. On the downside, you usually get a lower CTR with YPN, so overall your eCPM is often about the same. YPN doesn't have any minimum page view or unique visitor barriers, gives you 50 percent of the ad revenue, and pays out after you generate $100.

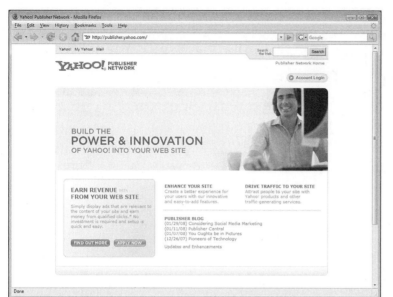

Figure 15.4

The Yahoo! Publisher Network.

Making Sense (and Cents) Out of Google AdSense

The biggest online ad network by a million miles (give or take) is Google's AdSense program. Anyone can join, as long as your site satisfies Google's easy-to-meet minimum requirements (more on that in a sec). I should mention, too, that you must be at least 18 years old to use AdSense.

AdSense places contextual ads on your site, so the come-ons are in some way related to the content of each page. This results in higher click-through ratios—since, presumably, if a person is interested in whatever's on your page, he or she should also be interested in whatever the ad is hawking—so you make more money than you would with noncontextual ads.

For a good example of contextual ads at work, check out Figure 15.5. This page from my Word Spy site is a post related to baby strollers. Of the four ads you can see—there are two at the top of the page and two on the right side of the page—three are directly related to strollers, and the fourth is related to baby products. Now *that's* targeted advertising.

Remember that Google is a CPC ad network, so just matching up ads and eyeballs doesn't do you any good. However, if the brain behind any pair of eyeballs commands the hand to click an ad, then your AdSense account gets richer by a few cents. If a few hundred or even a few thousand people click ads, you're on your way to a bit of extra cash.

Figure 15.5

Google AdSense serves up contextual ads targeted to your page content.

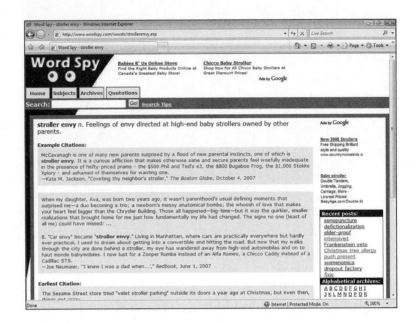

Because AdSense is so popular, I'm going to spend the rest of this chapter showing you how to set up an account, create the code that generates the ads, and tweak your site for maximum revenue generation.

Getting Started: Setting Up Your Account

Before you can take advantage of AdSense, you need to set up an account with Google. Anyone can join, although Google (like most ad networks) has a few restrictions on site content. That is, you can't run Google ads on a site that contains any of the following stuff:

- Violence, racial intolerance, or advocacy against any individual, group, or organization

- Pornography

- Hacking or cracking

- Illicit drugs and drug paraphernalia

- Excessive profanity

- Gambling or casino info

- Information on programs that compensate users for clicking on ads or offers, performing searches, surfing websites, or reading e-mails

♦ Excessive, repetitive, or irrelevant keywords in the text or code of web pages

♦ Deceptive or manipulative text or tags to improve your site's search engine ranking

♦ Sales or promotion of weapons or ammunition

♦ Sales or promotion of beer or hard alcohol

♦ Sales or promotion of tobacco or tobacco-related products

♦ Sales or promotion of prescription drugs

♦ Sales or promotion of products that are replicas or imitations of designer goods

♦ Sales or distribution of term papers or student essays

♦ Anything else that's illegal, promotes illegal activity, or infringes on the legal rights of others

This may seem like a long list, but of course there are a few million other topics out there, and I'm sure your site will qualify.

Here are the hoops you need to jump through to sign up with AdSense and get your own account:

1. Use your favorite browser to navigate to the AdSense home page: www.google. com/adsense (see Figure 15.6).

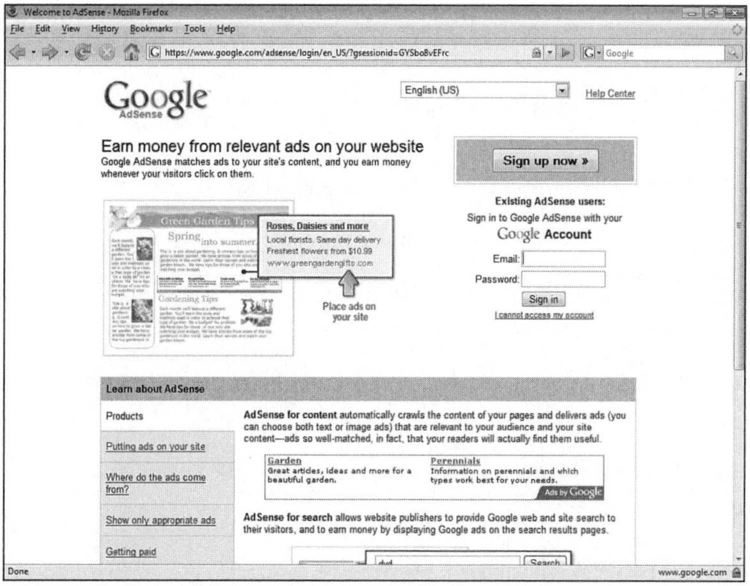

Figure 15.6

The starting point on your road to advertising riches: the Google AdSense home page.

2. Click **Sign up now.** You see the AdSense sign-up form, shown in Figure 15.7.

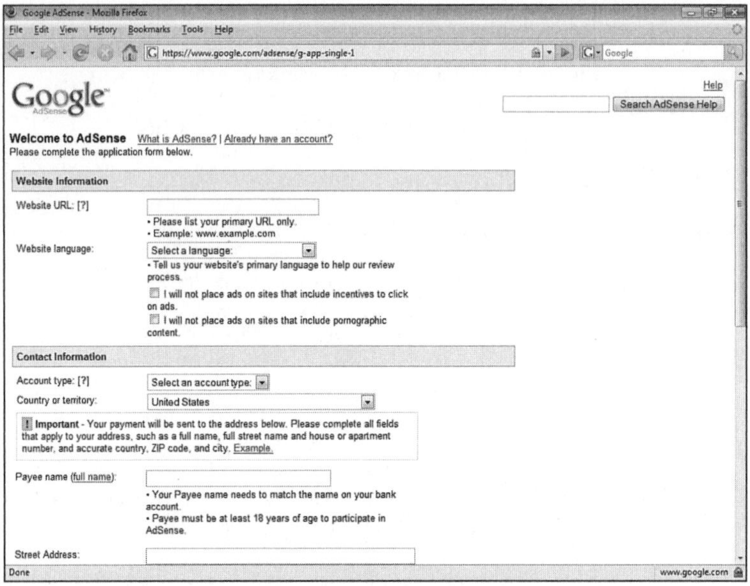

Figure 15.7

Fill in the fields on this form to set up your AdSense account.

3. Use the **Website URL** text box to type the address of your website.

4. Use the **Website language** list to specify the main language you use on your website.

5. Select the **I will not place ads on sites that include incentives to click on ads** check box.

6. Select the **I will not place ads on sites that include pornographic content** check box.

7. In the **Account type** list, select either **Individual** or **Business.**

8. Use the **Country or territory** list to select your country.

9. Use the **Payee name** text box to type your name (if you chose Individual in step 7) or your company name (if you chose Business in step 7).

10. Use the **Street Address, City/Town, State** (or Province), and **ZIP** (or Postal Code) controls (see Figure 15.8) to specify your postal address.

11. Select the **I agree that I can receive checks made out to the payee name I have listed above** check box.

12. Type your phone number in the **Phone** text box.

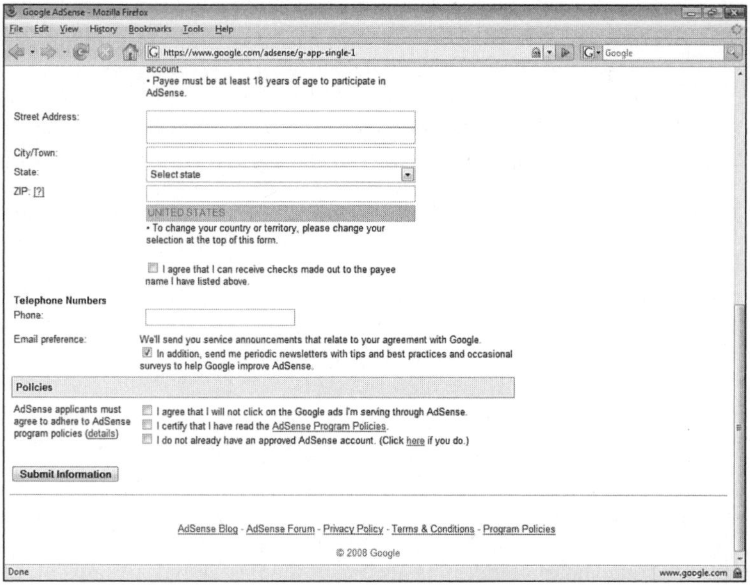

Figure 15.8

More fields to fill in to set up your AdSense account.

13. If you don't want to receive the AdSense newsletter, deselect the **In addition, send me periodic newsletters ...** check box.

14. Select the check boxes in the Policies section.

15. Click **Submit Information.** Google AdSense shows you a summary of the information you entered. Check the information to be sure it's accurate and then select one of the following options:

    ◆ Select **I have an email address and password (Google Account) ...** if you already have an account for other Google services. You then see the options shown in Figure 15.9, which enable you to either use your existing account with AdSense or to create a new account. If you select **I'd like to use my existing Google account for AdSense,** as shown in Figure 15.9, type your login data and skip to step 19; if you select **I'd like to choose a new login name and password just for AdSense,** proceed to step 16.

    ◆ Select **I do *not* use these other services. I would like to create a new Google Account** to set up a Google account, as shown in Figure 15.10, and continue with step 16.

16. Use the **Email** text box to type the e-mail address you want to associate with your Google account.

Figure 15.9

If you have a Google account already, you can either use it with AdSense or you can create a new account.

Figure 15.10

Fill in the fields shown here to create a new Google account.

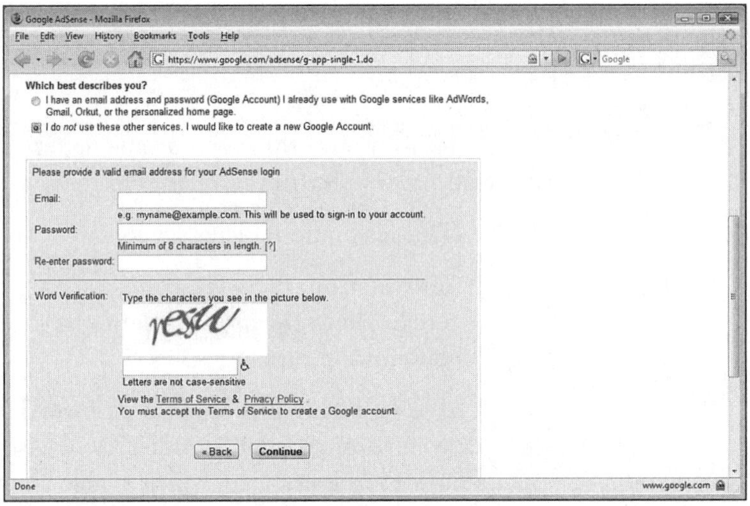

17. Use the **Password** and **Re-enter password** text boxes to type the password you want to use with your Google account.

18. In the **Word Verification** section, type the characters you see in the image.

19. Click **Continue.** After a short delay, Google sends you an e-mail message so you can verify your address.

20. Click the link in the e-mail message.

Now you sit back and wait for awhile. An actual person at Google will surf over to your site to check it out and be sure you're not up to any unsavory activities. This will take a day or two, after which you'll get a friendly e-mail welcoming you to the AdSense family.

Creating Ad Code for Your Site

With your AdSense account up and at 'em, it's time to put some ads on your website. Note, however, that with AdSense (like all other ad networks), you don't work with the ads directly. Instead, you need to inject a bit of programming code into your page tags. This programming code (it's JavaScript, in case you're wondering) contacts the AdSense server and asks it to deliver a fresh set of ads.

JavaScript? Groan! You mean I have to be a programmer to use AdSense? Not a chance, Vance. The Google AdSense site has an easy-to-use tool that generates the code for you automatically. You just copy the generated code from the AdSense site and paste it into your page source code. Nothing could be easier!

If there's a tricky part about AdSense, it's that you need to tweak the ad options to best suit your site and maximize revenue. It isn't always obvious how you do that, but I'll show you a few pointers in the next section (see "Taking AdSense to the Next Level").

For now, here are the steps to follow to generate the ad code for your site:

1. Use your favorite browser to navigate to the AdSense home page: www.google. com/adsense.

2. Use the **Email** text box to type your Google account e-mail address and the **Password** text box to type your Google account password. Click **Sign in** to get your Google AdSense page.

3. Click the **AdSense Setup** tab to get the AdSense Setup page, shown in Figure 15.11.

4. Click the type of AdSense product you want to add to your website:

   ◆ Click **AdSense for Content** to create code for contextual ads targeted at the content of your pages. The rest of the steps in this section assume you clicked this option.

   ◆ Click **AdSense for Search** to create code for a Google search box that enables your site visitors to search either your site or the entire web. The search results include targeted ads, and you get paid if visitors click any of those ads.

Figure 15.11

Use the AdSense Setup page to get started creating your AdSense code.

5. Now select the type of ad you want on your site. Click one of the following options (see Figure 15.12):

   ◆ **Ad unit** is an ad box that includes a title that links to the advertiser, the advertiser's ad text, and the URL of the advertiser's site.

   ◆ **Link unit** is a collection of links to advertiser sites.

Figure 15.12

Use this page to select the type of ad you want to place on your website.

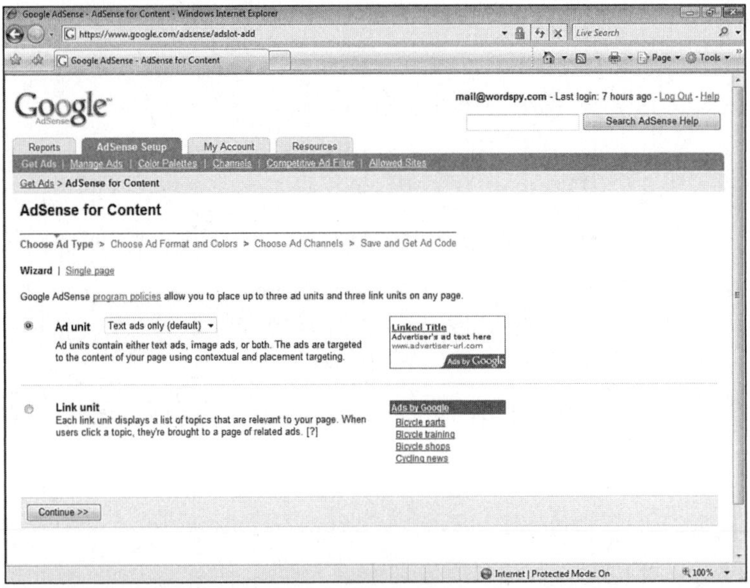

6. Click **Continue.** The Choose Ad Format and Colors page appears.

7. Use the **Format** list to choose the ad format you want to use (see Figure 15.13).

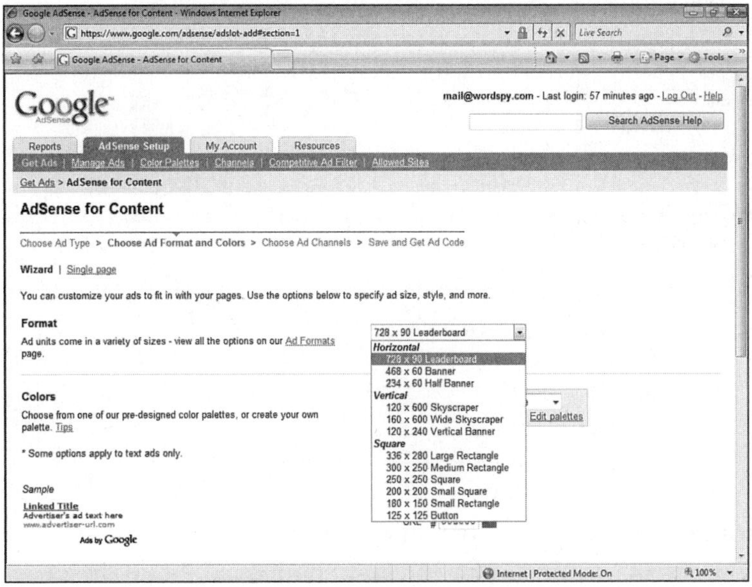

Figure 15.13

*Use the **Format** list to select the ad format you want to use.*

8. In the Colors section, use the **Palettes** list to select the color palette you want to use for the ad unit.

9. Use the following text boxes to customize the colors of the individual ad unit components (you can also click a color square and then click a swatch in the color palette that appears, as shown in Figure 15.14):

   ◆ **Border** is the color of the border that surrounds the ad unit.

   ◆ **Title** is the color of the linked title at the top of the ad unit.

   ◆ **Background** is the color of the ad unit's background area.

   ◆ **Text** is the color of the text that appears in the ad unit.

   ◆ **URL** is the color of the advertiser URL that appears at the bottom of the ad unit.

10. If you choose a visible border color, use the **Corner Styles** list to select the type of corners you want to use for the ad unit.

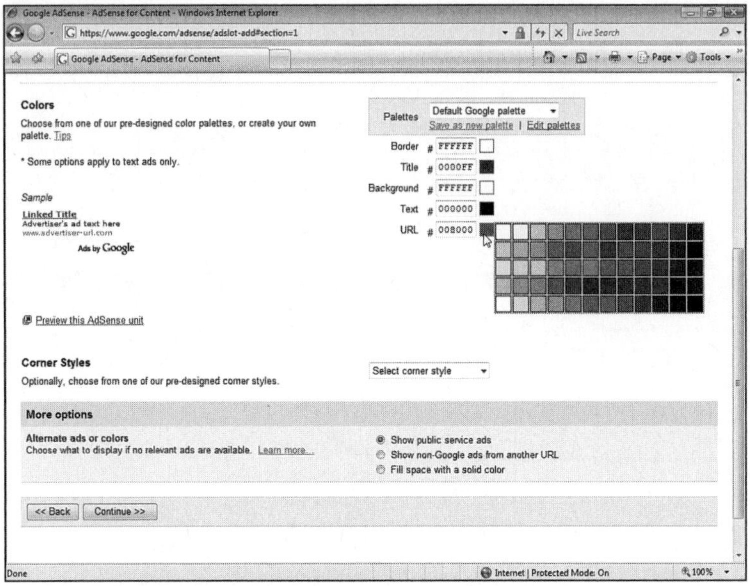

Figure 15.14

Click any color box to select from a palette of colors.

11. In the **More options** section, choose an option that specifies what you want AdSense to show if it doesn't have any relevant ads to display.

12. Click **Continue.** The Choose Ad Channels page appears. A *channel* is a kind of tag that AdSense applies to an ad unit, and in your reports AdSense will break down click-throughs, eCPM, and, of course, revenue, by channel.

Webmaster Wisdom

It's a good idea to create different channels for your site. If all your pages have more or less the same type of content, create a separate channel for each location on the page you use for ads (for example, the page header, the right column, the page footer, and so on). If your site has different types of content in different sections, set up a channel for each type of content.

---

13. Click **Add new channel,** type a name for the channel, and click **OK.** Figure 15.15 shows the Choose Ad Channels page with a few channels added.

14. Click **add** beside each channel you want to use for your ad unit.

15. Click **Continue.**

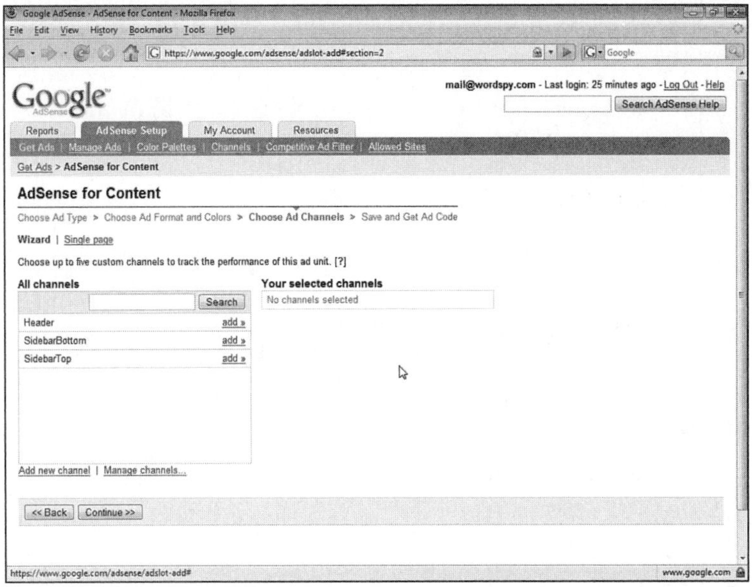

Figure 15.15

It's a good idea to set up a few channels to help you track the performance of your ad units.

16. Type a name for the ad unit and click **Submit and Get Code.** AdSense displays the ad unit code, as shown in Figure 15.16.

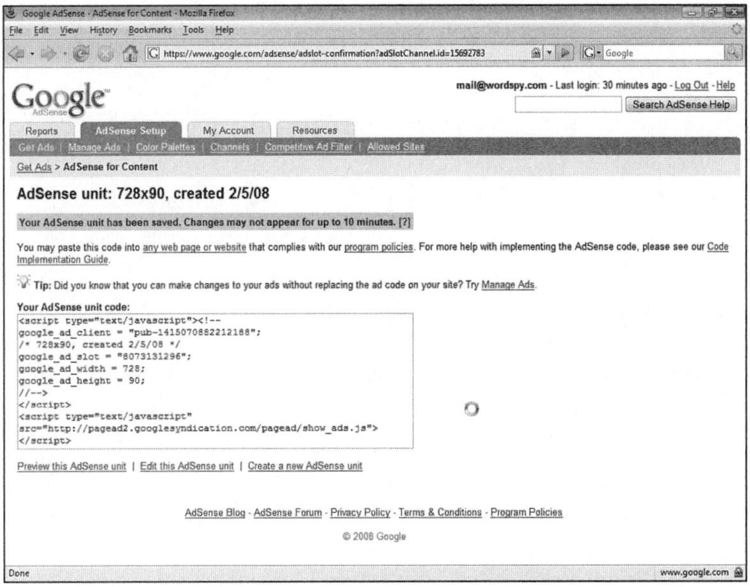

Figure 15.16

AdSense generates JavaScript code to display the ad unit on your site.

17. Click inside the script box to select the entire script, and press **Ctrl+C** (or ⌘+C on your Mac) to copy the code.

18. Switch to the page you want to use, position the cursor where you want the ad unit to appear, and press **Ctrl+V** (or ⌘+V) to paste the code.

19. Save the page and upload it to your site.

When your ad unit is in place, note that there are a few things that are against the rules in Googleland:

♦ You can't encourage users to click the Google ads by using phrases such as "Please click the ads," "Support our site by clicking an ad," or "I want money! Click an ad now, or else!"

♦ You can't direct the user's attention to the ads using arrows or other graphical gimmicks.

♦ You can't place misleading labels above Google ad units. For example, you can't say "My Favorite Sites" above an ad unit. A label such as "Sponsored Links" is okay, though.

♦ Similarly, you can't place misleading images alongside ad units.

♦ You can't promote your site's ads using spam, blog comments, or other or unsolicited content on third-party websites.

♦ You can't pay people to click your ads.

> **Webmaster Wisdom**
>
> Relevant ads likely won't appear right away on your page. When you first navigate to the page after the ad unit code is added, the code tells the AdSense server to send the AdSense crawler to examine the page content. Only after that's happened will you see relevant ads.

Taking AdSense to the Next Level

Just because you've plopped the code for some AdSense units onto a web page doesn't mean you'll soon be awash in cash. Like the web page itself, you need to tweak your AdSense units to attract eyeballs and get people to click those ads (without explicitly telling them to, of course). Fortunately, squeezing more bucks out of your AdSense units isn't rocket science. You can use a number of techniques, but a few have given me the most ad revenue jolts over the years.

One of the most important factors in how a block of ads performs is the location of those ads on the page. This makes sense, because you know that readers' eyes tend to gravitate to certain page "hot spots": the main content area, the navigation area, and, in general, things on the left rather than things on the right. In Figure 15.17, I've broken down a typical page into 13 areas, and I've given each area a rating of A, B, C, or D based on the amount of focus a typical reader gives each area—A gets the most focus, then B, then C, followed by the D areas, which get the least focus. In general, you want to place your ad units in high-focus areas.

After looking at Figure 15.17, you might realize that your own pages have two or three good areas to display an ad unit. How do you choose the area to use? Here's the short answer: you don't. There's nothing stopping you from using more than one ad unit on a page, so go ahead and experiment with multiple ad units in different places. (Note, however, that the maximum number of ad units you can shoehorn into a page is three.)

Page Pitfall

Just because an area generates high reader focus, it doesn't mean you must place an ad unit in that area. The number-one rule in the web ad game is to not let the ads get in the way of your content. Therefore, you should use most of the high-focus areas for content, and reserve one or two for ad units.

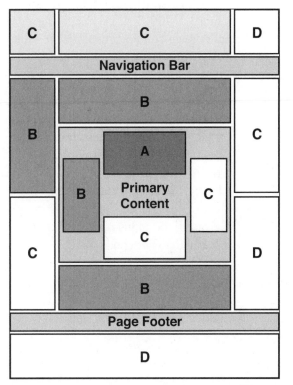

Figure 15.17

You can break down a page in terms of reader focus from highest (A) to lowest (D).

Webmaster Wisdom

To help measure the impact of the different locations, set up a separate channel for each location.

The classic banner ad format of 468×60 has been around forever and is a familiar feature of the web landscape. However, it seems as though the banner has become *too* familiar because surfers now routinely ignore *anything* that comes in the banner format. My guess is that the banner format is now indelibly imprinted in people's mind as an ad vehicle, so their minds simply tune out the banner automatically.

Remember that the goal of tweaking your ad units is to get people to click the links. To that end, it helps if the ads resemble site content instead of ads. One super-easy way to do that is to use one of the rectangle ad formats—either the medium rectangle or the large rectangle. Ads typically appear in thin strips (such as the leaderboard or the skyscraper format), and people have come to associate thin strips of text and links with ads. However, the medium rectangle and the large rectangle formats are more spacious, so they more closely resemble page content.

If the object is to make folks click your ads, you might be tempted to go with Google's image-based ads because they're more visually stimulating. However, image ads almost always generate *fewer* clicks, not more. Why? Because image ads always look like ads, while text ads look more like regular page content. Also, people inherently distrust image ads, so they don't click them. Text ads, on the other hand, seem more transparent, so people trust them more.

Page Pitfall

A border around an ad unit separates the ads from the rest of the page. This makes the ads look less like content and more like ads.

By far the most important thing you can do to make your AdSense units blend in with your site (and so, a bit paradoxically, make them more susceptible to being clicked) is to format the ads to resemble the formatting on your site. Most importantly, use a background color that matches the background of your page. Be sure the border matches the page background, too. This renders the border invisible, which is exactly what you want.

The Least You Need to Know

◆ Although a few doom-and-gloom types insist web advertising is dead, online ads are indeed alive and well and making people money. You may as well be one of them.

◆ Remember these terms: *impressions*—the total number of times that users see an ad—and *click-throughs*—the total number of times that users click an ad.

◆ If you want to attract more traffic to your site, choose a banner exchange network; if you have a reasonable amount of traffic, sign up with an ad network to start making money on your site right away.

◆ To get the most out of Google AdSense, place your ads in high-focus areas, avoid banners, and make your ad units resemble the rest of your page content.

Chapter 16

Working With Affiliate Programs

In This Chapter

- ◆ Understanding affiliate programs
- ◆ Choosing an affiliate program that's right for you
- ◆ How to make money selling other people's stuff!

In Chapter 17, you will learn how to put your widgets up for sale on the web. However, what if you don't have any widgets to sell? Surprisingly, that's not a major roadblock on your path to Internet semiriches! Why not? Because there are ways you can use your website to sell not only the widgets, but also the doodads and gizmos *other* people have cobbled together.

These are called *affiliate programs.* There are tons of them out there to choose from, and they're a great way to earn a bit of extra spending money. In this chapter, I give you the lowdown on setting them up on your site.

What's an Affiliate Program?

Did you read Chapter 15? No? Okay, go ahead and read it now. I'll wait.

I'm kidding! Anyway, the point is that in Chapter 15 I talked about various web advertising concepts. One was cost-per-thousand (CPM), where if you're a website publisher you get paid a certain amount for every 1,000 times an ad is viewed; another was cost-per-click (CPC), where you get paid a certain amount every time someone clicks an ad; finally there's cost-per-action (CPA), where you get paid each time someone clicks an ad *and* performs some action, such as purchasing a product, filling in a form, registering with the site, and so on.

Although all these programs pay money, the actual pay varies wildly. This makes sense given that each type of program demands quite a different amount of effort from the user:

- In a CPM program, the user only has to look at the ad. (Technically, the user doesn't even have to *see* the ad; an impression just means that the user was served a page that included the ad.)

- In a CPC program, the user must click the ad to go to the advertiser's site.

- In a CPA program, the user not only must click the ad, but once on the advertiser's site, he or she must perform some significant action.

Clearly we have an ascending amount of effort on the user's part. What does that mean to you as a publisher? Simple: your compensation is directly correlated to the amount of effort required by the user:

- A CPM system generally pays only a few cents per thousand impressions.

- A CPC system might pay a dollar or two per click.

- A CPA system might pay several dollars per action or, if the user is required to buy something, a percentage of the sale.

In other words, the big bucks can be found in a CPA system. However, most of the time the total compensation in these different systems evens out because it's relatively easy to generate impressions, a lesser number of users are willing to click an ad, and even fewer perform the necessary action when they get to the site.

That's generally true, but there's a special form of CPA program that's often the exception: an *affiliate program*. An affiliate program (also sometimes called a referral program) is a partnership with a site that sells stuff. The basic idea is that you put on your website links to specific products from the selling site. If someone clicks one of your links and ends up purchasing the product, you get a piece of the action—typically, a percentage of the selling price.

For example, the granddaddy of all affiliate programs is the Associates Program run by Amazon.com (see Figure 16.1). In the books portion of the program, if someone purchases a book after linking to Amazon through your site, you get a "referral fee," which starts at a cool 4 percent of the purchase price and can go as high as 8.5 percent. And the more you sell in a month, the higher the rate. For

def•i•ni•tion

An **affiliate program** is a CPA-based advertising program where you partner with a selling site by setting up product links and receiving a percentage of each sale.

example, if you sell at least 7 items, the rate goes up to 6 percent. So if someone buys a $30 book, your cut goes up to $1.80. It redefines the phrase "easy money"!

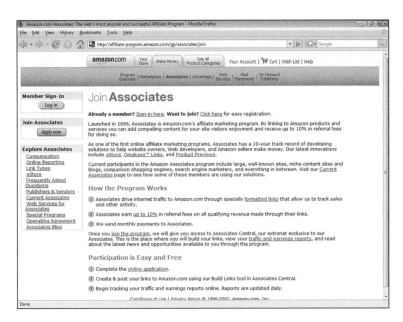

Figure 16.1

Amazon.com's Associates Program pays you boffo bucks for sending paying customers its way.

Even better, affiliate programs are available for more than just books. There are programs for CDs, videos, computer software and hardware, food, liquor, furniture, and even cars. So you can select a program that fits in with the type of site you have.

Webmaster Wisdom

Although most affiliate programs are commission-based, some are based on other criteria. For example, some programs pay a flat fee for each *new* visitor who purchases something. Other programs offer click-through incentives that pay for each new visitor sent to the site.

Choosing an Affiliate Program

The hardest part about setting up an affiliate program is choosing one. There are thousands available, and they all have different features. Here are a few things to watch for when choosing a program:

Commission rates. These vary widely. Amazon's 4 percent initial rate is pretty average, and most programs offer between 3 and 10 percent. Some programs offer a sliding scale where your commission goes up after the total sales attributed to your links goes over a certain amount.

Commission exceptions. Some programs offer their highest commission rate only on certain items. Amazon, for example, offers a 10 percent rate on Kindle and MP3 purchases. It's also typical to offer a reduced commission on products that are heavily discounted.

Direct versus general links. Most programs pay a much higher commission if a sale was generated from a direct link to a product (as opposed to linking to the program's home page, for example).

The commission base. Some programs base the commission on the selling price of the product; others base it on the profit earned by each sale.

Site restrictions. Many programs reject sites that have "unsuitable" themes such as sex, violence, discrimination, or the promotion of illegal activities.

Check thresholds. Many programs won't issue you a check until your commission reaches a certain threshold.

Exclusivity. Some program agreements demand exclusivity, meaning you can't also include a rival program on your site.

Researching Affiliate Programs

Whew! That's a lot to worry about. Fortunately, a few good people on the web have made it their full-time job to monitor and review these affiliate programs. The following are the sites I think do the best job:

◆ *100 Best Affiliate Programs* (www.100best-affiliate-programs.com) focuses on just the top programs and also offers tutorials and tips for getting more out of affiliates.

◆ *Affiliate Programs* (www.affiliateprograms. com) has an extensive directory of affiliate programs, terrific articles, forums, blogs, and a weekly newsletter.

◆ *Affiliates Directory* (www.affiliatesdirectory. com) offers capsule reviews of hundreds of programs, has lists of the most popular and highest rated programs, runs forums related to affiliate programs, and even offers free courses on getting the most out of affiliate programs.

> **Webmaster Wisdom**
>
> I've gathered all the sites listed in this chapter in a web page for your clicking convenience. See affiliates.htm on the CD.

◆ *Affiliate Programs Directory* (www.associateprograms.com) lists more than 10,000 programs, broken down into dozens of categories. It includes ratings from program users as well as a free newsletter.

◆ *ClickQuick.com* (www.clickquick.com) has excellent reviews of hundreds of affiliate programs. It also offers articles, tips, and a list of top-rated programs.

◆ *Webmaster-Affiliates* (www.webmaster-affiliates.net) has capsule reviews of an impressive number of programs. It's also bursting at the seams with affiliate resources, including a newsletter, articles, discussion forums, and much more.

Setting Up an Affiliate Program

Now that you've done all your research and know which affiliate program you want to use, here's how to set one up:

1. Go to the site offering the program and sign up for it.

2. Create a "store" on your site. This doesn't have to be anything elaborate, although most programs also offer program-related graphics and other helping hands.

3. For each product you want to feature, set up a link to the specific product on the program site. You usually include some kind of code in the link address that identifies your site as the referrer.

4. Sit back and wait for the checks to come rolling in.

Affiliate Program Pointers

To close this chapter, here are a few pointers for getting the most out of affiliate programs:

Choose a program that fits. Affiliate programs work best when you have lots of prospective buyers visiting your site. Therefore, always select a program that fits in with your site's theme. If you have a gardening site, for example, joining a CD-based program doesn't make much sense.

Sell your links. You want people to not only click the program links, but also buy the item on the other end of the wire. You can encourage people to do that by selling the product on your end: writing a review, listing the product's features, and so on.

Make your "store" attractive. Don't just slap up a few links. Use the HTML skills you've learned from this book to build a nice "store" that makes people come back for more. And don't forget to take advantage of whatever design help the affiliate program offers.

The Least You Need to Know

◆ An affiliate program is a CPA-based advertising program where you partner with a selling site by setting up product links and receiving a percentage of each sale.

◆ Before signing up with an affiliate program, do some homework. Study commission rates and learn how commissions are generated, when you get paid, and what restrictions the program insists upon.

◆ Choose a program that fits in with the content of your site, encourage visitors to buy the products, and make your store an attractive place to shop.

Chapter 17

Selling Stuff on Your Site

In This Chapter

♦ Using an e-commerce hosting service

♦ Creating an order form for your site

♦ Processing orders

♦ Pointers to e-commerce tutorials

Do you have a widget you want to sell on the web? Whether it's a painting, a pencil sharpener, or a paperback, there's a big, fat wired market out there, just waiting to clamor for your product. You already know more than enough HTML to put together a classy catalog that shows your wares in their best light. But what happens when someone takes a shine to one of your trinkets and says, "I'll take it!"?

Answering that question is the subject of this chapter. In the following pages, you'll learn about a few different ways to sell things online, including how to rent online retail space and how to cobble together an interactive order form that calculates the total automatically.

Renting Online Retail Space

In an ideal world, you'd do all your cyberselling directly from the comfy confines of your site. Unfortunately, doing this tends to be a complex and expensive business, so it's not for amateurs or the shallow pocketed. Don't despair, though, because I discuss some ways to sell things on the cheap directly from your site a bit later in this chapter. You should also check with your web hosting provider to see if it offers some kind of e-commerce package or a "virtual store" you can use.

Failing that, there are all kinds of businesses on the web whose job it is to host your online retail presence. This is a great way to go because the nasty details of things like shopping carts, payment authorization, and security are handled by the geeks at these companies.

The rest of this section takes you through a list of the e-commerce hosting companies that have the best reputations (at least as I write this). Here are a few things to look for when comparing the various services:

Store limitations   Most services place a limit on certain features, such as the number of products, the total disk space your pages use, and the amount of bandwidth your site serves. In most cases, you can increase those limits by spending more money.

Security   Web shoppers are getting more savvy every day, so there are fewer people around who will knowingly give out their credit card number over a nonsecure connection. Therefore, you should shun any service that doesn't offer a secure shopping cart and credit card transactions.

Domain name   Can you get your own domain name (such as www.yourdomain.com), or will you get a subdomain of the service (such as www.yourname.service.com)?

Residency requirement   Lots of services require that you be a resident of a particular country. (Because most of the services are U.S.-based, they require a U.S. address.)

Reports   What kinds of reports (orders, traffic, and so on) does the service send to you?

Set-up fee   Most sites charge a set-up fee not only for hosting your site, but also for setting up a *merchant account*. The latter is required if you want to handle credit card transactions.

Hidden fees   Most sites (or the credit card services they use, such as Cardservice International; www.cardservice.com) charge you an extra monthly fee for such an account and may also charge you extra fees for each transaction. Some services also charge a "revenue share" fee that's a percentage of your monthly sales. Find out about these fees up front.

Here are a few companies that rent online retail space or offer e-commerce hosting:

Webmaster Wisdom

I've collected all the resources I mention in this chapter and placed links for them in the file named selling.htm on the CD. Also, all prices quoted here are accurate as of when I hunted and pecked them into this chapter. Always double-check prices before signing up with any service.

◆ *CafePress* (www.cafepress.com) gives you an online store for selling customizable products such as T-shirts, posters, mugs, buttons, greeting cards, even books. You send your designs, set up a store, and CafePress takes care of everything else: payments, shipping, returns, even customer service.

◆ *eBay* (pages.ebay.com/storefronts/start. html; see Figure 17.1) is probably familiar to you, from the days you did some bidding, but the online auctioneer also runs stores for folks too impatient to wait. You get your very own storefront on one of the web's most popular sites, and eBay handles the shopping cart and payments. Plans start at $15.95 per month.

Figure 17.1

You can set up shop on the world's most popular auction site, eBay.

- *Etsy* (www.etsy.com) is dedicated to folks looking to sell handmade knickknacks and doohickeys. You create your own store on the Etsy site, and they take care of the shopping carts and payment processing. Best of all, you don't pay any set-up fees *or* any monthly fees. Instead, you pay a small charge to list an item (20 cents!), and then Etsy gets a cut of everything you sell (3.5 percent). Such a deal!

- *HostWay* (www.hostway.com/ecommerce/index.html) offers quite a few e-commerce packages, which start as low as $19.95 per month for an unlimited number of products. All packages offer a shopping cart, merchant account, and secure credit card transactions.

- *Network Solutions* (www.networksolutions.com/e-commerce/index.jsp), the world's biggest domain name registrar, also offers top-notch e-commerce hosting plans that include easy store setup, credit card payments, PayPal and Google Checkout support, and no transaction fees. Plans starts at $49.95 a month.

- *SiteGround* (www.siteground.com) offers an extensive e-commerce hosting service that includes a free domain, a shopping cart, a merchant account, PayPal support, and lots more, all for the low, low price of just $5.95 a month.

- *Yahoo! Small Business* (smallbusiness.yahoo.com/ecommerce; see Figure 17.2) offers a simple interface for building your store, a shopping cart, and secure credit card transactions. However, the big deal here is that you can choose to place your store in the Yahoo! Shopping section. This is one of the web's most popular shopping sites, so this gives you access to a huge number of potential customers. The basic price is $39.95 per month.

Figure 17.2

Yahoo! Small Business offers powerful and reliable e-commerce hosting with a store in the popular Yahoo! Shopping district.

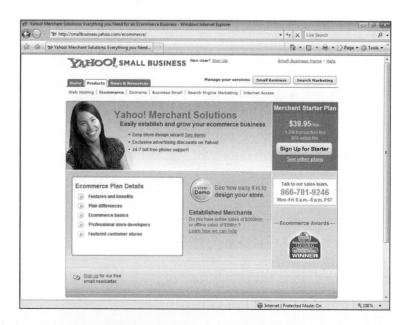

DIY: Selling Stuff from Your Site

If an e-commerce storefront seems like overkill for your small business, perhaps you should think about doing things "in house." I'm not talking here about building a full-fledged e-commerce system. As I explain a bit later, that's a tough row to hoe and requires lots of know-how and money. Instead, this section aims to show you that it's not very hard to set up a simple yet functional order-taking system using your HTML smarts and just a smidgen of JavaScript.

Creating an Order Form

The first thing you need to create is an order form your site visitors can use to specify what they want to purchase. This order form needs to have the following bits and pieces:

- A list of your products that includes the product name or description and the price of the product.

- Text boxes where the user can enter the quantity he or she wants to order for each item.

- Boxes that show the subtotal for each item (the price of the item multiplied by the quantity ordered).

- The overall total of the order.

- The user's personal data, including name, postal address, and e-mail address. This is vital information, particularly if something goes wrong with the order, because it enables you to contact the customer.

Figure 17.3 shows the top part of the form, which holds the list of products and the customer's order quantities. Note that the subtotals and order total are calculated automatically. That is, when the customer changes a quantity and moves to another field, the various totals are recalculated right away. Note, too, that things are set up so the user can't edit the subtotal or order total fields.

Webmaster Wisdom
If you have a large number of products, you may prefer to create a *shopping cart* that "remembers" customers' orders as they navigate through your site. That's a bit advanced for this book, but not for my *Special Edition Using JavaScript* (Que, 2001), which devotes an entire chapter to creating a shopping cart.

Figure 17.3

The top part of the order form.

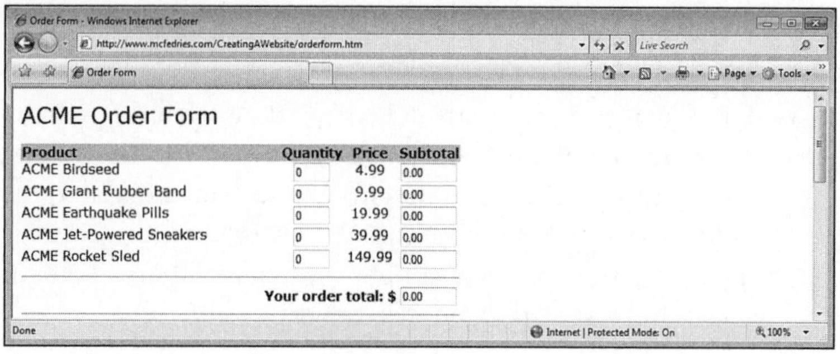

Here's the code that creates this part of the order form:

```
<body>

<div style="font-family: Verdana, sans-serif">
<div style="font-size: 20pt">
ACME Order Form
</div>

<form name="order_form"
      action="[Your form mailer script address goes here]"
method="post">
<table style="border-collapse: separate; border-spacing: 0px;
              padding: 5px" cellspacing="0">
<tr style="background-color: #cccccc">
<th style="text-align: left">Product</th>
<th>Quantity</th>
<th>Price</th>
<th>Subtotal</th>
</tr>

[Script that generates the product table goes here]

<tr><td colspan="4"><hr /></td></tr>
<tr>
<td colspan="3" align="right">
<b>Your order total: $</b></td>
<td align="center">
<input
    type="text"
    value="0.00"
    size="7"
    name="total"
    onfocus="document.order_form.elements[0].focus()"/>
```

```
</td>
</tr>
<tr><td colspan="4"><hr /></td></tr>
</table>
```

This is pretty standard stuff, except that bit about the script that generates the product table. I explain that in a second.

Figure 17.4 shows the bottom part of the form, which is where the user enters his or her personal data.

Here's the code that creates the bottom part of the order form:

```
Please fill in the fields below and then click the <b>Place Order</b>
button at the bottom of the form.<br />
Note that fields with <b>bold names</b> and red asterisks (<span
style="color: Red">*</span>) are mandatory.

<p>

<table border="0">

<tr>
<td>Salutation</td>
<td>
<select name="salutation">
<option value="none" selected>None</option>
<option value="dr.">Dr.</option>
<option value="miss">Miss</option>
```

```
<option value="mr.">Mr.</option>
<option value="mrs.">Mrs.</option>
<option value="prof.">Prof.</option>
</select>
</td>
</tr>

<tr>
<td><b>Name</b></td>
<td>
<input
    type="text"
    name="customer_name" />
<span style="color: Red">*</span>
</td>
</tr>

<tr>
<td><b>E-mail Address</b></td>

<td>
<input
    type="text"
    name="email" />
<span style="color: Red">*</span>
</td>
</tr>

<tr>
<td>Company Name</td>

<td>
<input
    type="text"
    name="company_name" />
</td>
</tr>

<tr>
<td><b>Phone Number</b></td>
<td>
<input
    type="text"
    name="phone_number" />
```

```
<span style="color: red">*</span>
</td>
</tr>

<tr>
<td><b>Fax Number</b></td>
<td>
<input
    type="text"
    name="fax_number" />
<span style="color: red">*</span>
</td>
</tr>

<tr>
<td><b>Address 1</b></td>

<td>
<input
    type="text"
    name="address_1" />
<span style="color: red">*</span>
</td>
</tr>

<tr>
<td>Address 2</td>

<td>
<input
    type="text"
    name="address_2" />
</td>
</tr>

<tr>
<td><b>City</b></td>

<td>
<input
    type="text"
    name="city" />
<span style="color: red">*</span>
</td>
```

```
</tr>

<tr>
<td><b>State/Province</b></td>

<td>
<input
    type="text"
    name="state" />
<span style="color: red">*</span>
</td>
</tr>

<tr>
<td><b>ZIP/Postal Code</b></td>

<td>
<input
    type="text"
    name="postal_code" />
<span style="color: red">*</span>
</td>
</tr>

<tr>
<td><b>Country</b></td>

<td>
<select name="country">
<option value="af">Afghanistan</option>
<option value="al">Albania</option>
<option value="dz">Algeria</option>
<option value="as">American Samoa</option>
<option value="ad">Andorra</option>
<option value="ao">Angola</option>
<option value="ai">Anguilla</option>
<option value="aq">Antarctica</option>
<option value="ag">Antigua and Barbuda</option>
<option value="ar">Argentina</option>
<option value="am">Armenia</option>
<option value="aw">Aruba</option>
<option value="au">Australia</option>
<option value="at">Austria</option>
```

```
<option value="az">Azerbaijan</option>
<option value="bs">Bahamas</option>
<option value="bh">Bahrain</option>
<option value="bd">Bangladesh</option>
<option value="bb">Barbados</option>
<option value="by">Belarus</option>
<option value="be">Belgium</option>
<option value="bz">Belize</option>
<option value="bj">Benin</option>
<option value="bm">Bermuda</option>
<option value="bt">Bhutan</option>
<option value="bo">Bolivia</option>
<option value="ba">Bosnia and Herzegovina</option>
<option value="bw">Botswana</option>
<option value="bv">Bouvet Island</option>
<option value="br">Brazil</option>
<option value="io">British Indian Ocean Territory</option>
<option value="bn">Brunei Darussalam</option>
<option value="bg">Bulgaria</option>
<option value="bf">Burkina Faso</option>
<option value="bi">Burundi</option>
<option value="kh">Cambodia</option>
<option value="cm">Cameroon</option>
<option value="ca">Canada</option>
<option value="cv">Cape Verde</option>
<option value="ky">Cayman Islands</option>
<option value="cf">Central African Republic</option>
<option value="td">Chad</option>
<option value="cl">Chile</option>
<option value="cn">China</option>
<option value="cx">Christmas Island</option>
<option value="cc">Cocos (Keeling) Islands</option>
<option value="co">Colombia</option>
<option value="km">Comoros</option>
<option value="cg">Congo</option>
<option value="cd">Congo, The Democratic Republic of the</option>
<option value="ck">Cook Islands</option>
<option value="cr">Costa Rica</option>
<option value="ci">Cote D'Ivoire</option>
<option value="hr">Croatia</option>
<option value="cu">Cuba</option>
<option value="cy">Cyprus</option>
<option value="cz">Czech Republic</option>
```

```
<option value="dk">Denmark</option>
<option value="dj">Djibouti</option>
<option value="dm">Dominica</option>
<option value="do">Dominican Republic</option>
<option value="tp">East Timor</option>
<option value="ec">Ecuador</option>
<option value="eg">Egypt</option>
<option value="sv">El Salvador</option>
<option value="gq">Equatorial Guinea</option>
<option value="er">Eritrea</option>
<option value="ee">Estonia</option>
<option value="et">Ethiopia</option>
<option value="fk">Falkland Islands (Malvinas)</option>
<option value="fo">Faroe Islands</option>
<option value="fj">Fiji</option>
<option value="fi">Finland</option>
<option value="fr">France</option>
<option value="gf">French Guiana</option>
<option value="pf">French Polynesia</option>
<option value="tf">French Southern Territories</option>
<option value="ga">Gabon</option>
<option value="gm">Gambia</option>
<option value="ge">Georgia</option>
<option value="de">Germany</option>
<option value="gh">Ghana</option>
<option value="gi">Gibraltar</option>
<option value="gr">Greece</option>
<option value="gl">Greenland</option>
<option value="gd">Grenada</option>
<option value="gp">Guadeloupe</option>
<option value="gu">Guam</option>
<option value="gt">Guatemala</option>
<option value="gn">Guinea</option>
<option value="gw">Guinea-Bissau</option>
<option value="gy">Guyana</option>
<option value="ht">Haiti</option>
<option value="hm">Heard Island and McDonald Islands</option>
<option value="va">Holy See (Vatican City State)</option>
<option value="hn">Honduras</option>
<option value="hk">Hong Kong</option>
<option value="hu">Hungary</option>
<option value="is">Iceland</option>
<option value="in">India</option>
```

```
<option value="id">Indonesia</option>
<option value="ir">Iran, Islamic Republic of</option>
<option value="iq">Iraq</option>
<option value="ie">Ireland</option>
<option value="il">Israel</option>
<option value="it">Italy</option>
<option value="jm">Jamaica</option>
<option value="jp">Japan</option>
<option value="jo">Jordan</option>
<option value="kz">Kazakstan</option>
<option value="ke">Kenya</option>
<option value="ki">Kiribati</option>
<option value="kp">Korea, Democratic People's Republic of</option>
<option value="kr">Korea, Republic of</option>
<option value="kw">Kuwait</option>
<option value="kg">Kyrgyzstan</option>
<option value="la">Lao People's Democratic Republic</option>
<option value="lv">Latvia</option>
<option value="lb">Lebanon</option>
<option value="ls">Lesotho</option>
<option value="lr">Liberia</option>
<option value="ly">Libyan Arab Jamahiriya</option>
<option value="li">Liechtenstein</option>
<option value="lt">Lithuania</option>
<option value="lu">Luxembourg</option>
<option value="mo">Macau</option>
<option value="mk">Macedonia, The Former Yugoslav Republic of</option>
<option value="mg">Madagascar</option>
<option value="mw">Malawi</option>
<option value="my">Malaysia</option>
<option value="mv">Maldives</option>
<option value="ml">Mali</option>
<option value="mt">Malta</option>
<option value="mh">Marshall Islands</option>
<option value="mq">Martinique</option>
<option value="mr">Mauritania</option>
<option value="mu">Mauritius</option>
<option value="yt">Mayotte</option>
<option value="mx">Mexico</option>
<option value="fm">Micronesia, Federated States of</option>
<option value="md">Moldova, Republic of</option>
<option value="mc">Monaco</option>
<option value="mn">Mongolia</option>
```

```
<option value="ms">Montserrat</option>
<option value="ma">Morocco</option>
<option value="mz">Mozambique</option>
<option value="mm">Myanmar</option>
<option value="na">Namibia</option>
<option value="nr">Nauru</option>
<option value="np">Nepal</option>
<option value="nl">Netherlands</option>
<option value="an">Netherlands Antilles</option>
<option value="nc">New Caledonia</option>
<option value="nz">New Zealand</option>
<option value="ni">Nicaragua</option>
<option value="ne">Niger</option>
<option value="ng">Nigeria</option>
<option value="nu">Niue</option>
<option value="nf">Norfolk Island</option>
<option value="mp">Northern Mariana Islands</option>
<option value="no">Norway</option>
<option value="om">Oman</option>
<option value="pk">Pakistan</option>
<option value="pw">Palau</option>
<option value="ps">Palestinian Territory, Occupied</option>
<option value="pa">Panama</option>
<option value="pg">Papua New Guinea</option>
<option value="py">Paraguay</option>
<option value="pe">Peru</option>
<option value="ph">Philippines</option>
<option value="pn">Pitcairn</option>
<option value="pl">Poland</option>
<option value="pt">Portugal</option>
<option value="pr">Puerto Rico</option>
<option value="qa">Qatar</option>
<option value="re">Reunion</option>
<option value="ro">Romania</option>
<option value="ru">Russian Federation</option>
<option value="rw">Rwanda</option>
<option value="sh">Saint Helena</option>
<option value="kn">Saint Kitts and Nevis</option>
<option value="lc">Saint Lucia</option>
<option value="pm">Saint Pierre and Miquelon</option>
<option value="vc">Saint Vincent and the Grenadines</option>
<option value="ws">Samoa</option>
<option value="sm">San Marino</option>
```

```
<option value="st">Sao Tome and Principe</option>
<option value="sa">Saudi Arabia</option>
<option value="sn">Senegal</option>
<option value="sc">Seychelles</option>
<option value="sl">Sierra Leone</option>
<option value="sg">Singapore</option>
<option value="sk">Slovakia</option>
<option value="si">Slovenia</option>
<option value="sb">Solomon Islands</option>
<option value="so">Somalia</option>
<option value="za">South Africa</option>
<option value="gs">South Georgia and the South Sandwich Islands
</option>
<option value="es">Spain</option>
<option value="lk">Sri Lanka</option>
<option value="sd">Sudan</option>
<option value="sr">Suriname</option>
<option value="sj">Svalbard and Jan Mayen</option>
<option value="sz">Swaziland</option>
<option value="se">Sweden</option>
<option value="ch">Switzerland</option>
<option value="sy">Syrian Arab Republic</option>
<option value="tw">Taiwan, Province of China</option>
<option value="tj">Tajikistan</option>
<option value="tz">Tanzania, United Republic of</option>
<option value="th">Thailand</option>
<option value="tg">Togo</option>
<option value="tk">Tokelau</option>
<option value="to">Tonga</option>
<option value="tt">Trinidad and Tobago</option>
<option value="tn">Tunisia</option>
<option value="tr">Turkey</option>
<option value="tm">Turkmenistan</option>
<option value="tc">Turks and Caicos Islands</option>
<option value="tv">Tuvalu</option>
<option value="ug">Uganda</option>
<option value="ua">Ukraine</option>
<option value="ae">United Arab Emirates</option>
<option value="gb">United Kingdom</option>
<option value="us" selected>United States</option>
<option value="um">United States Minor Outlying Islands</option>
<option value="uy">Uruguay</option>
<option value="uz">Uzbekistan</option>
```

```
<option value="vu">Vanuatu</option>
<option value="ve">Venezuela</option>
<option value="vn">Vietnam</option>
<option value="vg">Virgin Islands, British</option>
<option value="vi">Virgin Islands, U.S.</option>
<option value="wf">Wallis and Futuna</option>
<option value="eh">Western Sahara</option>
<option value="ye">Yemen</option>
<option value="yu">Yugoslavia</option>
<option value="zm">Zambia</option>
<option value="zw">Zimbabwe</option>
</select>
<span style="color: red">*</span>
</td>
</tr>


</table>

<input type="submit" value="Place Order" />


</form>

</div>
</body>
</html>
```

The order form is in a file named orderform.htm on the CD. There are two things you need to know right up front before you can think about customizing this file to suit your own site:

- The product list and ordering boxes are arranged in a table that's written automatically to the page using JavaScript. The item names and prices can be customized.

- The rest of the order form is a basic HTML table you can modify at will.

So the only bit of funny business here involves customizing the "database" of products. This is done as part of the script that sits near the top of the file. Here's the code that creates the database of products shown in Figure 17.3:

```
// Create the "database" of products
var database_records = new Array()
var i = 0
database_records[i++] = new database_record("ACME Birdseed", 4.99)
database_records[i++] = new database_record("ACME Giant Rubber Band",
➡ 9.99)
database_records[i++] = new database_record("ACME Earthquake Pills",
➡ 19.99)
database_records[i++] = new database_record("ACME Jet-Powered
➡ Sneakers", 39.99)
database_records[i++] = new database_record("ACME Rocket Sled", 149.99)

// This function creates a new database_record object.
function database_record(description, price) {
    this.description = description
    this.price = price
}
```

With this code, you're storing some data about each product in the computer's memory. The key here is each line that begins `database_records[i++]`. Here's the general format of this statement:

```
database_records[i++] = new database_record("Product Name", Price)
```

Here, you replace *Product Name* with the name or short description of the product, and you replace *Price* with the item's price. (Don't include a dollar sign or any other monetary symbol.)

Now here's the script that creates the table on the fly based on what's in the database:

```
<script language="javascript" type="text/javascript">
<!--

// Loop through the database_records array
for (var counter = 0; counter < database_records.length; counter++) {

    // Save the item's price
    item_price = database_records[counter].price

    // Add the item to the order form table
    document.writeln('<tr bgcolor="#ffffff" valign="top">')

    // Write the item's description
```

```
   document.writeln('<td width="320" align="left">')
   document.writeln(database_records[counter].description + '<\/td>')

   // Place the item's quantity in a text box
   document.writeln('<td width="75" align="center">')
   field_name = purge_characters(database_records[counter].
➦ description, " ")
   document.writeln('<input type="text" value="0"' +
                      ' size="3"' +
                      ' name="' + field_name + '"' +
                      ' onChange="calculate_total()"><\/td>')

   // Write the item's price
   document.order_form.elements[field_name].price = item_price
   document.writeln('<td width="65" align="center">')
   document.writeln(item_price + '<\/td>')

   // Write the item's total price
   field_name = "subtotal" + counter
   document.writeln('<td width="75" align="center">')
   document.writeln('<input type="text" value="0.00"' +
   ' size="7"' +
   ' name="' + field_name + '"' +
   ' onFocus="document.order_form.elements[0].focus()"><\/td>')

   document.writeln('<\/tr>')
}

document.close()

//-->
</script>
```

Processing Orders

The form from the previous section is designed to be e-mailed to you (using, for example, my MailForm service). When you receive the form data, you may need to finalize the order total to include extra charges such as shipping, gift wrapping, and taxes. When that's done, you have several choices:

◆ Contact the customer and ask him or her to send you a check or money order for the full amount.

◆ Use a third-party payment service such as PayPal (www.paypal.com) or Google Checkout (checkout.google.com/sell) to arrange a cash transfer from the customer's account to yours.

◆ Contact the customer and ask for his or her credit card (or debit card) information and use that info to process the payment.

How do you go about processing a credit card transaction? One easy way is to lease a *swipe terminal* that's normally used for swiping credit cards. You won't have access to the physical card, of course, but these terminals allow you to enter card numbers and expiration dates by hand. You can usually lease one for about $30 per month.

The next step up from there is to contract with a third-party payment service to handle the dirty work of each credit card transaction. This is called a *payment gateway*. Many of the companies I discussed at the start of this chapter also offer payment gateway services that let you add credit card processing to your pages.

Some companies will handle credit card transactions for you. Here are a few to check out:

◆ Authorize.Net (www.authorize.net)

◆ CCNow (www.ccnow.com)

◆ First Data (www.cardservicesales.com)

◆ Electronic Transfer (www.electronictransfer.com)

◆ Merchant Warehouse (www.merchantwarehouse.com)

When you're rummaging around in these sites, here are some questions to ask yourself when comparing sites:

◆ Which credit cards does the service handle?

◆ How can you send the orders (online, fax, e-mail, and so on)?

◆ Which currencies does the service support?

◆ How much does it cost to get your site set up with the service?

◆ How much does the service charge per transaction?

 Page Pitfall

Pay special attention to the transaction fees. Some can be quite exorbitant and may mean the difference between making a profit or breaking the bank. Avoid sites that charge both a percentage of the selling price and a dollar amount per transaction.

All About Big-Time E-Commerce

If you work for a medium or large company and some higher-up has told you to put together an in-house e-commerce system, things will get very complicated (and very expensive) in a hurry. A humble *Idiot's Guide* such as this is, unfortunately, not the place to delve into the details of planning for and setting up a full-blown e-commerce system. Fortunately, plenty of good e-commerce guides and tutorials are available on the web. Here are some to check out:

- *About.com E-Commerce Solutions* (onlinebusiness.about.com/od/shoppingcarts/ECommerce_Solutions.htm) offers a number of articles on various aspects of e-commerce, all put together with the quality that you've come to expect from the About.com family of sites.

- *Building Your First E-Commerce Site* (www.ecommerce-guide.com/solutions/building/article.php/10362_867521) offers Building Your First E-Commerce Site, a very thorough guide that takes you step by step through the process of getting an e-commerce site up and selling.

- *Online Commerce Introduction to eCommerce* (online-commerce.com/tutorial.html) offers the eCommerce Tutorial, a simple guide that gives you the basics of how e-commerce works.

- *Web Developer's Journal Electronic Commerce Tutorial* (www.webdevelopersjournal.com/columns/ecommerce1.html) isn't the best laid out article I've ever seen, but it's chock-full of useful information.

The Least You Need to Know

- If you decide to opt for an e-commerce host, be sure it supports secure shopping carts and credit card transactions.

- Before signing on the digital dotted line for any service that offers credit card transactions, find out what fees you'll be charged. It's common to have to pay a monthly fee and a per-transaction percentage. However, watch out for other "administrative" fees.

- Just in case anything goes wrong, you should always ask customers for contact information, particularly their address and telephone number.

Glossary

.asp   The extension used with Active Server Pages files.

.cgi   The extension used by a Common Gateway Interface script.

.php   The extension used by a PHP script. (Alternatives are .phtml and .php3.)

.pl   The extension used with Perl files.

404   Describes a person who is clueless. This comes from the following web server error message:

```
404 Not Found. The requested URL was not found on this
server.
```

above the fold   Sometimes called *above the scroll*, this describes a web page ad the user sees without having to scroll down. *See also* below the fold.

access counter   *See* counter.

action   Occurs when the user clicks an ad to visit the advertiser's site and then performs some action such as purchasing a product, filling in a form, registering, subscribing, or whatever.

Active Server Pages (ASP)   A web page technology that enables web designers to place scripts inside a page, and those scripts are executed by the web server before the page is sent to the user. *See also* .asp; PHP.

ad format   The dimensions of a web page ad.

ad network   A company that contracts with a number of advertisers to generate a pool of ads. It then uses an ad server to distribute those ads to sites that have signed up with the ad network.

advertiser   A company that creates ads for marketing its products or services. *Compare with* publisher.

affiliate program   A CPA-based advertising program where you partner with a selling site by setting up product links and receiving a percentage of each sale.

aggregator   A service that gathers headlines from blogs and news-related sites, usually by accessing each site's RSS feed.

ASP   *See* Active Server Pages.

bandwidth   A measure of how much stuff can be crammed through a transmission medium such as a phone line or network cable. Web hosting providers use this term to mean the amount of data that is sent to and from your site. Bandwidth is measured in bits per second (bps).

banner ad   An ad that appears in a web page as a rectangular, clickable image.

banner exchange network   A network in which sites submit their banner ads and agree to display the banner ads from the other sites in the network.

below the fold   Sometimes called *below the scroll*, this describes an ad that doesn't appear until the user scrolls down. *See also* above the fold.

billable hours   The hours a professional website designer actually works on a project.

bit   The fundamental unit of computer information (it's a blend of the words *binary* and *digit*). Computers do all their dirty work by manipulating a series of high and low electrical currents. A high current is represented by the digit 1 and a low current by the digit 0. These 1's and 0's—or bits—are used to represent absolutely everything that goes down inside your machine.

bits per second (bps)   A measure of bandwidth. Because it takes 8 bits to describe a single character, a transmission medium with a bandwidth of, say, 8bps would send data at the pathetically slow rate of 1 character per second. Bandwidth is more normally measured in kilobits per second (Kbps—thousands of bits per second). So for example, a 56Kbps modem can handle approximately 56,000 bits per second. With broadband connections, bandwidth is measured in megabits per second (Mbps—millions of bits per second).

body   The section of the web page in which you enter your text and tags. *See also* head.

bps   *See* bits per second.

breadcrumbing   A navigation feature that displays a list of the places a person has visited or the route a person has taken. The term comes from the fairy tale of Hansel and Gretel, who threw down bits of bread to help find their way out of the forest. If your website content is organized as a hierarchy or as a sequence of pages, you can use breadcrumb links to not only show people where they are now, but also to enable them to navigate your site hierarchy or sequence.

browser   The software you use to display and interact with a website.

byte   Eight bits, or a single character.

CGI   *See* Common Gateway Interface.

`cgi-bin`   A special directory your web host creates for you as a place to store your CGI scripts.

CGI-Joe   A programmer who specializes in the Common Gateway Interface (CGI) scripts that accept and handle input from most web page forms.

character reference   An HTML code that lets you insert special characters in your web pages (such as é). *See also* entity name.

click-through   When the user clicks an ad.

click-through ratio (CTR)   The rate at which users click an ad. It's calculated by dividing the number of click-throughs by the number of impressions.

client-side image map   An image map where the links are processed by the browser instead of the server. *See also* server-side image map.

comment   Text in a web page file that doesn't get displayed to the user or processed by the browser. Webmasters use comments to annotate a page's HTML code to make it easier to read and understand, and also to force the browser to bypass problematic code.

Common Gateway Interface (CGI)   A programming technology that enables a web server to accept data (usually from a form), process that data, and send the browser some kind of result. *See also* CGI-Joe.

contextual ad   A website ad that offers a product or service that's related to the content of the page on which the ad appears.

cost-per-action (CPA)   How much an ad costs you per action if you're an advertiser; how much an ad pays you per action if you're a publisher.

cost-per-click (CPC)   How much an ad costs you per click-through if you're an advertiser; how much an ad pays you per click-through if you're a publisher. This is calculated using the CTR (click-through ratio) and the CPM (cost-per-thousand): CPC = CPM ÷ CTR × 1,000.

cost-per-thousand (CPM)   How much an ad costs you per thousand impressions if you're an advertiser; how much an ad pays you per thousand impressions if you're a publisher. *See also* effective cost-per-thousand.

counter   A small script inserted in a web page that tracks the page's hits. Also referred to as an access counter.

CPA   *See* cost-per-action.

CPC   *See* cost-per-click.

CPM   *See* cost-per-thousand.

CTR   *See* click-through ratio.

cybersquatting   The practice of obtaining and holding an Internet domain name that uses another company's registered trademark name.

dedicated server   A web server run by a web hosting provider where a single website gets use of the entire computer. *See also* shared server.

deep link   A web page link that points to a file within a site rather than to the site's home page.

deprecated   Describes a tag or element that's no longer part of the HTML standard.

direct selling   Where you contact advertisers directly and ask them if they want to advertise on your site.

domain name   The part of your e-mail address to the right of the @ sign. The domain name identifies a particular site on the Internet.

e-commerce   The buying and selling of goods and services on the web.

e-tailer   A web-based retail operation.

effective cost-per-thousand (eCPM)   This is a measure of how much revenue an ad generates per 1,000 impressions. You calculate it using the ad's revenue (R) and its impressions (I): eCPM = R ÷ I × 1,000. You use eCPM to compare the performance of the ads on your site.

entity name   An HTML code that lets you insert special characters in your web pages. *See also* character reference.

FAQ (pronounced *FACK*)   *See* Frequently Asked Questions (FAQ) list.

favicon   A "favorite icon," or an icon that identifies a website in the browser's address bar and tabs.

File Transfer Protocol (FTP)   The usual method for sending HTML files to your web server. Note that it's okay to use FTP as both a noun (a method for transferring files) and a verb ("Your images aren't showing up because you forgot to FTP the graphics files to your home directory.").

footer   An area at the bottom of each page you use for things like your copyright notice, contact information, and less important links you want to appear on each page. *See also* header.

form   A web document used for gathering information from the reader. Most forms have at least one text field where you can enter text data (such as your name or the keywords for a search). More sophisticated forms also include check boxes (for toggling a value on or off), radio buttons (for selecting one of several options), and command buttons (for performing an action such as submitting the form).

frames   Rectangular browser areas that contain separate chunks of text, graphics, and HTML. You can use frames to divide the browser window into two or more separate pages.

Frequently Asked Questions (FAQ) list   A list of questions that have come up most often. If you want to send a question to a newsgroup or to a website's administrator, it's proper "netiquette" to read the group's FAQ list to see if you can find the answer there first.

FTP   *See* File Transfer Protocol.

GIF (Graphics Interchange Format)   One of the two most commonly used graphics format on the web. *See also* JPEG.

head   The top part of an HTML file. This is like an introduction to a web page. Web browsers use the head to glean various types of information about the page (such as the title). *See also* body.

header   An area at the top of each page you use for stuff like your site's title and icon, links to the main areas of your site, and perhaps some ads. *See also* footer.

hit   In general, a single access of a web page. That is, a hit is recorded for a particular web page each time a browser displays the page. Technically, however, it's a request to a web server for data. This means that a request for an HTML file is a hit, but so are any requests for supporting files, such as images, Java applets, external style sheet files, and so on. Therefore, may people prefer to use the more accurate term *page view*.

hosting provider   *See* web host.

HTML   *See* Hypertext Markup Language.

HTML editor   A program that makes it easier to mark up a document by using menu commands and toolbar buttons to insert tags.

hypertext link   *See* link.

Hypertext Markup Language (HTML)   The collection of tags used to specify how you want your web page to appear.

image map   A clickable image that takes you to a different link, depending on which part of the image you click. *See also* client-side image map; server-side image map.

impression   An instance of an ad being displayed to a user. For example, if a person views one of your pages that has an ad and then a second person views the same page, you chalk up two impressions. Similarly, if one person views that page and then returns to the page an hour later, that would also count as two impressions because the ad was displayed to the user twice. This is also called an *ad view*.

index   A list of words that appear in a site's web pages and that's used by a search engine to find all the pages that match a user's search query.

Internet service provider (ISP)   A company that offers access to the Internet.

interstitial   An ad that appears in a separate browser window, especially one that appears while the regular page is loading.

intranet   A website designed to operate and be accessible only over a network.

ISP   *See* Internet service provider.

JPEG   A common web graphics format developed by the Joint Photographic Experts Group. *See also* GIF.

Kbps   Kilobits per second (thousands of bits per second).

link   A word or phrase that, when selected, sends the reader to a different page or to an anchor.

link rot   The gradual obsolescence of the links on a web page as the sites they point to become unavailable.

Mbps   Megabits per second (millions of bits per second).

microbrowser   *See* mobile browser.

mobile browser   A web browser used on small-screen devices such as pocket PCs, personal digital assistants, and cell phones.

mouse potato   The computer equivalent of a couch potato.

news aggregator   *See* aggregator.

page jack   To steal a web page and submit it to search engines under a different address. Users who run a search and attempt to access the page are then routed to another site.

page view   An instance of a user viewing a web page. *See also* hit.

Perl   A programming language used to create CGI scripts. *See also* .pl.

PHP   A web page technology that enables web designers to place scripts inside a page, which are then executed by the web server before the page is sent to the user. PHP is used primarily on Unix or Linux servers. *See also* .php; Active Server Pages.

pixel shim   A small, transparent, image (usually 1 pixel wide by 1 pixel tall) web page designers use to achieve exact placement of text and images.

plug-in   A program that attaches itself to a web browser so the functionality of the program then becomes an integral part of the browser.

pop-under   An ad that appears in a separate browser window that gets displayed "under" the user's current browser window.

pop-up   An ad that appears in a separate browser window that gets displayed "on top of" the user's current browser window.

portal site   A website that combines a wide array of content and services in an effort to convince users to make the site their home page.

publish   To make a web page available to the World Wide Web community at large.

publisher   A person or company that creates a website on which an advertiser or ad network can display one or more ads.

run-of-site   This means that an ad can appear on any page of your site and not just a specific page (such as your home page).

search engine   A resource that indexes web pages and then enables the user to search for those pages that contain a particular word or phrase.

server   A computer that sends out stuff. *See also* web server.

server-side image map   An image map where the links are processed by the server. *See also* client-side image map.

server-side include (SSI)   A special HTML tag that enables the page designer to "include" an external text file or to "echo" certain types of data to the page.

shared server   A web server run by a web hosting provider where each website shares the server with other websites; there could be dozens or even hundreds of them. *See also* dedicated server.

shovelware   Content from an existing medium such as a newspaper or book that's been dumped wholesale into another medium such as a web page.

sitemap file   An XML file that lists all the files on a website.

skyscraper ad   An advertisement that runs vertically down the side of a web page.

spamdexing   To repeat a word dozens or even hundreds of times at the top of a web page. The word is usually indicative of the subject matter of the site, and repeating it so many times is an attempt to fool web search engines into thinking the site is a good representation of that subject. However, most search engines recognize this and refuse to index such a site.

sticky   Describes a website that encourages visitors to spend long periods of time visiting its various pages.

surf   To leap giddily from one web page to another by furiously clicking any link in sight; to travel through cyberspace.

syndication   The distribution of website content in a format that enables others to gather and read that content.

tags   HTML commands, in the form of letter combinations or words surrounded by angle brackets (< and >), that tell a browser how to display a web page.

title   A short description of a web page that appears at the top of the screen.

typosquatter   A person who registers one or more domain names based on the most common typographical errors a user might commit when entering a company's registered trademark name (for example, amazon.com).

Uniform Resource Locator (URL)   A web addressing scheme that spells out the exact location of a Net resource. For example, my home page's URL is www. mcfedries.com.

unique users   The number of separate individuals who have viewed a page or ad.

upload   To send files from your computer to a remote location such as your web host's server.

uptime   The percentage of time a web hosting provider's server is up and serving.

URL   *See* Uniform Resource Locator.

validator   A website that validates HTML or CSS code.

vaporlink   A link that points to a nonexistent web page.

web host   A company that provides you with storage space (usually for a fee) for your website. The company runs a web server that enables other people to view your site. Also called *web hosting provider.*

web server   A computer that stores your website's pages and hands them out to anyone with a browser who comes calling.

World Wide Web Consortium (W3C)   The organization that maintain the various standards—such as HTML and CSS—you have to wrestle with to build your website.

What's on the CD

The purpose of this book is to be a one-stop shop for budding websmiths. To that end, the text is geared toward getting you up to speed with this website rigmarole without a lot of fuss. But fine words butter no parsnips, as they say (no, they really do), so you'll also find tons of stuff on the CD in the back of the book. The CD is jammed full of handy references, files, and other documents that should provide everything you need to get your website authorship off to a rousing start. This appendix describes what's on the CD and tells you how to install it.

Accessing the CD's Contents

To get to the sections on the CD, there are two routes you can take. The simplest and most straightforward is to use your browser to open the file named index.html in the main folder of the CD. (That's if your computer doesn't take you there automatically.) This gives you a nice, clickable interface to everything that's on the CD. The other way is to open the CD and access the files directly.

CSS

Style sheet properties are even harder to keep straight than tags because there are more than 140 properties in existence! Not to worry, though: see the CD's CSS section, which contains a CSS property reference that runs through a complete list of the available style sheet properties. For each property, you get a description of the property, notes on using it, a list of the property's possible values, a link to the property's official W3C page, and an example that shows how the property works.

Examples

Many of this book's chapters are sprinkled with examples showing HTML tags on the go. If you'd like to incorporate some of these examples into your own website work, don't bother typing your poor fingers to the bone. Instead, all the example files are sitting on the CD, ready for you to copy and paste in the Examples section. And note that the examples are organized by chapter.

Goodies

To round out the CD, I've also included a Goodies section, which contains three more references I hope you find useful.

The 216 "safe" web colors page shows you all the 216 so-called "safe" web colors to use on your pages. ("Safe" means these colors display well on almost all screens.) One table shows you the colors, and another table shows you the corresponding RGB values.

The X11 color set page runs through all the colors that have defined names (such as "red," "blue," and "chartreuse").

Finally, the *HTML Code for Cool Characters* page lists all the HTML codes and entity names you can use to incorporate characters such as ¢ and © in your pages.

Tags

With more than 100 HTML tags to keep track of, you are forgiven if you forget one or can't remember which attribute goes with which tag. To help you out, check out the Tags section, which contains a complete HTML tag reference. This gives you the nitty-gritty on all the HTML tags. For each tag, you get a description of the tag, notes on using the tag, a complete list of the tag's attributes, a link to the tag's official W3C page, and an example that shows the tag in action.

Templates

In various places throughout the book, I showed you templates that implement common site structures such as headers and footers, columns, margins, RSS feeds, order forms, and more. See the Templates section for these and other templates you can use as starting points for your site's pages.

Index

X–Y–Z

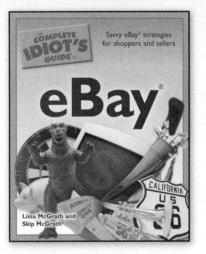
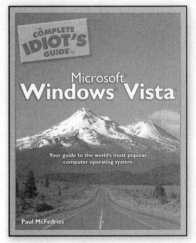